Intermediate Conversational Sign Language

American Sign Language
with English Translations

Intermediate Conversational Sign Language

American Sign Language
with English Translations

Willard J. Madsen

Illustrated by
Lois A. Lehman

Clerc Books
Gallaudet University Press
Washington, D.C.

COVER: Conversation in Sign Language is basically dependent upon a number of handshapes which communicate symbol after symbol. Handshapes are a primordial key to this vibrant, visual form of language. Equally important are the variable lines of movement which may indicate size or shape and direction or location. The cover illustration of this book is analogous to the historical enlightenment of deaf people through meaningful communication. This analogy is abstracted from the arms and hands reaching out to convey a message to one another which is not readily discernible. There is further abstraction in the eye-like shape of the background which would symbolize the importance of the visual aspects. Perhaps, to the student of Sign Language who has come this far, that is what it is all about—arms and hands reaching out, begging to be seen or "heard," hands constantly changing shape, and each shape, each change, becoming significant in the message intended, although not all of it is quite easily grasped as yet. Then, too, there is the concrete in the specific handshapes, combinations of which do, in fact, say something to one who knows and understands handshapes, positions, and movements.

Clerc Books
An imprint of Gallaudet University Press
Washington, DC 20002-3695

Library of Congress Catalog Card Number 82-81440
International Standard Book Number 0-913580-79-1

Dedicated to Sign Language teachers
everywhere

Contents

Foreword

In 1960, when Dr. William C. Stokoe's *Sign Language Structure: An Outline of the Visual Communication System of the American Deaf* was published, people in the embryonic Sign Language field were just starting to seriously and systematically analyze what makes Sign Language tick. In recent years, Sign Language teaching has begun to emphasize utilization of second language teaching methodology, techniques, and technology as well as newly gleaned linguistic discoveries that pertain to Sign Language. But there is sometimes a problem of translating this information into manageable instruction in the classroom.

Many Sign Language books are written in a more-or-less traditional format. They primarily present lists of English words and lists of signs. This traditional format has its place and value. But there is more to the teaching and learning of Sign Language than vocabulary, and many of these texts are not broad enough.

Intermediate Conversational Sign Language: American Sign Language with English Translations by Willard J. Madsen is indeed a welcome addition to the field of Sign Language teaching. This new book allows students to systematically analyze the mysteries of Sign production and grammar and learn signs in manageable chunks. For teachers, it presents an approach to systematic instruction that can be adapted for use on several Sign Language training levels.

The book should also be useful to Sign Language students and teachers interested in exploring new methods of learning and teaching the language of Sign.

Besides illustrating individual signs and signed sentences quite clearly, the author uses a unique system for writing signs with words and symbols. It takes into consideration a number of major elements of the linguistic terminology pertaining to Sign Language and presents the essential information about sign production and grammar in a straightforward, not-too-technical manner.

The technical terms that are introduced in the book are both useful and well-explained. The terms are necessary if teachers and students alike are to share a clear, concise, objective way of discussing language. Teachers and students will also find that the terms and definitions in this book will help them understand the ever-increasing number of linguistically oriented books and articles relevant to Sign Language.

The illustrator, Lois Lehman, has also made her mark in her attention to details of Sign production: shift in body posture for a clearer view of the sign being formed instead of the traditional frontal illustrations; additional circled or boxed illustrations showing the sequences of movements instead of relying entirely on directional arrows. The artist also purposely attended to detailed expressions on the face with sharp attention being given to the forehead, eyebrows, eyes, nose, lips, and mouth. This, in itself, is no easy task for any artist rendering Sign Language into illustrations.

Examples of how signs are used in sentences are worked out as completely as possible to show the intermediate signer each step of the sign formation. The author has made it easy for the reader to follow, in some detail, novel concepts and signing procedures.

Readers will find this book well-organized and well-written, useful either as a resource handbook or as a text in courses in Sign Language.

H. P. Menkis
Assistant Professor
Department of Sign Communication
Gallaudet University
Washington, D.C.

Preface

This book is a product of the phenomenal growth in texts dealing with American Sign Language (ASL) in the 1980s. Earlier sign communication books were often little more than collections of selected sign vocabulary, or dictionaries, with little or no explanation about the grammar or use of ASL as a language. These books were usually arranged in topical units, or even by handshape, and the signs were presented in alphabetical order within each unit. More recent sign language texts are a far cry from these earlier books.

In 1972, my book, *Conversational Sign Language II: An Intermediate-Advanced Manual*, marked the *first* attempt to develop a text that would help students gain some understanding of colloquial American Sign Language and idiomatic expressions used by the Deaf community. This work included very few illustrations. Rather, it relied on synonyms and detailed explanations of how to produce specific signs and expressions. Some of these could not be explained with English equivalents. This book also contained the first attempt to translate common English idioms into ASL. Though the book was well received, many teachers and students have complained that it does not have enough illustrations.

An initial attempt at revising this earlier work to include illustrations soon led to the obvious need for a new work which would be more in keeping with current research into American Sign Language or ASL. Hence, *Intermediate Conversational Sign Language: American Sign Language with English Translations*, a fully illustrated text, came into being. The format of this text has been modeled somewhat after current foreign language textbooks. Sentence patterns, illustrated in the target language, are glossed to show syntactical relationships and some of the grammatical features. Grammatical notes help to clarify usage and English translations are also included for comparative purposes. Appropriate practice material further gives the student opportunities to achieve some competence in the target language along with an increased awareness of cultural implications. Linguistic information was purposely kept simple and limited so as not to overburden the student. The introduction and explanation of such information is left to the discretion of the teacher.

Perhaps the biggest problem encountered in producing this text has been the development of a glossing system and the selection of glosses to represent specific signs. Because this work is so new within the field, there are bound to be differences in the way the glossing is carried out in this text as compared to the way it is carried out in other new texts in American Sign Language. It will be some time before complete uniformity occurs. We will welcome suggestions from researchers, from teachers, and from students on how improvements and revisions might be handled in future editions of this work.

We are confident, however, that for the time being users of this book will find many practical applications for the material included herein.

Acknowledgments

The author wishes to thank the following people for their advice, assistance, and encouragement in the production of this book:

- Lois Lehman, the artist, for her creative suggestions and hard work in providing the illustrations and layout of the original art work.

- Kitty Dillman and Bob Seremeth for their help in critically reviewing the illustrations and written text and for making numerous suggestions for improving the overall content.

- Dr. Robbin Battison for helping me develop the transcription system and write the grammatical notes.

- Paul Menkis for his suggestions and encouragement from the start of the project.

- Larry Baker, Gallaudet student, for assisting me and the artist during the formative stages of production.

- Dennis Cokely and Charlotte Baker for their interest, suggestions, and encouragement, especially in the early stages of developing the book.

- Gallaudet officials, particularly Dr. John S. Schuchman, Dr. Doin Hicks, and Dr. Thomas A. Mayes, for their support of the project.

- The Gallaudet University Press for its assistance in making possible the publication of this book, and Dr. Elaine Costello, Director of the Press, for her timely and helpful suggestions.

- Jan-Lee Music, Beverly Hills, California, for permission to use the words of the song "Let There Be Peace on Earth . . ." by Sy Miller and Jill Jackson.

- The many other individuals and friends who offered suggestions or expressed interest in the work.

- And, finally, members of my family for helping to see me through.

Intermediate Conversational Sign Language

American Sign Language
with English Translations

Introduction

Intermediate Conversational Sign Language: American Sign Language with English Translations is an illustrated text primarily designed to assist students in developing some proficiency in the use of conversational ASL. It is arranged by topics based on everyday occurrences. The topics cover food shopping, eating, clothing, medical situations, home care (inside and outside), death, babysitting, driving, travel, sightseeing, engagements, elections, Christmas planning, school reunions, and poetry and song. All but one of the characters depicted in this book are representative of deaf persons in a typical Deaf community.

The section, How to Use This Book, gives an explanation of the format of the book. It contains a detailed explanation of how the signs are written in the book with selected English **glosses** (words) and special symbols. The section includes a Key to Gloss Symbols which categorizes the various types of glosses used throughout the text. This key gives examples of how the glosses are used and translated.

The key is followed by an explanation of the various types of arrows and other marking symbols found in the illustrations, which helps provide information on how to produce the signs. This is an important introduction to understanding sign formation, movement, directionality, degree of emphasis, repetitions, and complex executions such as those found in alternate hand movements or in signs which combine with other signs in some special way.

Then follows an introduction to the seven deaf characters in the book and to the additional characters which are depicted in specific lessons: Lesson 15 deals with babysitting a grandson; Lesson 16 introduces a state police officer, the son of deaf parents, who appears briefly on the scene; and Lesson 19 brings in a deaf couple who are visiting from another part of the country.

Finally, students are presented with suggestions for solving translation problems and for understanding variations of certain sign vocabulary which they will come across as they progress through this book.

Another section gives a summary review of fingerspelling principles and practices to help the intermediate student improve this necessary skill. Fingerspelling is used only when necessary in this text, but it is an essential skill needed by the student of American Sign Language as he or she advances towards fluency in communicating with deaf persons. Fingerspelling practice is referred to only in the suggested activities at the end of each lesson.

Following the fingerspelling review, there is also a review of numbers and counting which is illustrated along with helpful hints to the student for improving skills in understanding and using numbers in Sign communication. This review is a prelude to Lesson 1, which focuses on the subject of numbers and counting. The majority of sentences in this lesson are unrelated; however, dialogue is used in Lessons 2 through 24; and Lesson 25 deals with the problems of translating songs or poems originally written in English.

Each lesson contains a glossed introductory paragraph, with only the title illustrated, followed by an illustrated dialogue. Opposite each page of illustrated ASL dialogue are glossed sentences with English translations and grammatical notes that explain the significance of specific signs from a linguistic point of view. Sometimes, a given thought can be expressed in a number of ways, but such variations are left to the discretion of the teacher since no text can cover every possible way in which a specific thought might be expressed in a given language. A vocabulary review of glossed sign words and phrases follows the dialogue in each lesson and translation exercises are provided both for ASL>English and English>ASL practice. In addition, substitution drills and a list of suggested activities are provided for most lessons.

The purpose of the glossed introductory paragraph to each lesson is to provide the teacher with material for comprehension practice before the dialogues are studied. Students may not understand everything in the paragraph when it is first signed, but repeated exposure to this type of activity will enhance their comprehension skills over time. The dialogue sentences, the translation exercises, and the substitution drills should enable students to practice thinking in the target language, gradually developing proficiency in both comprehension and expression of ASL. The vocabulary review can serve as a checklist for the students to quickly find out their understanding and retention of the signs used in the lesson. And, finally, the suggested activities may be randomly used to provide real-life experience and practice in acquiring proficiency at the intermediate level.

At the end of the text are vocabularies of the glosses representing ASL signs and their English translations or equivalents to serve as a reference.

Whatever the purpose in using this book, it is hoped that students will come away with a clearer understanding of ASL and the community of deaf people who use it, and that they will want to continue studying the language and the culture surrounding it.

How to Use This Book

How the Signs Are Written in This Book

It is very difficult to write signs in a Sign Language book so that the reader knows exactly what the sign is and how it is made. A combination of pictures, words, and other symbols to represent signs on paper were chosen for this book. Since pictures take a lot of space and can sometimes be misleading, the words and symbols are also necessary.

Signs are written here with *glosses* and other printed symbols. *A gloss is an English word that represents the sign by naming it.* The same gloss is always used to represent the same sign, and the gloss is written in capital letters, for example, TRUE.

Usually, the English word chosen for the gloss of a sign is also one of the most frequent translations of that sign. For example, the sign TRUE can sometimes mean "true," or sometimes it can mean "real" or "sure." It may also have other translations, but the single word chosen to represent this sign is TRUE.

To keep this system simple, an effort was made to gloss each sign with a single English word, but this was not always possible. Sometimes there is no single English word that is adequate to name the sign and distinguish it from other signs that are similar in meaning or form. In these cases, several capitalized words, separated by hyphens, were used. For example, the sign TIME-PERIOD is different from the sign TIME. But the sign TIME-PERIOD is still just a single sign because there is no part of it that means just "time" and no part of it that means just "period." Another example of this is the sign NEW-YORK, which is also just a single sign; no part means just "new" and no part means just "York."

Other signs are glossed with more than one English word because they are *complex* signs, with many meaningful parts; each part has to be named. In these cases, other symbols are usually added to the basic gloss to show how it is made. These complex signs are generally a basic sign plus some modifications that change the meaning of the sign, or change how it can be used in a sentence. For example, the sign don't=KNOW is not a combination of the sign DON'T and the sign KNOW; rather, it is the sign KNOW made with an additional twisting movement that changes the meaning of the verb to a negative. Likewise, the sign we=TWO is the basic sign TWO, made with a directional movement that clearly specifies that it is about "you" and "me," or "we"; the sign WE is a separate sign that is not related. But both WE and we=TWO can be translated as "we".

In some cases, simply repeating the sign with small, abrupt movements can change a verb into a noun. These signs are always marked with the word "noun." For example, KNOW = noun + means "knowledge" and FLY = noun + means "airplane." The + sign shows repetition; the word "noun" in the gloss shows the grammatical result. In a few cases, these glosses may seem a bit peculiar. For example, American Sign Language has a sign that means "store" and the sign could have been called STORE to make things easy for the students. But one of the goals of this book is to draw attention to the relationships among different signs; therefore, this sign was written as SELL = noun +, since it is really a repeated form of the verb sign SELL. The same relationship is true of EAT (which means "eat") and EAT = noun + (which means "food").

The following key explains the method of using glosses (English words) to represent ASL signs. The students should spend a few minutes becoming familiar with the symbols in this table and how they are used to represent signs. The teacher will demonstrate the signed sentences. After a few lessons, students will probably be quite skilled in reading Sign sentences and will only have to refer to this key occasionally.

After some sentences in the lessons, there are brief grammatical notes. These notes explain

1. complex transcription symbols when they are used for the first time;

2. any large differences between the words of glosses and the words of translation;

3. the relationships (and differences) between signs to help prevent confusion or to present a larger pattern of how signs are made;

4. nuances of meanings to help in using the sign properly in conversation.

Key to Gloss Symbols

Gloss	Translation	Explanation
FATHER	"father"	Single sign.
EAT	"eat"	Single sign.
TIME-PERIOD	"period of time"	A hyphen (-) between all-CAP words shows that two or more words represent a single sign and a single unit of meaning.
LET'S-SEE	"we will see," "wait and see"	
KNOW+	"I know."	The plus sign (+) by itself shows that the sign is repeated once. A double plus sign (+ +) shows the sign is repeated two or more times. In the illustrations, we also use these symbols.
KNOW+ +	"I know about that."	
KNOW = noun +	"knowledge" or "familiarity"	A short, abrupt repetition of a verb will change it into a noun.
KNOW	"know"	*Italic type* shows that the sign is made with the nondominant hand—that is, the hand that usually does not move much when making signs. For a right-handed signer, the right hand is dominant and the left hand is nondominant.
TEACH	"teach"	
BLUE *RED* GREEN	"blue and red and green"	
KNOW$_2$	"know"	The symbol $_2$ indicates that the sign is made with both hands
KNOW$_A$	"know-it-all"	The symbol $_A$ indicates that the sign is made first with one hand, then with the other. These "alternating" signs are almost always repeated.
MANY$_1$, $\wedge$	"how much?"	The symbol $_1$ means a sign normally made with two hands is made with only one hand; compare with the sign that means "how many?" in the section explaining directional markers. The symbol $\wedge$—in this case—means the movement of the sign is directly upward.
"WHIFF"	"get a whiff of"	A nonstandard sign or mime-sign is shown in all-CAPS with quotation marks.
"PALM-SIZE"	"small" or "hand-sized"	

Gloss	Translation	Explanation
HELP = me	"help me" or "lend a hand"	*Complex signs* have more than one part, and each part has a meaning. Each part is labeled with a word, and the words are separated by equal signs (=). The principal part of each sign is capitalized, and the other parts that modify or change it in some way are printed in lower case letters, e.g., two = WEEK, which means "two weeks."
near = PAST	"recent past" or "very recently"	
she = GIVE = you	"she gave to you" or "she gives to you"	
two = WEEK	"two weeks"	
don't = KNOW	"don't know"	
we = TWO	"we" or "the two of us"	
KNOW = noun +	"knowledge" or "familiarity"	
EAT = noun +	"food"	
MOTHER‿FATHER	"parents"	A curve that joins the tops of two glosses (‿) shows a *compound* sign made of two or more single signs in *sequence;* the "pronunciation" and the meaning of these signed compounds are usually different from the two signs made separately. These will be explained in the grammatical notes. The first part of a compound sign usually has a very reduced movement.
MIND‿FREEZE	"shocked" or "speechless"	
COAT‿PANTS	"suit"	
KNOW	"I know!"	A sign printed in **boldface** type shows that its meaning is emphasized, usually by changing its movement. The exact changes will be explained in the grammatical notes.
FINISH	"stop that!" "that's enough!"	
		These symbols indicate a movement *added* to the sign or overlaid on the sign's basic movement.
MANY₂ ∧	"how many?"	*Upward* movement.
JOT-LIST ∨	"make a list of" or "a list"	*Downward* movement.
ASIDE >	"move or put out of the way"	Movement to signer's *right.*
ASIDE <	"move or put out of the way"	Movement to signer's *left.*
me = APPROACH = you ⊥	"I went up to you"	*Forward* movement, away from signer.
you = APPROACH = me ⊤	"you came up to me"	Movement *toward* signer.

Gloss	Translation	Explanation
this = SAME = that >	"these two are alike" or "this is just like that"	These glosses are directional; that is, the first part begins in one location and moves to the other according to the symbol used.
here < = NEXT-TURN = there >	"after this, then that" or "then"	
S-C-R-A-M-B-L-E	"scramble"	Letters separated by hyphens indicate fingerspelled words and abbreviations. Each letter represents a different fingerspelling handshape.
V-E-G	"vegetable"	
B-B-Q	"barbecue"	
R-X	"prescription"	
#DO +	"what will (we) do?"	A gloss preceded by a crosshatch (#) shows a fingerspelled word that is MADE LIKE A SIGN and that usually has a special meaning. These will be explained in the grammatical notes.
#IF + +	"if" or "suppose"	
EAT + ROOM	"dining room"	The curve joining the bottoms of two words (‿) means a slight blend or contraction of two signs. They are made so that they influence each other, but they do not have a special meaning. A part of one sign may still be visible while the second sign is beginning. Blends are *not* compounds. This symbol is only added as an additional clue to "pronouncing" signs fluidly and fluently.
WIRE T-T-Y	"call via a teletype machine"	
NEW DIFFERENT	"changing" or "completely different"	
BLUE *GREEN* RED	"blue and green and red"	

Explanation of Arrows and Symbols

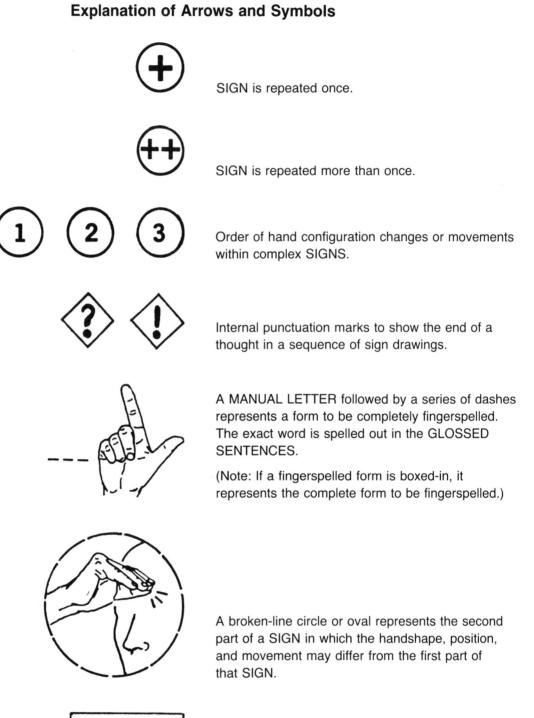

SIGN is repeated once.

SIGN is repeated more than once.

Order of hand configuration changes or movements within complex SIGNS.

Internal punctuation marks to show the end of a thought in a sequence of sign drawings.

A MANUAL LETTER followed by a series of dashes represents a form to be completely fingerspelled. The exact word is spelled out in the GLOSSED SENTENCES.

(Note: If a fingerspelled form is boxed-in, it represents the complete form to be fingerspelled.)

A broken-line circle or oval represents the second part of a SIGN in which the handshape, position, and movement may differ from the first part of that SIGN.

A boxed-in SIGN is used primarily to conserve space or to meet spatial requirements or limitations within an illustrated line. These are used only for commonly known signs for which body position is already known.

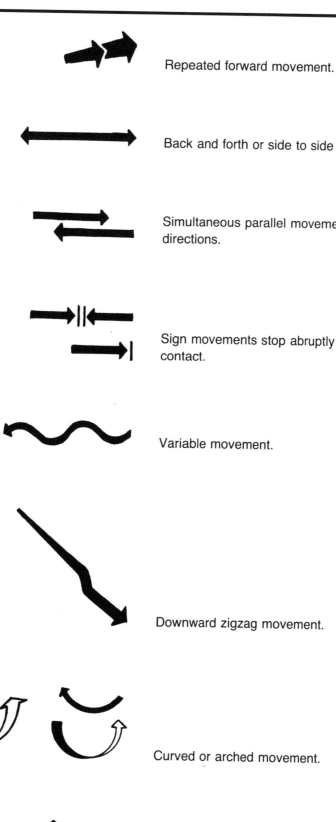

Repeated forward movement.

Back and forth or side to side movement.

Simultaneous parallel movement in opposite directions.

Sign movements stop abruptly short of actual contact.

Variable movement.

Downward zigzag movement.

Curved or arched movement.

Repeated upward curved or arched movement.

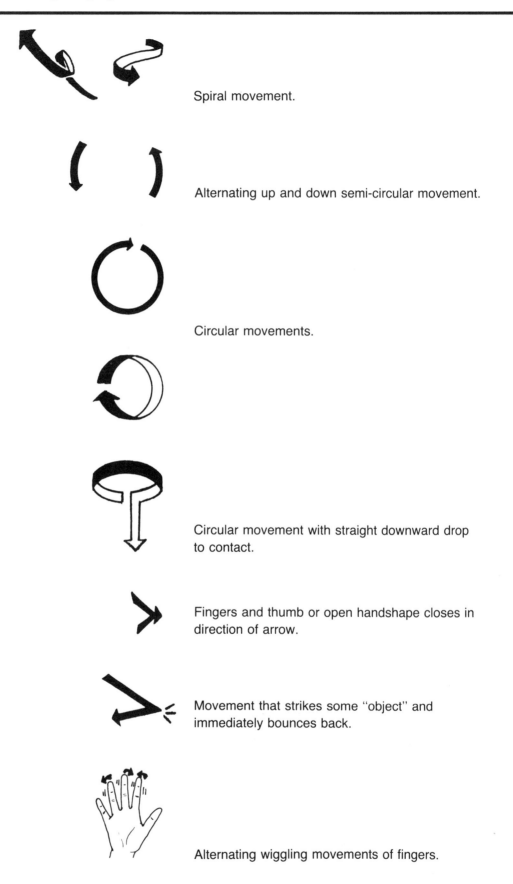

Spiral movement.

Alternating up and down semi-circular movement.

Circular movements.

Circular movement with straight downward drop to contact.

Fingers and thumb or open handshape closes in direction of arrow.

Movement that strikes some "object" and immediately bounces back.

Alternating wiggling movements of fingers.

Introduction to Characters

In this book, seven deaf characters have been created to represent some typical deaf people in a given community, in this case, the Washington, D.C., area. These characters are Benny, Gloria, Alexander, Jennifer, Lawrence, Jane, and Kee Kong. Any resemblance to actual people, either in name or in appearance in the illustrations, is purely coincidental.

Since this text is designed to help students of Sign Language, the characters portray deaf people and, thereby, something of the deaf culture that exists today. Deaf people do things much the same as do other groups in society, but some cultural differences do exist. They are found largely in language differences and in the fact that many deaf people are actually bilingual. Differences also exist in their general orientation to their surroundings, to the way they monitor their environment.

Here are the characters who appear again and again throughout the lessons.

Benny and Gloria Buetchel are exemplary of a successful, middle-aged, white, deaf couple, married 29 years with two grown children who are hearing. Like many such deaf people, Benny and Gloria are models for younger deaf people who see in them possibilities for successful lives also.

Alexander Armstrong is a young, single, black deaf man who is a successful mechanic. His girl friend, Jennifer Fowler, works as a keypunch operator. Alexander and Jennifer are good friends of Lawrence Larsen and Jane Bowman who are sweethearts and are engaged to be married. Jane lives next door to Alexander who often helps her when she has problems with her car. Jane works in a large insurance company office. Lawrence, her fiancé, is a draftsman who is also going to night school to improve his skills so he can obtain a better job.

Then there is Kee Kong, a young Oriental deaf woman in her early 20s. Kee is a commercial artist and shares an apartment with Jennifer. All these people are graduates of the Pine Ridge School for the Deaf (PRSD).

Because they live in the same community and share a common alma mater, they occasionally get together socially in either formal or informal settings. Each has a name sign from school days; however, like many deaf people their names are also sometimes fingerspelled for identification, and the student may wish to use fingerspelling from time to time for practice purposes.

In addition to these people, this text also includes Jimmy, the Buetchel's grandson (Lesson 15); a state police officer, the son of deaf parents (Lesson 16); and Barbara and Tom, a deaf couple from San Francisco who visit Benny and Gloria (Lesson 19).

Students will learn more about these people—their lives, their hopes, their dreams, their families, and their friends—as they journey through this book. Now, meet individually the seven main characters.

HI ! ME B-E-N-N-Y , BENNY ; WORK CARPENTER .

Hi, I'm Benny; I work as a carpenter.

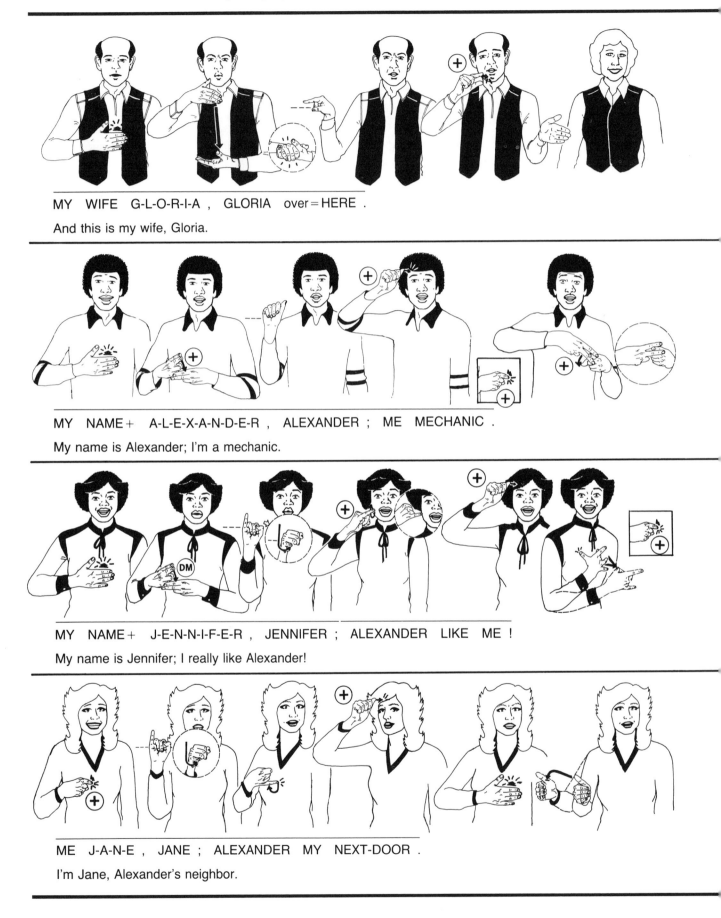

MY WIFE G-L-O-R-I-A , GLORIA over=HERE .

And this is my wife, Gloria.

MY NAME+ A-L-E-X-A-N-D-E-R , ALEXANDER ; ME MECHANIC .

My name is Alexander; I'm a mechanic.

MY NAME+ J-E-N-N-I-F-E-R , JENNIFER ; ALEXANDER LIKE ME !

My name is Jennifer; I really like Alexander!

ME J-A-N-E , JANE ; ALEXANDER MY NEXT-DOOR .

I'm Jane, Alexander's neighbor.

ME L-A-W-R-E-N-C-E , LAWRENCE ; JANE MY SWEETHEART !

I'm Lawrence; Jane is my sweetheart!

ME K-E-E K-O-N-G , KEE-KONG ; WORK C-O-M-M-E-R-C-I-A-L ART+ .

I am Kee Kong; I work as a commercial artist.

Hints to the Student

If you have difficulty in translating an English sentence, try paraphrasing it or writing a different version of it which will retain the original meaning. Then try translating the new version of this sentence.

For example, you might come across a translation exercise with the sentence, "How much money did you spend on groceries last week?" You say to yourself, "But I don't know what the sign for *groceries* is. I can't translate the sentence."

In this case, paraphrase the sentence. For example, "How much money did you spend on *food* last week?" means the same thing, and you *do* know the sign for *groceries*.

It will be helpful for you to learn to think in terms of basic concepts because ASL is a visual-gestural language that contains many conceptually based signs, like the example above with *food* and *groceries*. Such words are related to the basic sign concept of EAT; in exploring further, we find ASL signs meaning *breakfast, lunch, dinner, meal*, and *banquet* are also conceptually related to this one sign.

You may also occasionally experience difficulty or confusion over certain sign variations. It is important to become acquainted with the transcription symbols which will help you overcome some of this confusion. For example, take the following glosses: COST, COST+, and **COST.** The first gloss may mean "cost," "price," "fee"; the second, because it is repeated, may mean "being charged over and over," but it also may mean "taxes" and the meaning may be derived from contextual clues; the third gloss is the emphatic form and it usually means an arbitrary charge or a "fine." There is another sign that may sometimes mean "cost" or "price" and that is WORTH. Variations such as these usually have to be memorized. A simple rule is just to remember that in ASL, as in any other language, you will find variations which must be learned according to usage.

These suggestions are only intended to serve as a general guide to the kinds of situations you will encounter in this book from time to time.

Review of Fingerspelling Problems

Students invariably express frustrations and anxieties when it comes to reading fingerspelling. Sometimes these feelings lead to the formation of a kind of mental block in some individuals. Trying to learn to read fingerspelling becomes a painful experience for them. What can be done to help avoid or alleviate such problems? For one thing, being aware of the basic guidelines for fingerspelling and reading fingerspelling should help.

First and foremost of the guidelines are hand position and palm orientation in fingerspelling. The palm of the fingerspeller or communicator should always face outward. It is important also that the hand be positioned just below chin level or at shoulder level so that facial information is not blocked. The arm should remain stationary while the fingers execute a spelled word. If the fingerspeller is right-handed, movement will naturally be from left to right, and from right to left if left-handed. The arm and hand should be in a comfortable position.

Fluency and rate are also significant factors for the fingerspeller and the receiver or "listener." Fingerspelling should be done smoothly and at a rate of speed that is neither too slow nor too fast for comfortable expression or reception. It is important to maintain an even, steady pace. Words should never be fingerspelled at an extremely slow pace, even to a beginner. Such practice will only create more problems for the receiver in the long run. In using fingerspelling drills, the material should be presented at a normal pace. If it is not understood on the first try, it should be repeated at a slightly slower pace. If the material is still not understood, it should be tried a third time at a slightly slower pace. More repetitions than that are not recommended because they actually become a crutch, and the aim in receptive fingerspelling skills should be to challenge the receiver consistently. With practice it should not be necessary to repeat material more than once, if at all.

When fingerspelling, avoid mouthing of letters. Practice instead mouthing and fingerspelling syllables simultaneously. If done regularly, this will make fingerspelling more readable, and the receiver should begin to recognize fingerspelled words by their shape. The listener or receiver should focus on the face of the person communicating, not on the hands. The eyes will then receive important cues from the facial expressions and non-manual behaviorisms of the fingerspeller which aid in comprehension of the total message. If the person communicating does not mouth the syllables or words being fingerspelled, some attention must be given to the hand movements. However, the receiver should never focus solely on the fingerspeller's hands.

It is essential for the communicator to maintain firm, almost stiff, control of the hand and fingers, allowing crisp, clear finger movements in a slight left to right hand movement, somewhat similar to hand movements in writing. Other factors to be aware of are separation of words fingerspelled in sequence and the inclusion of all letters in a fingerspelled word. In fingerspelling two or more words in sequence, minute pauses are necessary so that the words are clearly distinguishable as individual words and not as run-ons or single words. Except for fingerspelled loan signs (which are identifiable in this text such as #JOB, #DO, #LUCK), all letters in a word must be clear. Occasionally, the communicator or fingerspeller may "stutter" or omit a letter. This is as natural as slips of the tongue in speaking, which do not interfere with complete understanding of the message. It is only when this is done repeatedly that problems are created for the receiver. Above all, avoid bouncy or jerky hand movements by keeping the arm steady. Sometimes it helps to grasp the dominant arm just below the wrist to hold it steady. Experienced fingerspellers do this as a technique that will force them to slow down a bit for emphasis.

Visual memory exercises or drills in real or nonsensical combinations are helpful in the development of receptive fingerspelling skills. In the American Manual Alphabet, letter handshapes vary from closed, to open vertical, to open horizontal, to open inverted forms. Becoming familiar with these will enable the receiver eventually to understand what is fingerspelled through the visual picture a complete fingerspelled word represents.

Closed letters: A, E, O, M, N, S, T
Open vertical letters: B, D, F, I, K, L, R, U, W, X
Open horizontal letters: G, H
Open inverted letters: P, Q

While material presented out of context is more difficult to receive, it is necessary for classroom drill to focus on simple elements in the basic and perhaps early intermediate levels. Drills can be based on material grouped by syllable count, i.e., one-syllable words, then two-syllable words, and on to three- and four-syllable words. Proper names—names of well-known personalities, large cities, major rivers, local communities, and the like—also make good drill practice material. It is helpful to master reading single items, but occasionally students should work with two- or three-word phrases until some proficiency is obvious. Only through regular practice with various drills will students develop fingerspelling receptive skills.

Students must also recognize that most fingerspelling normally occurs as part of a larger signed context. At the intermediate level, they should eventually arrive at the point where such fingerspelling activities happen regularly. Contextual clues play a large part in understanding the overall thought expressed. That is why, in the suggested activities in each lesson, students are asked to use random selections from the sentences in the English to ASL translation exercises for fingerspelling practice.

When fingerspelling is used along with signing, it is helpful to provide the receiver with some visual cue to indicate that fingerspelling is going to occur. A quick glance by the communicator toward his or her hand is sufficient. The eyes should immediately move back toward the listener so that eye contact is not lost. This kind of cueing is most beneficial when a complex word or a proper name is about to be introduced. It is helpful, too, to slow down finger movements to a steady, even pace until the complete word is fingerspelled.

Remember that by regular practice through short-term drills, students will develop proficiency in both expressive and receptive fingerspelling.

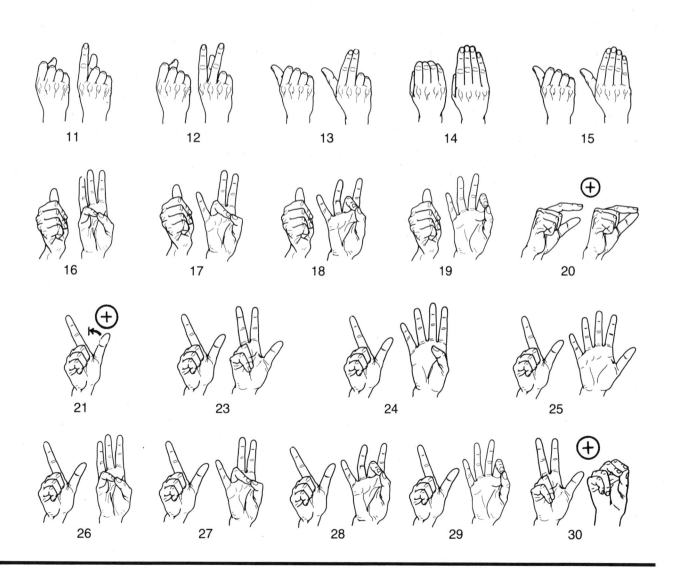

Double digits are formed simply by moving the number from left to right in a gentle arc. The numbers, 66, 77, 88, and 99 require a short, quick break between the digits for clarity.

In signing numbers, such as the ones illustrated here, it is important to follow one simple "rule" for clarity, that is, to avoid confusing numbers which might look alike from a distance. The "rule" is when the *smaller* digit is first, the hand position is slightly downward to the right and it moves up left to the larger digit. Conversely, when the *larger* digit is first, the hand position is straight up and it drops down slightly to the right as it forms the second or smaller digit.

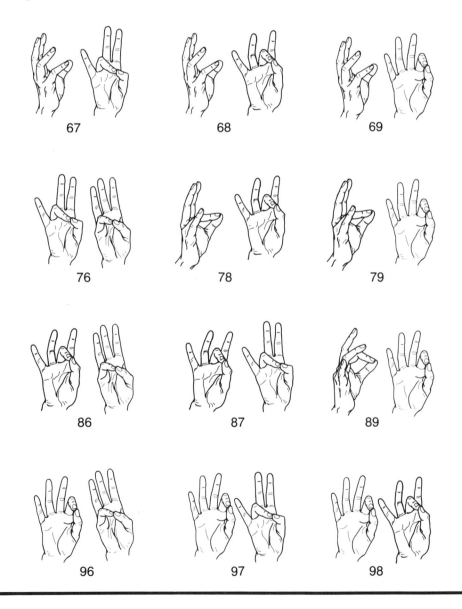

The hundreds are generally formed with the number of hundreds, followed rapidly by the "C" handshape. Learn the abbreviated form as well as the more formal one. The abbreviated form is generally used in everyday conversations, the formal one before audiences where distance may require concise clarity.

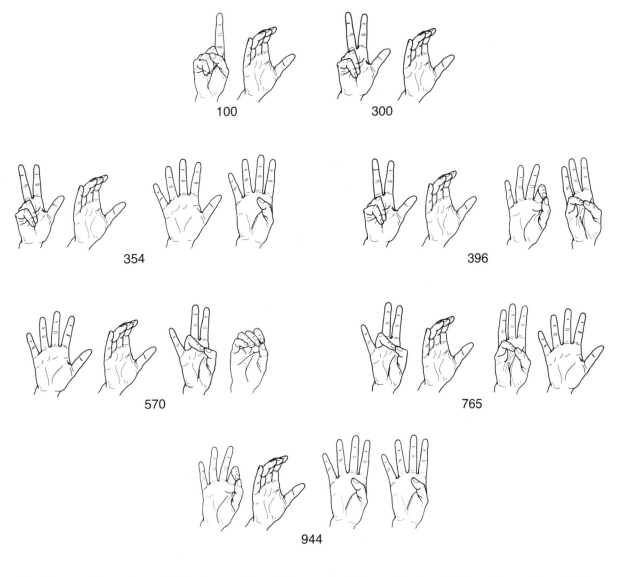

100   300

354   396

570   765

944

The thousands are formed with the number of thousands, followed by the "M" handshape brought down against the opposite palm, fingertips touching palm.

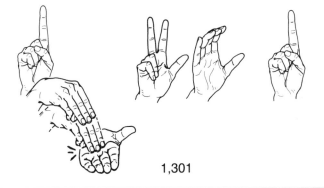

1,301

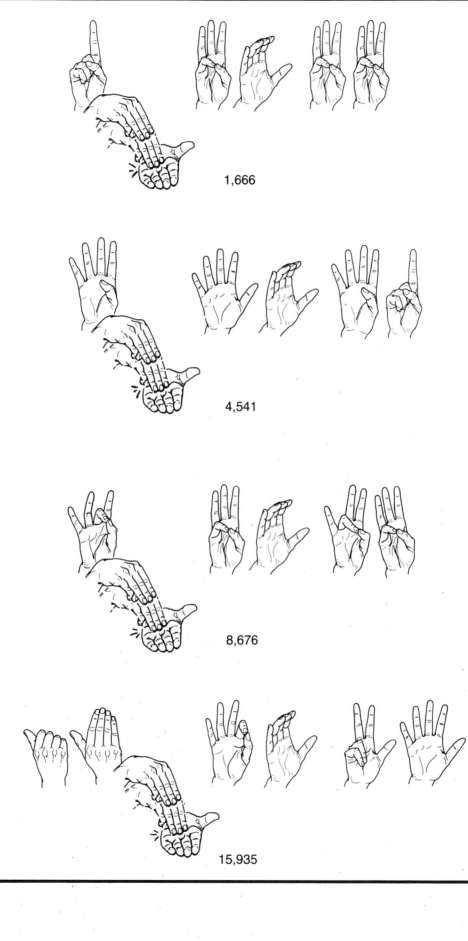

1,666

4,541

8,676

15,935

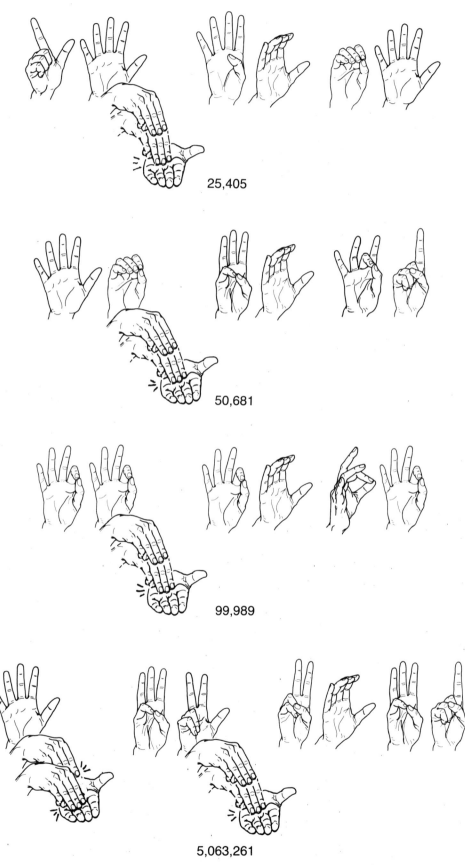

25,405

50,681

99,989

5,063,261

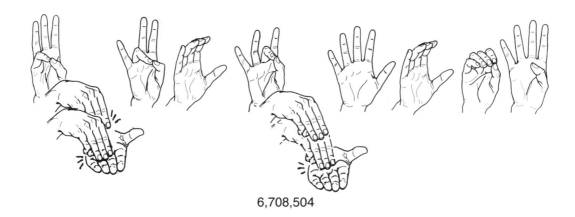

6,708,504

Percentages are formed by using the number needed, followed by an oval handshape, made by tips of fingers and thumb touching and moved in the same way the percentage symbol would be written.

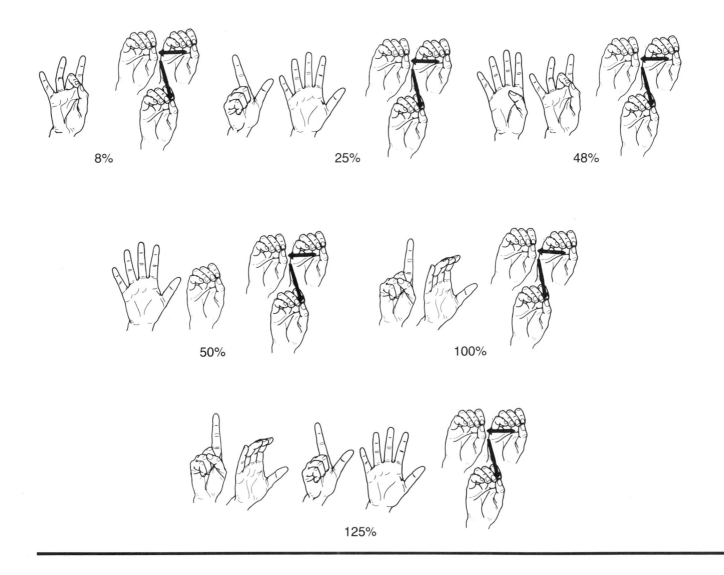

8%   25%   48%

50%   100%

125%

Time signs are generally prefaced by an abbreviated form of TIME, followed by hour. Numbers are signed the same way in which they are spoken.

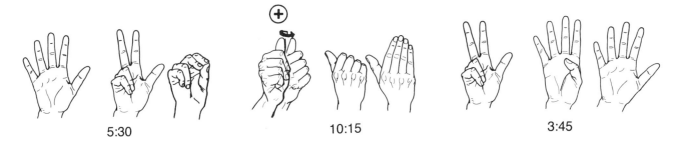

5:30   10:15   3:45

Signs representing years are likewise formed in the same manner in which they are spoken.

1492   1776

1813   2001

Street numbers or house numbers are generally signed in the same manner in which people normally say them when speaking.

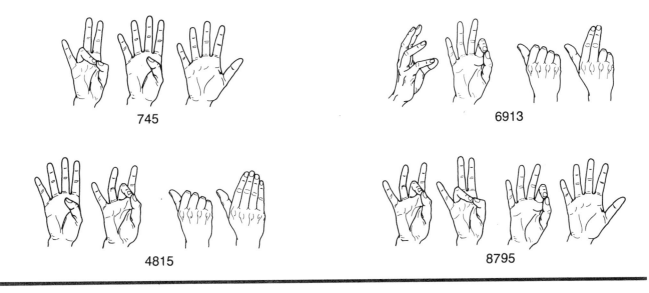

745   6913

4815   8795

Telephone numbers, like street or house numbers, are also signed the same way in which they are spoken.

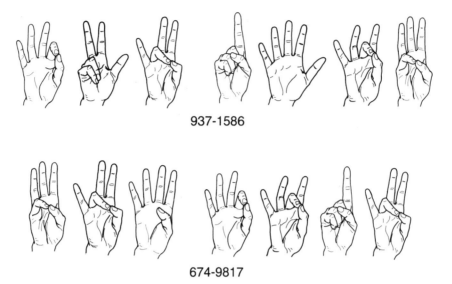

937-1586

674-9817

Fractions are formed by signing the numerator and then dropping the hand downward while signing the denominator.

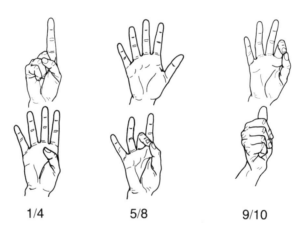

1/4   5/8   9/10

The sign TWICE is made by sweeping the tip of the middle finger down against the opposite palm in a twisting motion. ONCE, THRICE, FOUR-TIMES, and FIVE-TIMES would be signed likewise with the last finger making the contact.

TWICE/TWO TIMES

Dollars and cents may be formed in one of two ways: (1) for denominations one through nine, a sharp twist of the hand indicates "dollars," followed by whatever amount of "cents" is to be given; (2) for all denominations, one may indicate the number followed by a period followed by whatever number is needed for "cents." The latter is useful when money is clearly the subject. DOLLAR and CENTS are signed only when there is need for clearly stating such.

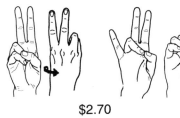

$2.70

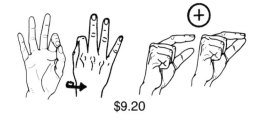

$9.20

$196.79

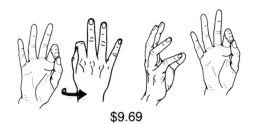

$9.69

Numbers and Counting

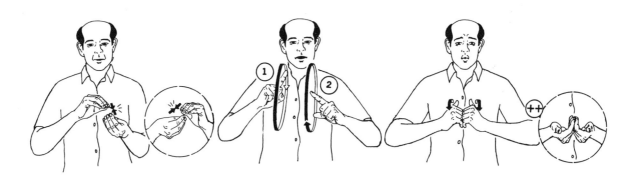

NUMBER   SIGN   HOW+ + ?

COUNT+   NUMBER SOMETIME PROBLEM LEARNER THEIR=around . FEW SAME
FINGERSPELLING . SHOW SOMEONE SIGN YEAR , SIGN CLEAR 19>30 **NEED** . SIGN
1-9-3-0 CAN'T , WRONG+ . #IF+ + NUMBER CLEAR SIGN , EASY READ=*my-finger*+
WANT YOU , PRACTICE+ REQUIRE . FRIEND ADDRESS HIS+ GIVE₂ WANT+ , NUMBER
"SPELL-OUT" SAME+ 6-1-1-7 OR SIGN CAN 61>17 , PLUS STREET NAME+ ITS+
"SPELL-OUT" . #IF+ + STORY-TALK IDEA SAME 25 DOLLAR AND FIFTEEN CENT , SIGN
25 DOLLAR AND FIFTEEN CENT **DON'T** ! BETTER SIGN 25 PERIOD 15 ENOUGH .
IMPORTANT LEARN+ NUMBER SIGN SAME 2-0-0 , 3-0-0 . EVERYDAY DEAF SIGN 2-C ,
3-C NOT ! TEND DEAF FAST SIGN "200" , "300" up=LIMIT "500" . WATCH DEAF
NEED , WILL "OH-I-SEE" . POINT OTHER : NUMBER SAME F-I-R-S-T , S-E-C-O-N-D ,
VARIOUS DEPEND MEAN "WHAT" , RACE , LIST . REMEMBER PRACTICE+ + SMOOTH
WILL YOU !

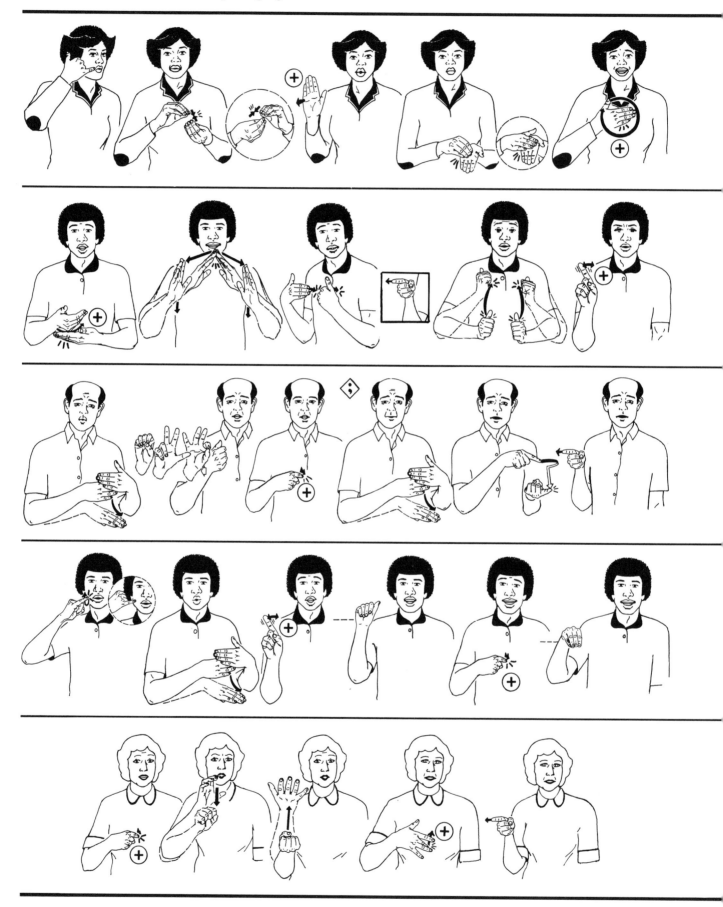

Glossed Sentences, Translations, and Grammatical Notes

1. TELEPHONE   NUMBER   YOUR+   JOT-DOWN   PLEASE+ .

Please write down your telephone number.

A possessive sign usually is repeated in a request or a command. JOT-DOWN may also be translated as "put down" or "jot down."

2. NEW+   HOUSE   HAVE   YOU .   ADDRESS   WHERE ?

You have a new house, right? What's the address?

HAVE YOU after NEW+ HOUSE indicates acknowledgment of the fact before asking where the house is. WHERE is the appropriate sign because the question is about location or place.

3. BORN   19>30   ME+ .   BORN   WHEN   YOU ?

I was born in 1930; when were you born?

ME+ is repeated but YOU is not because it ends a question.

4. SHE=jennifer   BORN   WHERE   A-L-A-B-A-M-A ;   ME+   M-I-S-S-I-S-S-I-P-P-I .

Jennifer was born in Alabama; I was born in Mississippi.

Name signs in ASL are generally used only when the person named is not present. If present, the signer indicates the person by pointing, and we would write the sign SHE=jennifer (the pointing is the sign SHE; the direction of the point gives the information "jennifer"). Even if a person is not present, he or she can be given a location in space instead of being named.

5. ME+   OLD   MANY, ∧ ,   FEEL+   YOU ?

Guess how old I am!

The sign FEEL, translated into "guess," represents an estimate or guess based on subjective judgment or feelings.

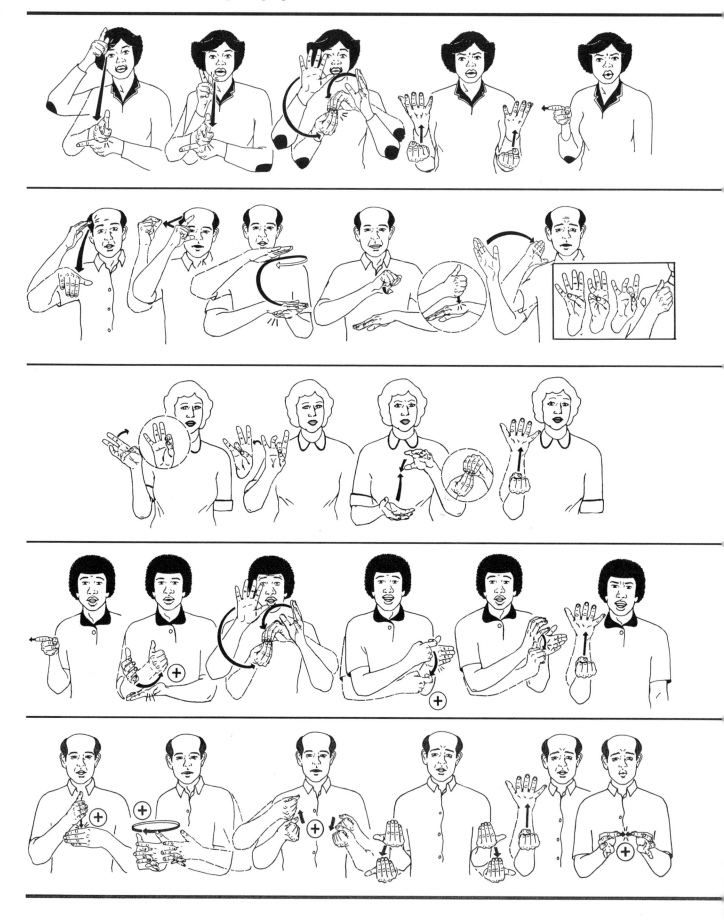

6. BROTHER , SISTER ALTOGETHER MANY₂ ∧ YOU ?

How many brothers and sisters do you have in all?

7. KNOW‿THAT GALLAUDET UNIVERSITY ESTABLISH **LONG-AGO** 18>64 ?

Did you know that Gallaudet University was founded way back in 1864?

There are no tense markers in ASL; past and present are indicated by context or by specific time signs. KNOW‿THAT is blended so closely that the handshape does not visibly change into the usual hand configuration for THAT. The emphatic form **LONG-AGO** is produced with a slow, deliberate backward movement past one's head.

8. 69 , 87 ADD-UP MANY₁ ∧ ?

What is the sum of 69 and 87?

ADD-UP could also be translated as "total" or "sum."

9. YOU EARN+ ALTOGETHER , COST+ SUBTRACT MANY₁ ∧ ?

How much of your income is withheld in taxes?

EARN+ repeated may mean "earnings" as well as "income." COST, by itself, may mean "cost," "price," or "charge." In repeated form, it may be translated as "taxes." SUBTRACT is translated as "withheld" because of the context in which it is used.

10. AVERAGE AMERICAN CAR NOW MANY₁ ∧ WORTH ?

How much does the average American car cost now?

11. Z-I-P C-O-D-E ITS S-F+ KNOW+ YOU ?

Do you know the zip code for San Francisco?

ITS is the possessive sign used here to establish reference to place rather than to person as in sentence 1.

12. SUPPOSE 65 DOLLAR WALLET‿IN HAVE YOU ;

Let's say you have $65.00 in your wallet;

SUPPOSE is like the sign IMAGINE, but the movements are very short and repeated. This sign could also be translated literally as "suppose" or as "if," as well as "let's say." WALLET‿IN is blended; only the dominant hand moves after referent is established.

38.35 SPEND FOR GIFT$_2$, LEFT MANY$_1$ $\wedge$?

you spend $38.35 for a gift. How much will you have left?

The decimal point in the figure, 38.35, is signed "point" or "period" to separate dollars from cents.

13. 25 DOLLAR OWE=her=jane JANE ; PAY=her=jane **FINISH$_2$** ME !

I have paid Jane back the $25.00 I owed her!

PAY=her indicates sign is made towards another person, whom the signer has already "established" in a position in space. The emphatic form **FINISH$_2$** is produced with a firm, but not vigorous, single movement.

14. STRIKE-CHANCE ONE THOUSAND DOLLAR , **#DO**+ THINK YOU ?

If you won $1,000 by a lucky chance, what do you think you would do with it?

#DO is a fingerspelled form which has become a common sign: the letters are closely blended, the movement is repeated, and the meaning is restricted to "what (would you) do?"

Vocabulary Review

Test your ability to produce the following signs or sign phrases.

ADDRESS	HOW + +	"SPELL-OUT"
ADD-UP	#IF + +	SPEND₂
ALTOGETHER **MANY₂** ∧	IMPORTANT	STORY-TALK
AVERAGE	JOT-DOWN	STRIKE-CHANCE
COST +	KNOW THAT	SUBTRACT
COUNT +	up = LIMIT	SUPPOSE
DEAF	LIST	TELEPHONE NUMBER
DEPEND	**LONG-AGO**	TEND
#DO +	"OH-I-SEE"	VARIOUS
DOLLAR	OLD MANY₁ ∧	WALLET
EARN +	OWE = her/him	WANT +
ESTABLISH	PAY = her/him	WANT YOU
EVERYDAY	RACE	WHAT ?
FINGERSPELL	READ = my-finger +	"WHAT"
GALLAUDET COLLEGE	REQUIRE	WORTH MANY₁ ∧
GIFT₂	SMOOTH	WRONG +

Notes

Translation Exercises—ASL to English

Translate the following glossed sentences into appropriate English equivalents.

1. BROTHER+ MY+ ALTOGETHER SIX ; SISTER+ THREE .
2. BROTHER , SISTER ALTOGETHER MANY$_2$ ∧ YOU ?
3. COLOR TV AVERAGE NOW WORTH MANY$_1$ ∧ ?
4. 3/16 , 5/8 ADD-UP MANY$_1$ ∧ ?
5. SIT-DOWN=opposite$_2$ "SPELL-OUT"=each-other$_2$ NUMBER PRACTICE we=TWO , O-K ?
6. NEW+ ADDRESS YOUR+ JOT-DOWN PLEASE+ .
7. "SPELL-OUT"=me TELEPHONE NUMBER YOUR+ .
8. SUPPOSE+ 300 CHICKEN HAVE YOU ; SELL FINISH$_2$ 228 , LEAVE+ MANY$_2$ ∧ ?
9. Z-I-P C-O-D-E YOUR+ "SPELL OUT"=me AGAIN PLEASE , FORGET ME !
10. 45 DOLLAR WALLET IN HAVE ME ; EAT=noun+ SPEND$_2$ ALTOGETHER 42.58 . MONEY LEAVE SMALL+ !
11. #IF++ L-O-T-T-E-R-Y STRIKE-CHANCE 500 DOLLAR+ , #DO+ YOU ?
12. 439 SUBTRACT 278 MANY$_1$ ∧ ?

Translation Exercises—English to ASL

Translate the following sentences from English into ASL equivalents.

1. Where were you born?
2. My wife won $100 by a lucky chance playing bingo!
3. How much does the average house cost in this area?
4. Suppose you lost $25.00, what would you do?
5. Can you read my fingerspelling?
6. This book cost $15.95; that book was $12.50.
7. How much do I owe you?
8. How many classes are you taking now?
9. Please write down your address and phone number.
10. The zip code for my hometown is 20801.
11. What is the sum of 48 and 67?
12. You must practice your numbers and counting.

Single-Slot Substitution Drills

Practice signing the following target sentences, substituting the suggested vocabulary in each slot. If you have problems with any of the vocabulary, consult your instructor for help.

1. BOOK   COST   MANY$_1$ $\wedge$?   <u>$12.95</u> .

                       3.45

                    15.75

                    21.50

                    10.95

                    12.95

2. EAT=noun+   BUY+   SPEND   ALTOGETHER   <u>$38.27</u> .

                                      71.03

                                      64.48

                                    15.63

                                107.12

                                    38.27

3. <u>$25.00</u>   OWE=him   B-O-B ,   PAY=him   **FINISH$_1$**   ME !

   5.00

   1.00

   4.50

  15.00

   6.00

 25.00

4. ME+   BORN   WHERE ,   <u>K-A-N-S-A-S</u> .

                         CALIFORNIA

                         A-R-K-A-N-S-A-S

                         NEW-YORK

                         TEXAS

                         K-A-N-S-A-S

5. <u>BROTHER</u>   ALTOGETHER   MANY$_2$ $\wedge$ YOU ?

  SISTER

  CHILDREN

  COUSIN

  NIECE

  BROTHER

6. <u>TELEPHONE NUMBER</u> JOT-DOWN PLEASE .

ADDRESS

LICENSE NUMBER

Z-I-P C-O-D-E

NAME +

WORK WHERE

TELEPHONE NUMBER

7. RACE HORSE MY + <u>FIRST = place</u> .

                    THIRD = place

                    FOURTH = place

                    SECOND = place

                    LAST = place

                    FIRST = place

8. MONEY <u>EARN</u> ALTOGETHER , MANY$_1$ ∧ YOU ?

        SPEND

        LOSE

        FIND

        SAVE

        HAVE

        EARN

9. NEW CAR MANY$_1$ ∧ WORTH ? <u>$8,295</u> WHEW !

                    4,995

                    6,575

                    10,695

                    12,849

                    25,450

                    8,295

10. STRIKE-CHANCE <u>$1,000</u> , #DO + YOU ?

                5,000

                10,000

                50,000

              100,000

            1,000,000

                1,000

Suggested Activities

1. Make up a short paragraph about your family, tracing your background and including numerical information on birthdates, numbers of brothers and sisters, sons and daughters, etc. Bring this paragraph to class to share with other members of the class.

2. Pair off in class and ask your partner questions which will require numerical responses, e.g.,
   BORN   WHEN   YOU ?
   OLD   MANY$_1$ $\wedge$ YOU ?
   TELEPHONE   NUMBER   YOUR+   "WHAT" ?
   HOME   YOUR+   ADDRESS   WHERE ?
   BROTHER ,   SISTER   ALTOGETHER   MANY$_2$ $\wedge$ YOU ?
   GALLAUDET   UNIVERSITY   ESTABLISH   LONG-AGO ,   "WHEN" ,   KNOW   YOU ?
   (Additional questions can be made up and added to the list for more number practice.)

3. Each student may bring to class sentences patterned after sentences 8, 12, 13, and 14, substituting other numbers or figures for those given. Use these substitutes in pairing-off exercises or small-group practice.

4. For additional receptive practice with numbers, have a deaf person from a local organization of the deaf visit your class and give a treasurer's report from his/her organization.

5. For fingerspelling practice, you may use some of the sentences or selected phrases from the sentences in the English to ASL translation exercises in this lesson. Pair off in class. Partners may then take turns randomly selecting two or three sentences or phrases to fingerspell to each other while the instructor observes.

Supermarket Blues

EAT = noun +   BUY +   head = PAIN

EAT = noun +   BUY +   head = PAIN   ALWAYS   WHY + +   MONEY   WORTH   UP   DOWN !   SAVE
MONEY +   WANT   YOU ,   **NEED**   LOOK-AT + + >   ADVERTISE = noun +   EAT = noun +   ITS + ;   SEE
FIND   EAT = noun +   MONEY   REDUCE ,   CUT = coupon + .   SUPPOSE +   ENTER   LARGE
SELL = noun +   EAT = noun +   ITS ,   NEED +   TIME   ENOUGH   LOOK-AT = around$_2$ MEAT ,   NEW
V-E-G ,   EAT = noun +   ITS   tin = CAN + + > .   WHAT-FOR ,   LET'S-SEE   BEST   VALUE   MONEY
ITS   WHICH .   SOMETIMES   EXAGGERATE   TIME +   LOOK-AT + + ,   SEARCH ,   STRIKE-CHANCE
CORRECT   EAT = noun + .   TRUE   WISE +   JOT = list   EAT = noun +   NEED +   BEFORE   GO-OUT
SELL = noun +   WHY + +   SAVE   TIME + .   SAME   WISE   SMALL   "PALM-SIZE"   CALCULATOR
BRING ⊥   WHAT-FOR   COUNT +   ALTOGETHER   MANY,∧   PAY   **NEED** .   AVOID   GO
LINE = forward$_2$ EAT = noun +   PAY   SHOCK   TOO-MUCH .   TRUE   WORTH   LOOK-AT$_2$
ADVERTISE = noun +   EAT = noun +   ITS   MONEY   REDUCE   PLUS   CUT = coupon + +   HELP = you
MONEY   **SAVE** !

Glossed Sentences, Translations, and Grammatical Notes

1. near = RECENT   WIRE = her͜ T-T-Y   JENNIFER ,   ME   ASK = her = jennifer   COME = here ,

   I just called Jennifer on the TTY to ask her to come over.

   The blended signs WIRE͜ T-T-Y represent the way in which deaf people make telephone calls with telecommunication devices, such as teletypewriters (TTYs) or other keyboard and display machines. ASK = her is a directional verb directed towards Jennifer's location in space.

   WHAT-FOR ,   we = TWO   GO-OUT   EAT = noun +   BUY + .

   Why? So the two of us could go shopping for groceries.

   The sign WHAT-FOR is actually the sign FOR made with a short, rapidly repeated movement. It is translatable either as "what for?" or "why?" we = TWO is a complex directional sign; the sign TWO is moved back and forth between signer and the second party. The sign BUY + may represent "shopping" or "buying" while EAT = noun + represents the noun form of "eat," which is "food."

2. HI !   READY   NOW   GO-OUT   EAT = noun +   BUY + ?

   Hi, Jane! Are you ready to go shopping for food now?

   HI! in translation becomes "Hi, Jane!" because Sign Language uses name signs only in the absence of the person indicated.

3. YES ,   JOT = list   NEED +   BUY +   FINISH₁ +   ME .

   Yes, and I have made a shopping list of what I need.

   JOT = list is another form of JOT-DOWN; the downward movement represents "making a list." FINISH₁ + indicates some action completed and is, therefore, equivalent to the perfect tense form in English.

4. **me = SAME = you₂** !   BUY   HEAP₂   **NEED**   ME   WHY + + ,

   Me, too! I have to buy a lot of food because

   me = SAME = you₂ moves between the signer and the other person. This sign is also sometimes made with one hand. HEAP₂ can be translatable as "a lot of," "a pile of," or "a stack of," depending upon context. WHY + + is used as a connective, which we translate as "because."

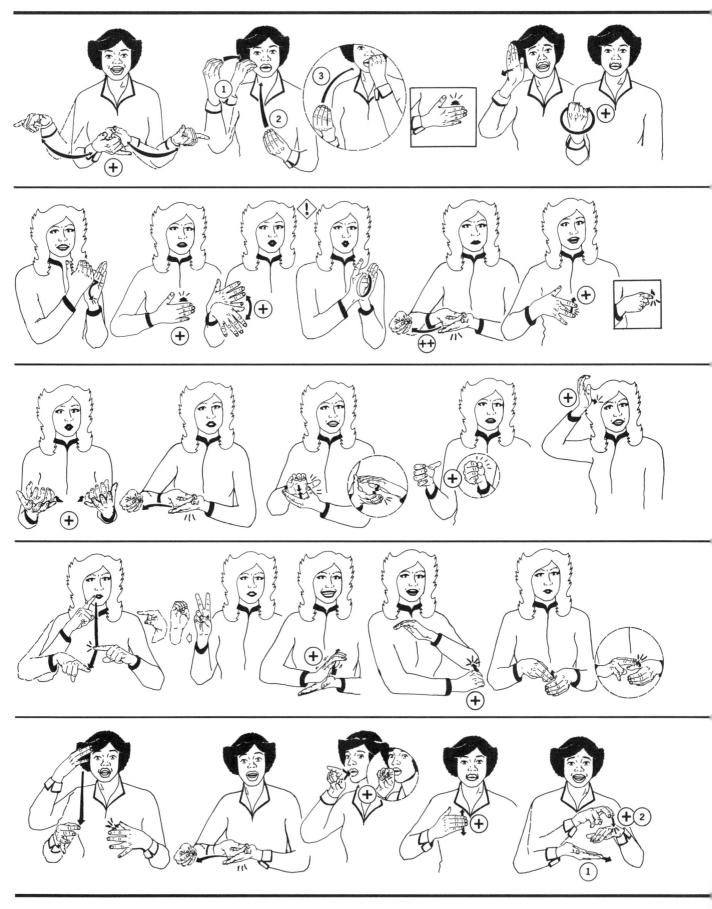

PARTY EAT_A MY+ WILL‿SATURDAY .

of that dinner party of mine this Saturday.

WILL‿SATURDAY is a blend that may be translated as "this Saturday" or "next Saturday."

---

5. LIST MY+ WHEW ! **one=HOUR** BUY++ FEEL+ ME .

My list is rather long! I feel it will take a good hour to shop.

WHEW is often used to indicate an exclamation or to emphasize one. It is also translatable in some contexts as "very," "very much," or as the "super"-superlative form of a word.

WANT+ BUY HAMBURGER , MILK , LETTUCE ,

I want to buy hamburger, milk, lettuce,

TOMATO , V-E-G , CHEESE , CRACKER , MUSTARD .

tomatoes, vegetables, cheese, crackers, and mustard.

MUSTARD is an old sign, rarely seen in the U.S. now, but still quite commonly used in European countries.

---

6. DECIDE BUY CHICKEN BREAST , PUT-IN-OVEN‿POTATO .

I've decided to buy chicken breasts and baking potatoes.

WHISKEY SELL=noun+ GO CAN we=TWO ?

Can we also go to the liquor store?

WHISKEY is translatable as "whiskey," "liquor," and sometimes other hard-liquor beverages; "beer" and "wine" have their own signs. When repeated, SELL is translated as "store," or "a place where things are sold."

KEE-KONG TELL=me PLEASE BOTTLE WINE BUY .

Kee Kong told me to please buy a bottle of wine.

TELL=me is made in the direction of the signer.

7. FINE ! WINE FRENCH ITS BUY ME⌣WANT .

That's fine with me! I want to get some French wine.

In ME⌣WANT, ME is blended so well into the next sign, WANT, that a separate handshape with the index finger pointing toward the subject is not really visible.

8. WORRY ME MONEY MANY$_1$ $\wedge$ SPEND$_2$;

I'm worried about how much money I'll spend;

SPEND, made with two hands, has the meaning of "lots of spending" in this sentence. Degree of emphasis with which the sign is made can vary the connotation.

SMALL "PALM-SIZE" CALCULATOR FORGET BRING , "NO-NO" .

don't forget to bring your small pocket calculator.

"PALM-SIZE" is a mime sign used to describe a small calculator which ordinarily fits into the palm or hand. FORGET must be accompanied by a clear and firm negative headshake. "NO-NO" represents the common negative gesture of waving one's index finger to indicate that something is not desired or is "taboo."

Vocabulary Review

Test your ability to produce the following signs or sign phrases.

ADVERTISE = noun +

AVOID

BOTTLE

BUY +

tin = CAN + +

CHEESE

CHICKEN BREAST

CRACKER

CUT = coupon

EAT = noun +

FRANCE

GO-OUT

HAMBURGER

HEAP$_2$

one = HOUR

JOT = list V

LET'S-SEE

LETTUCE

LINE = forward$_2$

LOOK-AT = around$_2$

ME WANT

MUSTARD

NEED +

NEED

"NO-NO"

NOW DAY

head = PAIN

"PALM-SIZE" CALCULATOR

PUT-IN-OVEN POTATO

READY< >

near = RECENT

me = SAME = you$_2$

SELL = noun +

SHOCK

SHRIMP

SMALL

TOMATO

TOO-MUCH

we = TWO

UP DOWN +

WHAT-FOR ?

WHISKEY/LIQUOR

WILL SATURDAY

WINE

WIRE = her T-T-Y

WISE +

Notes

Translation Exercises—ASL to English

Translate the following glossed sentences into appropriate English equivalents.

1. EAT = noun + NEED + JOT = list FINISH, YOU ?
2. NO , LATE . TIME + NONE$_2$; BUSY all = MORNING !
3. WIRE = me T-T-Y WILL SATURDAY YOU ; you = WITH = me BUY + + we = TWO , O-K ?
4. SATURDAY all = DAY BOWLING TOURNAMENT ; me = WITH = you BUY + CAN'T ME .
5. SMALL "PALM-SIZE" CALCULATOR YOUR + , BORROW ME ?
6. NOW WEEK CUT = coupon **GOOD** ; MONEY **SAVE** WHEW !
7. CUT = coupon SEARCH + EXAGGERATE TIME WHEW , BUT WORTH TRUE !
8. WINE FRENCH THEIR , LIKE YOU ?
9. WEEK = past ME + BUY BOTTLE WINE ITS ITALIAN .
10. MONEY SPEND EAT = noun + , WORRY ME , WHEW !
11. NOW WEEK S-T-E-A-K MONEY REDUCE .
12. TRUE ? RUN BUY ME !

Translation Exercises—English to ASL

Translate the following sentences from English into ASL equivalents.

1. When you go to the store, do you take a pocket calculator?
2. Read the food advertisements, and cut out the coupons you want.
3. Do you make a shopping list before going to the food store?
4. The two of us shopped for more than an hour at the new Safeway.
5. We are having a dinner party this Friday.
6. How much does hamburger cost this week?
7. Please buy some baking potatoes and some milk.
8. We try to clip food coupons or advertisements to help save money on food.
9. How much money did you spend on groceries last week?
10. Call me on the TTY when you are ready to go grocery shopping with me.
11. What was the name of that bcttle of French wine you showed me?
12. Tell me what you have on your grocery list.

Single-Slot Substitution Drills

Practice signing the following target sentences, substituting the suggested vocabulary in each slot. If you have problems with any of the vocabulary, consult your instructor for help.

1. near = <u>RECENT</u>   WIRE = her   T-T-Y   GLORIA .

   WEEK = past

   YESTERDAY

   TOMORROW

   NOW DAY

   near = RECENT

2. JOT = list   NEED +   BUY +   <u>FINISH$_1$ +</u>   ME .

   　　　　　　　　　　　　　LATE

   　　　　　　　　　　　　　WILL

   　　　　　　　　　　　　　LOSE

   　　　　　　　　　　　　　CAN'T

   　　　　　　　　　　　　　FINISH

3. EAT = noun +   ITS   FREEZE ,   EAT = noun   ITS   tin = CAN ,   <u>BETTER</u>   WHICH ?

   　　　　　　　　　　　　　　　　　　　　　　　　　　　　　　MONEY **SAVE**

   　　　　　　　　　　　　　　　　　　　　　　　　　　　　　　MONEY   REDUCE

   　　　　　　　　　　　　　　　　　　　　　　　　　　　　　　PREFER

   　　　　　　　　　　　　　　　　　　　　　　　　　　　　　　DELICIOUS

   　　　　　　　　　　　　　　　　　　　　　　　　　　　　　　BETTER

4. ME WANT   BUY   <u>HAMBURGER</u> .

   　　　　　　　　　CHICKEN   BREAST

   　　　　　　　　　PUT-IN-OVEN POTATO

   　　　　　　　　　CHEESE ,   CRACKER

   　　　　　　　　　WINE   WHITE +

   　　　　　　　　　HAMBURGER

5. <u>C-E-R-E-A-L</u>   MONEY REDUCE   CUT = coupon ,   HAVE   ME .

   MILK

   BREAD

   ORANGE   J-U-I-C-E

   HOT   DOG

   COFFEE

   C-E-R-E-A-L

6. PARTY EAT_A MY+ WILL SATURDAY .

     two = WEEK

     WEEK = ahead

     TOMORROW +

     FRIDAY NIGHT

     DAY-AFTER-TOMORROW

     SATURDAY

7. TOMORROW BUY EAT = noun+ HEAP$_2$ **NEED** ME .

      NEED +

      NOT NEED +

      MAYBE

      WILL

      NEED

8. SELL = noun+ ITS+ EAT = noun+ GO-OUT WHY+ + COFFEE ALL-GONE .

          MILK

          BREAD

          MEAT

          POTATO

          BUTTER

          COFFEE

9. BUY COFFEE NEED+ , me = SAME = you .

  MILK

  BREAD

  MEAT

  POTATO

  BUTTER

  COFFEE

10. SMALL "PALM-SIZE" CALCULATOR HAVE YOU ?

      WANT ME .

      HAVE NONE$_2$+ .

      HAVE ME .

      BORROW ME ?

      NEED+ ME .

      HAVE YOU ?

Suggested Activities

1. Make a grocery list of food, drink, and sundry items you might need for a dinner party you are "planning." Figure how much of each item you might need and approximately what each item will cost. Use this information to create a paragraph you can share with the class.

2. See if your instructor can arrange a TTY or TDD hookup in class for practice in "calling a deaf friend" to plan a grocery shopping trip together. In this TTY/TDD practice conversation, you might ask questions about coupons, which store(s) to shop in, and what time you will meet to go shopping.

3. Tell about a recent food shopping trip in which the items you selected totaled more than you had expected to pay. Describe your feelings when you went through the checkout line.

4. Act out the dialogue used in this lesson. Class members may pair off and take turns in role playing the characters, substituting male names in place of the female names.

5. For fingerspelling practice, you may use some of the sentences or selected phrases from the sentences in the English to ASL translation exercises in this lesson. Pair off in class. Partners may then take turns randomly selecting two or three sentences or phrases to fingerspell to each other while the instructor observes.

6. Write an English version of the glossed introductory paragraph.

SUNDAY   EAT_A   late = MORNING

those = TWO BENNY , GLORIA LIKE INVITE_A FRIEND + SAME + THEY JANE , LAWRENCE ,
ALEXANDER , JENNIFER , KEE-KONG WHAT-FOR , EAT_A late = MORNING SUNDAY . ALL
LIKE SLEEP SUNRISE LITTLE-BIT #IF + +   GO-OUT PARTY + , DANCE + PAST NIGHT
SATURDAY . SOMETIMES BENNY , GLORIA those = TWO SATURDAY NIGHT GO-OUT MASS
FINISH₂ WHY + + , OFF-WORK SUNDAY . GLORIA TELL = them FRIEND + COME AROUND
TIME 10:30 , EAT_A AROUND 11:00 . those = TWO = benny = gloria GET-UP 9:00 AROUND ,
COFFEE DRINK_A , FUNNY₂ , NEWSPAPER READ FINISH₂ , DRESS_A **ENOUGH** TIME + .
START EAT = noun + PLAN + those = TWO WORK + , COOK , READY< > EVERY THING .
FRIEND + ARRIVE + AT-LAST GLORIA = she ASK = them + +   WANT + EGG + +   FLIP = over ,
SCRAMBLE , SOFT BOIL WHICH . BENNY = he POUR + COFFEE , TEA TASTE +
THEIR + + . FINISH₂ ALL SIT = around₂ EAT_A + + , CHAT + +   **ENOUGH** TIME + ...
PLEASE = noun₂ THEY !

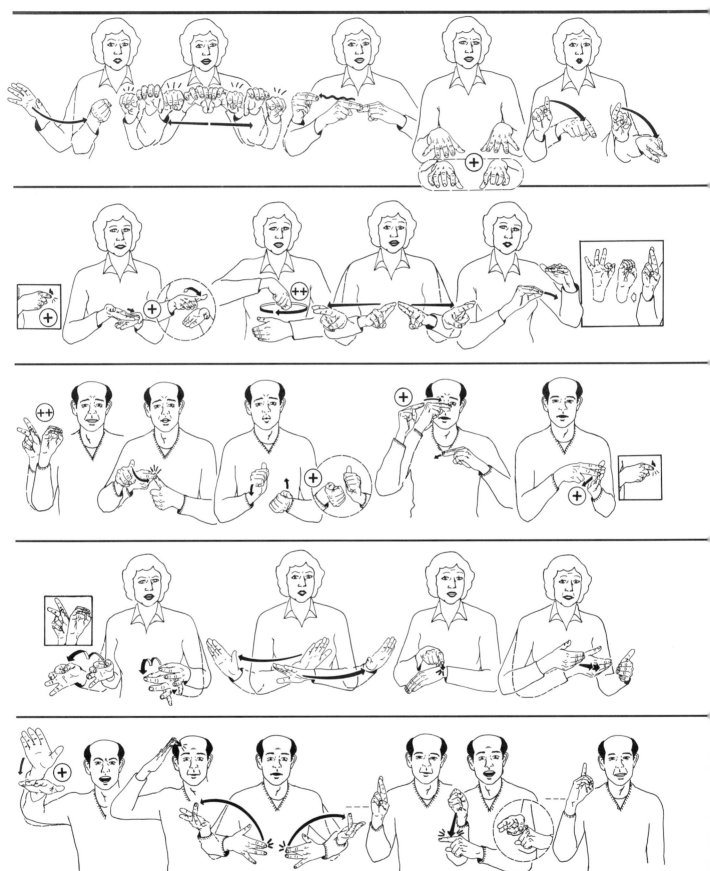

Glossed Sentences, Translations, and Grammatical Notes

1. FETCH   SAUSAGE ,   BACON   FREEZE + +   GO = down .

Go downstairs to the freezer and get some sausage and bacon.

The repetitive form of FREEZE is equivalent to "freezer."

ME   PANCAKE +   STIR + +   READY< >   PUT-IN   R-E-F .

I will prepare the pancake mix and put it in the refrigerator.

The sign PANCAKE could also be used for "turning over" other food items, such as an egg. Fingerspelled abbreviations such as R-E-F are frequently used for everyday objects for which there is no specific sign.

---

2. O-K + + ,   FIRST   RACE = noun ,   FUNNY$_2$ READ +   ME .

OK, but first let me finish reading the sports and comics.

The sign RACE = noun can also be translated as "sports," "race," or "competition." FUNNY$_2$ is translatable as "comics"; the movement of each hand is parallel over the nose rather than downward as in "funny."

---

3. O-K ,   POSTPONE + +   DON'T ;   TIME   NEAR + .

OK, but don't put it off too long; time is getting short.

---

4. "HEY" ,   KNOW   WHAT'S-UP ,   R-E-D-S-K-I-N-S   **BEAT**   D-A-L-L-A-S !

Hey, do you know what? The Redskins beat Dallas!

"HEY" is a call for attention with a wave of the hand. It looks like the common gesture for "goodbye." WHAT'S-UP may be translated literally, but in this example, raised eyebrows are indicative of the question, "Do you know what?" The variant of the sign BEAT shown here can also be translated as "better than."

5. TRUE ? we = TWO BEAT TIME+ HOPE ME !

Really, I hope the two of us can beat the clock!

6. FREEZE + + EAT = noun + FETCH FINISH$_1$; WANT ME #DO+ ?

I got the food from the freezer; what do you want me to do now?

EAT = noun + means "food." (See Lesson 2.) See sentence 14 in Lesson 1 for an explanation of #DO + .

7. TABLE NOW PUT = around$_2$ PLEASE .

Please set the table now.

PUT = around$_2$ is equivalent to "putting objects around a surface."

NAPKIN PUT = around$_2$ FORGET **DON'T** ; IMPORTANT !

Don't forget to place napkins around. It's important!

8. LIGHT-OFF-ON + DOOR SOMEONE , WHO WONDER ME .

There go the lights; someone is at the door; I wonder who?

LIGHT-OFF-ON + here refers to doorbell lights or telephone-TTY lights mounted on walls that deaf people use. Changing the position of the hands can depict "ceiling lights" or "table lamps."

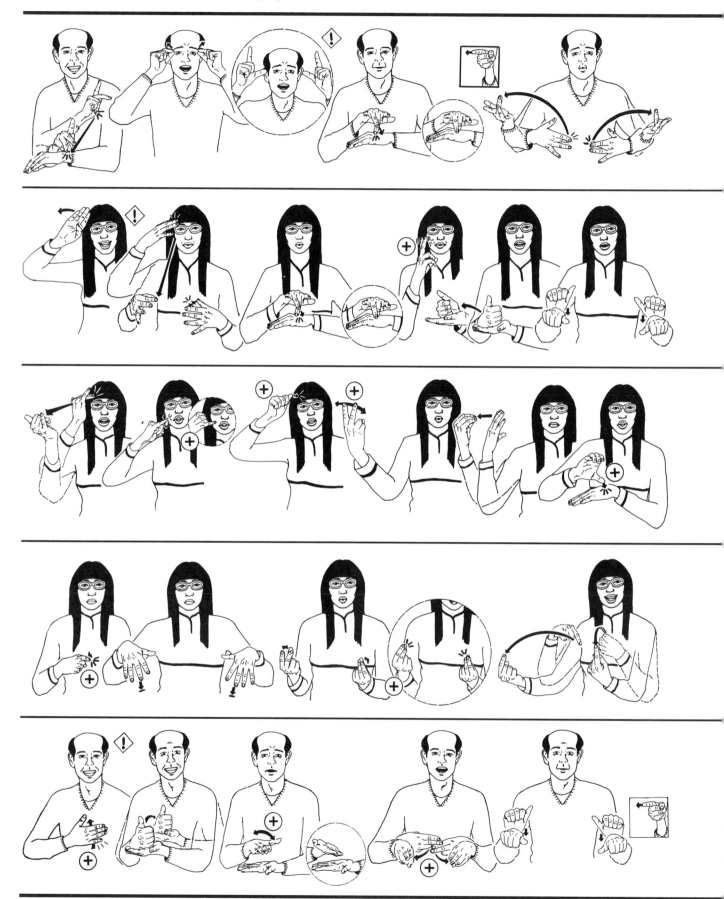

KEE-KONG SURPRISE ! EARLY YOU , WHAT'S-UP ?

Kee Kong, what a surprise! You're early, what's up?

9. HI ! DECIDE EARLY LET'S-SEE HELP = you CAN .

Hi, I decided to come early to see if I could help you.

LET'S-SEE is a variation of the sign SEE which can be translated as "We'll see about that" or "Let's wait and see."

WHY + + , JENNIFER , ALEXANDER those = TWO GO-OUT CHURCH ,

The reason why is that Jennifer and Alexander went to church,

ME IDLE #DO + , COME .

and I had nothing to do so I came over.

10. HAPPY . HELP = me COOK + EGG + CAN YOU .

I'm glad. You can help me cook the eggs.

Vocabulary Review

Test your ability to produce the following signs or sign phrases.

AROUND 11:00	FREEZE + +	PLAN +
ARRIVE	FUNNY$_2$ +	PLEASE = noun$_2$ +
ASK = them + +	13GET-UP	POSTPONE + +
AT-LAST	GO = down	PUT = around$_2$
BACON	HELP = me	RACE = noun/SPORTS
BEAT	HELP = you	SAUSAGE
CHAT + +	"HEY"	SCRAMBLE EGG +
CHURCH	IDLE	SIT = around$_2$
COFFEE	INVITE$_A$	SLEEP SUNRISE
COOK	LIGHT-OFF-ON$_2$ +	SOMEONE
DANCE	LITTLE-BIT	STIR + +
EARLY	catholic = MASS	TABLE
ENOUGH	NAPKIN	TASTE +
FETCH	NEWSPAPER	**TIME** NEAR + T
FETCH FINISH$_1$	OFF-WORK	TIME 10:30
FLIP = over	PANCAKE +	those = TWO

Notes

Translation Exercises—ASL to English

Translate the following glossed sentences into appropriate English equivalents.

1. FRIEND+ INVITE=here$_A$ EAT$_A$late=MORNING SUNDAY , LIKE YOU ?

2. EAT$_A$ late=MORNING SUNDAY WANT+ YOU , PLAN+ **NEED** .

3. PAST+ GO HOUSE FRIEND HIS EAT$_A$ late=MORNING SUNDAY .

4. FRIEND FIRST GIVE-OUT DRINK ITS BLOODY M-A-R-Y .

5. DRINK$_A$ FINISH , EAT=noun+ HEAP$_2$ DIFFERENT++> , "FINE" !

6. LOOK-AT=past$_2$ WIFE we=TWO PLEASE=noun .

7. early=MORNING REQUIRE "WHAT"$_1$ ME , COFFEE , READ NEWSPAPER .

8. NEWSPAPER READ FINISH , READY< > HELP=her WIFE COOK+ .

9. COOK+ BACON , SAUSAGE , POTATO , EGG+ , **LIKE** ME .

10. ONCE-IN-AWHILE FRIEND APPEAR EARLY , EAT=noun+ READY< > NOT !

11. SUPPOSE+ FRIEND EARLY , ME+ #DO+ , "COME-ON" WORK HELP=me !

12. SUGGEST WHY͡NOT we=TWO EAT$_A$ late=MORNING SUNDAY PLAN+ near=FUTURE+ ?

Translation Exercises—English to ASL

Translate the following sentences from English into ASL equivalents.

1. Put the milk and cheese in the refrigerator, please.

2. We must buy a new freezer.

3. What's wrong with the freezer we have now?

4. It's not working right; the food doesn't stay frozen.

5. We'll see what we can do about it.

6. Can you help me cook for this Sunday's brunch?

7. I'll help you if you let me read the Sunday comics first.

8. I like the way you made the omelets last time.

9. Maybe I should go into the restaurant business.

10. You're dreaming again! Let's take care of the Sunday business first.

11. Sunday is my day to oversleep and watch the football game on TV.

12. It isn't when we have people coming over for brunch.

Mixed-Slot Substitution Drills

Practice signing the following target sentences, substituting the suggested vocabulary in each slot. If you have problems with any of the vocabulary, consult your instructor for help.

1. <u>BACON , SAUSAGE</u> FETCH‿FINISH$_1$.

   MILK , BREAD

   BUTTER , JELLY

   CREAM , SUGAR

   SALT , PEPPER

   BACON , SAUSAGE

2. EGG+ LIKE HOW++ , <u>SCRAMBLE</u> ?

                         FLIP=over

                         HARD‿BOIL

                         O-M-E-L-E-T

                         SCRAMBLE

3. <u>PLATE+</u> NOW PUT=around$_2$, PLEASE .

   NAPKIN

   GLASS+

   KNIFE , FORK

   SPOON

   PLATE+

4. ME IDLE #DO+ , <u>COME</u>.

                     GO-OUT

                     READ

                     SWIM

                     COOK+

                     COME

5. HELP=you COOK+ <u>EGG+</u> SCRAMBLE , HAPPY ME .

                         BACON

                         SAUSAGE

                         G-R-I-T-S

                         H-A-M

                         EGG+ FLIP=over

                         EGG+ SCRAMBLE

6. SOMEONE DOOR ONE=approach=me , DEAF KNOW HOW++ , <u>LIGHT-OFF-ON+</u> .

    DOG BARK++

    FEEL++

    HAPPEN LOOK=at= window

    LIGHT-OFF-ON+

7. COME AROUND TIME <u>10:30</u> , EAT+ AROUND <u>11:00</u> .

10:00	10:30
9:30	10:00
11:00	11:30
11:30	12:00
10:30	11:00

8. SATURDAY NIGHT GO-OUT <u>DANCE</u> FINISH , WHY++ <u>PLEASE=noun$_2$</u> .

EAT$_A$	COOK+ BORED
MOVIE	NONE$_2$ #DO+
VISIT FRIEND	LONESOME
MASS	SUNDAY OFF-WORK
DANCE	PLEASE=noun$_2$

9. <u>EAT$_A$++</u> FINISH , SIT=around$_2$ <u>COFFEE DRINK$_A$</u> .

COFFEE DRINK	CHAT++
CHAT++	REST
REST	MEETING
MEETING	TALK$_A$
EAT$_A$++	COFFEE DRINK$_A$

10. INVITE$_A$ FRIEND <u>late=MORNING SUNDAY</u> WHAT-FOR <u>EAT$_A$ HEAP$_2$</u> .

SATURDAY NIGHT	PARTY
WEDNESDAY NIGHT	MOVIE‿CAPTION
TOMORROW NIGHT	MEET$_A$ NEW FRIEND
SATURDAY AFTERNOON	OUT COOK+
FRIDAY NIGHT	DANCE++
late=MORNING SUNDAY	EAT$_A$ HEAP$_2$

Suggested Activities

1. Break up into small groups of threes to plan a menu for a Sunday brunch. When each group is finished, select one person to relate to the rest of the class what that group has planned.

2. Act out the dialogue used in this lesson. Three persons may volunteer or be selected from the group to role play each character.

3. Invite a TTY/TDD repair person or representative from your community (if one is available) to tell your class about the light relay systems that deaf people use with telephone-TTY/TDD hookups. You might also inquire about doorbell light relay systems that are used in private homes or apartments, both "homemade" and sophisticated systems.

4. Find out from deaf people you know how *they* know if someone is at the door or if the telephone is ringing. Share your findings in class discussion.

5. For fingerspelling practice, you may use some of the sentences or selected phrases from the sentences in the English to ASL translation exercises in this lesson. Pair off in class. Partners may then take turns randomly selecting two or three sentences or phrases to fingerspell to each other while the instructor observes.

6. Write an English version of the glossed introductory paragraph.

A Dinner Party

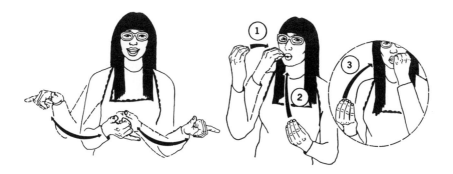

PARTY EAT$_A$

KEE-KONG , JENNIFER those = TWO DECIDE FINISH$_2$ PARTY EAT$_A$ THEIR + A-P-T near = FUTURE . those = TWO INVITE ALEXANDER , OF-COURSE , PLUS those = TWO LAWRENCE , JANE . PLAN + + EAT = noun + WHAT ? those = TWO = kee-kong = jennifer AGREE FINISH$_1$, SERVE "WHAT"$_1$ CHICKEN BREAST BROIL , PUT-IN-OVEN POTATO , BEANS ITS GREEN MIX BACON TINY-BIT + + , ONION CREAM POUR = around STIR , APPLE PIE WITH CHEESE . ALSO those = TWO THINK GOOD IDEA "WHAT"$_1$ ADD WINE ITS WHITE + WITH EAT = noun + . SHE = jennifer SAY WILL HERSELF BUY two = BOTTLE WINE ITS WHITE "KNOW YOU" L-I-E-B-F-R-A-M-I-L-C-H GERMAN ITS FAMOUS , DELICIOUS ! SHE = kee-kong WANT + SMALL SHRIMP SALAD FOR START . BOTH GIRL + those = TWO EXCITED + PLAN + PARTY EAT$_A$, FRIEND INVITE$_A$.

Glossed Sentences, Translations, and Grammatical Notes

1. **TIME** EAT=noun+ COOK+ READY< > PARTY NIGHT .

It's time to prepare the food for our party tonight.

The sign COOK+ can mean "prepare food" (with or without heat). The hands do not touch and multiple movements may occur.

LUCKY EAT=noun+ BUY++ FINISH₂ DAY-BEFORE-YESTERDAY .

It's a good thing I finished shopping for the food the other day.

DAY-BEFORE-YESTERDAY may be translated as "the other day," "two days ago," or "the day before yesterday." This sign can be modified to mean "three days ago," "four days ago," etc., depending on how many fingers are extended.

---

2. SHRIMP COOK PUT-IN FREEZE++ FINISH₂ ME ;

I've already cooked the shrimp and put it in the freezer ;

PROCEED SALAD FIX NOW CAN .

I can go ahead and fix the salad now.

PROCEED can mean "proceed," "go on," "go ahead," or "move on." FIX is very similar to MAKE: the fists of FIX remain in contact, one atop the other, but in MAKE there is a break between the movements.

---

3. PROCEED ! ME+ APPLE PIE P-A-S-T-R-Y ROLL=pastry .

Go ahead! I'm going to roll the pastry to make my apple pie.

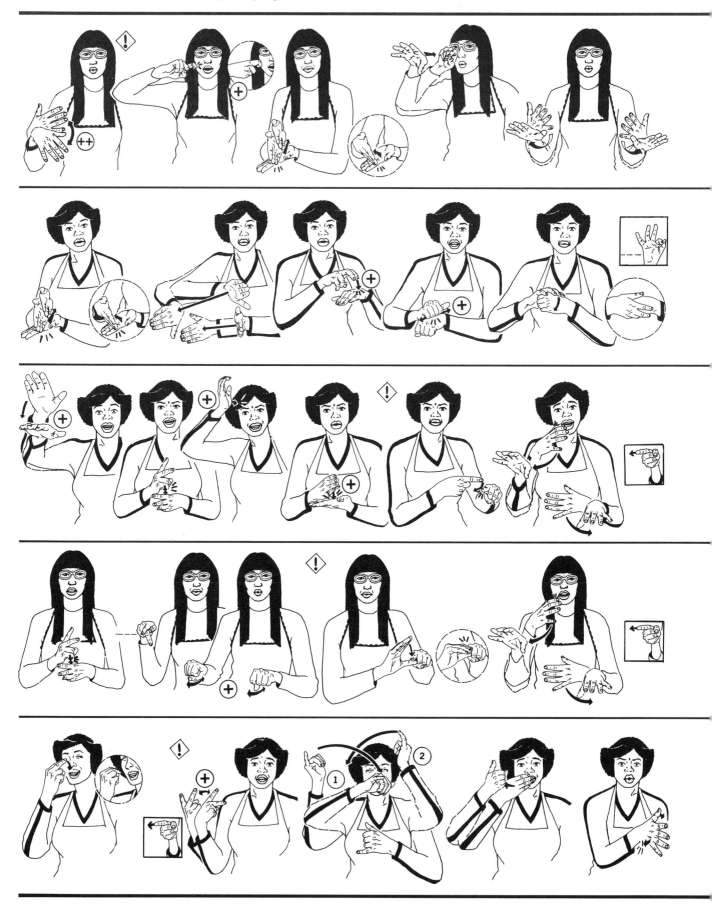

4. WHEW ! APPLE PIE **"WHIFF"** FINISH₂ !

Oh boy! I can just smell that apple pie right now!

5. PIE ASIDE< , POTATO WASH = object WRAP = object F-O-I-L .

When I get the pie out of the way, I'll wash the potatoes and wrap them in foil.

ASIDE < is a directional sign which is translatable as "put aside," "push aside," or "out of the way." Both the WASH and WRAP signs are modified to incorporate the idea of a small object, represented by the hand that does not move (in this case, a potato).

"HEY", **CAREFUL** LETTUCE CHOP+ ! CUT = finger **don't = WANT** YOU !

Be careful chopping that lettuce! You don't want to cut your finger!

CUT = finger is a modification of the sign CUT in which the nonmoving index finger represents the thing being cut.

6. **CAREFUL** P-A-S-T-R-Y ROLL ! FLAT = finger **don't = WANT** YOU !

Be careful rolling that pastry! You don't want to smash your finger!

FLAT = finger, like CUT = finger above, incorporates a specific body part.

7. **FUNNY** YOU ! we = TWO SILLY_A BETTER **FINISH₁** + .

You are the funny one! We better stop fooling around now.

The emphatic form, **FUNNY**, is produced with one firm movement rather than with a repeated movement as in the regular form. SILLY_A is one of the repeated forms of the sign which can mean "foolish." Alternating (A) signs always have two hands and are almost always repeated.

8. O-K₂ . SALAD FINISH₂ ; WANT ME #DO+ ?

OK. The salad is finished; what do you want me to do next?

9. CHICKEN BREAST WASH=object READY< > BROIL .

Wash the chicken breasts and get them ready to broil.

The sign WASH incorporates the idea of an object.

10. FINE ! FINISH₂ TABLE PUT=around₂ WILL ME .

That's fine! When I'm through, I'll set the table.

11. ME+ THINK EAT_A PLAN+ we=TWO **HARMONIZE** .

I think the two of us plan a dinner very well together.

The sign **HARMONIZE** is also translatable as "work out," or "fall into place," "mesh," "integrate," etc.

12. SECOND=you ! NOW ONION PEEL WHO , YOU‿ME ?

I agree with you! Now who's going to peel the onions, you or me?

SECOND is a verb meaning to "show support" or "to agree" in the parliamentary sense; it is directional and thus usually incorporates a person as the object. ASL has several ways to show choices and rarely uses a separate sign that means "or." One way is to string the items together, as in YOU ME (which may be repeated). If the signer intended "you *and* me," she would have used we=TWO.

Vocabulary Review

Test your ability to produce the following signs or sign phrases.

AGREE‿FINISH₁

ALSO

APPLE   PIE

ASIDE<

BROIL

CAREFUL

CHOP+

CUT=finger

DAY-BEFORE-YESTERDAY

DECIDE

DELICIOUS

EAT_A

EXCITED

FAMOUS

"FINE"

FINISH₁+

FLAT=finger

FUNNY‿YOU

near=FUTURE

GERMAN

HARMONIZE

IDEA   GOOD

LUCKY

NOW‿NIGHT

OF-COURSE

ONION

PARTY   EAT_A

PEEL

PLAN+

POUR=around++

PROCEED

PUT-IN   FREEZE++

ROLL=pastry

SALAD

SATURDAY

SECOND=you

SERVE

SILLY_A

START

TIME

TINY-BIT++

don't=WANT

WASH=object=chicken-breast

WASH=object=potato

WHEW

"WHIFF"

WINE   ITS   WHITE

WRAP=object=potato

Notes

Translation Exercises—ASL to English

Translate the following glossed sentences into appropriate English equivalents.

1. FRIEND COME PARTY EAT_A ALTOGETHER MANY₂ ∧ ?
2. REMEMBER INVITE=here ALTOGETHER SIX .
3. PARTY EAT_A PLAN+ COOK+ NOW **NEED** we=TWO .
4. RIGHT , FORGET ME ! EAT=noun+ PLAN+ #WHAT ?
5. F-R-Y CHICKEN HEAP₂ , PUT-IN-OVEN POTATO , SALAD , ENOUGH+ THINK YOU ?
6. **ENOUGH** WHEW ! FRIEND COME **FULL=eat** WILL THEY !
7. FINE+ . NOW START COOK++ CHICKEN , ME+ .
8. F-R-Y CHICKEN "WHIFF" FINISH₂ , DROOL ME !
9. DROOL **FINISH₁** ! PROCEED SALAD FIX NOW YOU .
10. SALAD FIX FINISH ; NOW WANT ME #DO+ ?
11. POTATO WASH=object , WRAP=object F-O-I-L READY> PUT-IN-OVEN .
12. WORK me=COOPERATE=you HARMONIZE we=TWO !

Translation Exercises—English to ASL

Translate the following sentences from English into ASL equivalents.

1. It is exciting to plan a dinner party for friends.
2. Planning what you will serve and buying the food is half the fun.
3. Preparing the food can be a lot of fun, too.
4. Some foods, such as salads and, perhaps, pies, can be finished first.
5. I just love the smell of fresh pies baking in the oven!
6. Do you know how to make a good apple pie?
7. You can buy good pastry mixes that are easy to roll.
8. I wish I could make pastry like my mother did, but I don't know how.
9. When you get your salad and pie out of the way, you can go ahead with the meat and vegetables.
10. Setting the table for a dinner party is fun, too.
11. You want your table to look attractive; candles and cloth napkins help.
12. What would you like to eat at my dinner party?

Single-Slot Substitution Drills

Practice signing the following target sentences, substituting the suggested vocabulary in each slot. If you have problems with any of the vocabulary, consult your instructor for help.

1. PARTY   EAT$_A$ PLAN+   <u>near = FUTURE</u> .

   WILL‿SATURDAY

   WEEK = past

   TOMORROW‿NIGHT

   WILL   one = MONTH

   near = FUTURE

2. EAT$_A$ START   "WHAT"$_2$,   <u>SMALL   SHRIMP   SALAD</u> .

   TOMATO   J-U-I-C-E

   CHICKEN   SOUP

   A-V-O-C-A-D-O   SALAD

   ONION   SOUP

   SMALL   SHRIMP   SALAD

3. DRINK   "WHAT"$_2$ WINE   RED   ITS+   <u>FRENCH</u> .

   GERMAN

   ITALIAN

   CALIFORNIA

   NEW-YORK

   FRENCH

4. MEAT   GIVE-OUT   "WHAT"$_1$,   <u>S-T-E-A-K</u> .

   CHICKEN   BREAST   BROIL

   FISH   ITS   T-R-O-U-T

   PUT-IN-OVEN   F-L-O-U-N-D-E-R

   HAM

   S-T-E-A-K

5. POTATO   COOK+   HOW++ ,   <u>BOIL</u> .

   PUT-IN-OVEN

   FRENCH   FRY

   MASH

   BOIL

6. PROCEED <u>SALAD</u> FIX NOW CAN ME .
    APPLE PIE
    SHRIMP SALAD
    CAKE
    SOUP
    CHERRY PIE
    SALAD

7. <u>SHRIMP</u> COOK+ PUT=in FREEZE++ FINISH ME .
 MEATBALL
 APPLE PIE
 S-T-E-W
 CHICKEN
 SHRIMP

8. <u>APPLE PIE</u> ASIDE> , #DO+ ME ?
 SALAD
 SOUP
 SHRIMP COOK+
 TABLE PUT=around$_2$
 WASH=object=dishes
 APPLE PIE

9. **CAREFUL** <u>LETTUCE</u> CHOP , CUT=finger **don't-WANT** YOU !
    ONION
    C-E-L-E-R-Y
    M-U-S-H-R-O-O-M
    APPLE
    LETTUCE

10. EAT=noun+ BUY+ FINISH$_2$ <u>DAY-BEFORE-YESTERDAY</u> .
      YESTERDAY
      PAST⌣SATURDAY
      THREE-DAY-AGO
      PAST⌣NIGHT
      WILL TOMORROW
      DAY-BEFORE-YESTERDAY

Suggested Activities

1. Act out the dialogue used in this lesson. Two persons may volunteer or be selected from the group to role play each character.

2. Use the ASL to English translation exercises to create an additional dialogue between two other people in your class. Act out this dialogue giving particular attention to emotions and to facial expression.

3. Plan a silent class potluck dinner. One person may be elected to coordinate what each member of the class volunteers to bring. During the actual potluck, talk about the various dishes; exchange recipes; ask questions about who made what; comment on what you liked best and why; compliment one another on the dishes you liked. (If it is successful, maybe you'll want to plan another at a later time.)

4. Ask anyone in your class to volunteer to bring a recipe he/she may have created for a special dish. Share it with the class by explaining *how* to make it, giving ingredients, measurements, directions for preparing, cooking, etc.

5. For fingerspelling practice, you may use some of the sentences or selected phrases from the sentences in the English to ASL translation exercises in this lesson. Pair off in class. Partners may then take turns randomly selecting two or three sentences or phrases to fingerspell to each other while the instructor observes.

6. Write an English version of the glossed introductory paragraph.

Having a Picnic

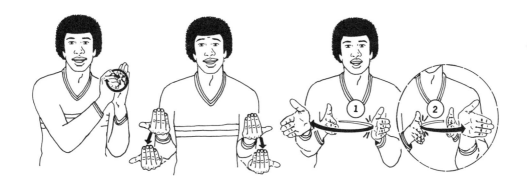

PICNIC TIME-PERIOD

two = WEEK = past those = TWO ALEXANDER , JENNIFER INVITE_A FRIEND THEIR WHAT-FOR , PICNIC GO L-A-K-E-W-O-O-D P-A-R-K NEAR B-E-A-C-H AROUND . those = TWO = alexander = jennifer ASK = them + + LAWRENCE , JANE , KEE-KONG , GLORIA , BENNY group = TOGETHER group = GO . ASK = them + + HOW + + , WIRE = them T-T-Y . those = FIVE AGREE ALL ! STRIKE-CHANCE PRETTY DAY , SUNSHINE , WARM . those = TWO LAWRENCE , JANE BRING = here TWO D-O-Z HOT-DOG . KEE-KONG MAKE EGG "ROLL" , CAKE object = TWO , BOTH DELICIOUS . BENNY , GLORIA BRING HAMBURGER , PICKLE , POTATO C-H-I-P . ALEXANDER , JENNIFER BRING HOT-DOG HAMBURGER B-U-N-S PLUS SALAD , BEER , AND POP . all = GROUP PLEASE = noun₂ + all = DAY SWIM , LIE-DOWN B-E-A-C-H , EAT_A HAMBURGER , HOT-DOG , COOK B-B-Q PLUS SALAD , EGG "ROLL" , CAKE . ALL **FULL = eat** EAT_A TOO-MUCH ! LATER group = TOGETHER PLAY VOLLEYBALL , C-R-O-Q-U-E-T . GO-OUT HOME GROUP TIRED , HAPPY !

Glossed Sentences, Translations, and Grammatical Notes

1. SUNSHINE   DAY   JUMP=up+   ME ,   WHY++

   I'm so happy it's such a bright, sunshiny day because

   JUMP=up+ means "happy" or "filled with joy," as in the English expression, "jump for joy."

   NEWSPAPER   YESTERDAY   FORESEE   RAIN ,   **RELIEVED** !

   the newspaper yesterday was forecasting rain; I'm so relieved!

---

2. DEPEND   NEWSPAPER   CAN'T ;   50>50   CORRECT>WRONG .

   You can't depend on the newspapers; half the time they're right and half the time wrong.

---

3. **SECOND=you** !   WORRY   WHAT-FOR ,   PROCEED   PLEASE=noun$_2$+ !

   I agree with you 100% on that! Why worry, let's enjoy ourselves!

   The emphatic form **SECOND=you** means "agree with 100%"; the movement is much sharper than normal. (See Lesson 4, sentence 12.) PLEASE=noun$_2$+ is a variant of PLEASE with a slower and stronger movement. It may be translated as "pleasure" or "enjoy."

---

4. WISH   LAWRENCE   HURRY   BRING   HOT-DOG .

   I wish Lawrence would hurry up and bring the hot dogs.

   WISH has a shorter downward movement than hunger; the two signs are otherwise identical. BRING is a directional sign which incorporates a location; in this case, the hands move to position very close to the body.

5. EGG "ROLL" MY+ DELICIOUS .

My egg rolls are delicious.

"ROLL" is not a standard sign; some people would fingerspell R-O-L-L.

6. **FINISH=you** ; DROOL NOW ! EVERY⌒THING READY< > ?

Stop that, you're making my mouth water! Is everything ready?

The emphatic sign **FINISH** has a very sharp, abrupt, single movement; in this case this command is also made in the direction of a particular person. DROOL is often used to signify strong likes, cravings, and desires.

7. YES , ALEXANDER PUT-IN$_A$ CAR FINISH$_2$.

Yes, Alexander finished packing everything in the car a while ago.

The two-handed alternate form of PUT-IN means "to put in many different things" or "to pack."

8. LAWRENCE ARRIVE **AT-LAST** ! BENNY , GLORIA COME=here ?

Lawrence has finally arrived! Are Benny and Gloria coming over?

AT-LAST has one sharp movement; the related sign SUCCEED is repeated as it moves upward.

9. NO , GLORIA WIRE=me T-T-Y , TELL=me MEET THERE .

No, Gloria called me on the TTY and told me they would meet us there.

WIRE is a directional verb that can mean "send a telegram" as well as "make a call (on a TTY)."

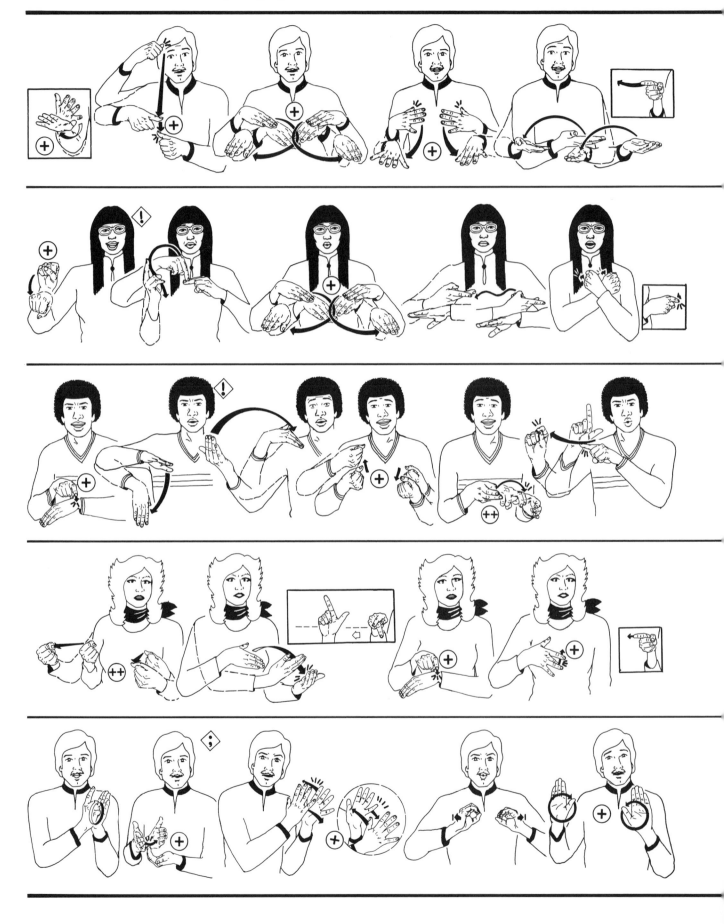

10. FINISH₂ REMEMBER SWIM CLOTHES BRING ⊤ , YOU = around ?

Did you all remember to bring your swim clothes?

In YOU = around, the index finger moves in an arc to point at everyone the signer includes.

11. YES ! DIVE , SWIM , lie-down = FLOAT , LOVE ME .

Yes! I just love to dive, swim, and float.

12. TIME **LATE** ! "COME-ON" GET-IN-VEHICLE + + **ZOOM** !

It's getting late! Come on everybody, get in the car and away we go!

GET-IN-VEHICLE is used for entering or boarding cars, trains, buses, boats, and planes. **ZOOM** can also mean "leave quickly" or "disappear rapidly into the distance."

13. DRIVE + + ⊥ , ARRIVE L-A-K-E-W-O-O-D P-A-R-K TIME + , FEEL‿YOU ?

How long do you think it will take us to get to Lakewood Park?

Repeated short movements of DRIVE give the idea of "an extended period of time."

14. ONE-HOUR EASY ; TRAFFIC NONE₂ SUNDAY .

In an hour easily; there's no traffic on Sunday.

TRAFFIC is the general sign for "movement of many vehicles or persons in a confined path"; there are other signs for "traffic" that specify the number of lanes in each direction.

Vocabulary Review

Test your ability to produce the following signs or sign phrases.

AFRAID	FORESEE	PUT-IN$_A$ CAR
BEER	FULL = eat	RAIN
BRING ⊤	GET-IN-VEHICLE + +	RELIEVED
BRING ⊥	group = GO	SUNDAY
CAKE DELICIOUS	all = GROUP	SUNSHINE
"COME-ON"	HAPPY	SWIM +
CORRECT > WRONG	HOT-DOG	TELL = me
all = DAY	HURRY	over = THERE
DEPEND‿CAN'T	JUMP = up +	group = TOGETHER
DIVE	**LATE**	TRAFFIC
DRIVE + + ⊥	NONE$_2$	you = TWO
DROOL	PICKLE	VOLLEYBALL
EGG "ROLL"	PICNIC	two = WEEK = past
EVERY‿THING	PLAY	YESTERDAY
FIFTY>FIFTY (50-50)	PLUS	YOU = around
lie-down = FLOAT	POP	**ZOOM**

Notes

Translation Exercises—ASL to English

Translate the following glossed sentences into appropriate English equivalents.

1. two = WEEK = ahead   FRIEND   group = TOGETHER   group = GO   PICNIC .
2. group = GO   PICNIC   WHERE ,   CAPTAIN   C-O-V-E   B-E-A-C-H .
3. **THAT = place**   "FINE"   WHY + + ,   B-B-Q   AROUND   HAVE .
4. COOK +   HAMBURGER ,   HOT-DOG ,   CHICKEN ,   VARIOUS   CAN   YOU .
5. PLUS   OTHER   AROUND   WHAT-FOR ,   PLAY   ALSO   VOLLEYBALL ,   SOFTBALL .
6. PEOPLE   WANT + + ,   DIVE ,   SWIM ,   lie-down = FLOAT   CAN   THEY .
7. B-E-A-C-H   ITSELF   **CLEAN** ;   MAN   DUTY   HIS   LOOK-AT = around$_2$ HAVE .
8. #IF + +   PREFER ,   LIE-DOWN   sun = SHINE +   TAN   CAN .
9. OTHER   PLACE   GOOD   HAVE ;   **THAT = place**   ONE   **BEST** !
10. group = GO   PICNIC   CAPTAIN   C-O-V-E   PLEASE = noun$_2$ +   WILL   THEY .
11. DRIVE + + ,   ARRIVE   CAPTAIN   C-O-V-E   TIME +   MANY$_1$ ∧ ?
12. AROUND   ONE-HOUR ,   UNDERSTAND +   TRAFFIC   SMOOTH .

Translation Exercises—English to ASL

Translate the following sentences from English into ASL equivalents.

1. Let's plan a picnic for next weekend, OK?
2. I agree with you. Let's hope there's no forecast for rain!
3. You bring the hamburgers and hamburger rolls.
4. I'll bring a potato salad and baked beans.
5. Who will bring the charcoal and the grill for cooking?
6. Let him bring that; I'll bring the pop and beer.
7. Fine! Then we can pack everything in our van, OK?
8. All of you bring your swimwear; the lake is good for swimming.
9. We can also play volleyball and maybe water basketball.
10. Let's meet here at 8:30 next Saturday morning.
11. It's a little over an hour's drive to the lake.
12. We forgot something. Will you bring catsup, mustard, pickles, and potato chips?

Single-Slot Substitution Drills

Practice signing the following target sentences, substituting the suggested vocabulary in each slot. If you have problems with any of the vocabulary, consult your instructor for help.

1. PICNIC   group = GO   AGREE   <u>we = FIVE</u> .
                                 those = FIVE
                                 those = FOUR
                                 we = THREE
                                 those = THREE
                                 we = FIVE

2. PICNIC   group = GO   WHERE ?   <u>G-R-E-A-T   F-A-L-L-S</u> .
                                     R-O-C-K   C-R-E-E-K   P-A-R-K
                                     S-H-E-R-W-O-O-D   F-O-R-E-S-T
                                     P-A-L-M   B-E-A-C-H
                                     L-A-K-E   P-O-N-T-C-H-A-R-T-R-A-I-N
                                     G-R-E-A-T   F-A-L-L-S

3. #IF + +   RAIN ,   PICNIC   <u>CANCEL</u> .
                         POSTPONE
                         "SAME"$_2$
                         WHERE ?
                         CAN'T
                         CANCEL

4. SUNSHINE   DAY   JUMP = up +   ME   WHY + + ,   <u>PICNIC</u> !
                                                            B-E-A-C-H
                                                            PLAY   VOLLEYBALL
                                                            SWIM +
                                                            BASEBALL
                                                            FISHING
                                                            PICNIC

5. <u>EGG   "ROLL"</u>   MY +   DELICIOUS !
   HAMBURGER
   CAKE
   BEER
   EGG   "ROLL"

6. B-B-Q HAMBURGER **"WHIFF"** , DROOL ME !
    HOT-DOG

    CHICKEN

    S-T-E-A-K

    P-O-R-K C-H-O-P

    HAMBURGER

7. FINISH REMEMBER SWIM+ CLOTHES BRING YOU = around ?
    HAMBURGER , HOT-DOG

    POP , BEER

    GAME+

    OLD CLOTHES

    UMBRELLA

    SWIM+ CLOTHES

8. DRIVE++ , ARRIVE G-R-E-A-T F-A-L-L-S TIME+ FEEL YOU ?
    L-A-K-E

    B-E-A-C-H

    PICNIC

    S-K-Y-L-I-N-E D-R-I-V-E

    G-R-E-A-T F-A-L-L-S

9. SWIM+ LIKE YOU ?
    DIVE

    lie-down = FLOAT

    VOLLEYBALL

    PICNIC

    COOK+

    SWIM+

10. PICNIC FINISH group = GO HOME TIRED .
    HAPPY

    EXHAUSTED

    HUNGRY

    sun = SHINE+ **RED**

    FULL = eat

    TIRED

Suggested Activities

1. Break up the class into small groups to plan a hypothetical picnic or outing to a nearby state park in your region. Assign each group specific responsibilities, e.g., food, recreation or activities, transportation, etc. When the groups complete their planning, select one person from each group to report back to the entire class.

2. Act out the dialogue used in this lesson. Five persons may volunteer or be selected from the group to role play each character. Give particular attention to emotions and to facial expressions.

3. Plan a silent cookout and invite a deaf group to participate. Ask the deaf group to share in the food planning and to plan for some of the activities for the group. Suggested activities: games, stories, jokes, skits, etc.

4. Tell about an outing you and your family or group participated in. It may include something humorous, or something sad, or something exciting.

5. For fingerspelling practice, you may use some of the sentences or selected phrases from the sentences in the English to ASL translation exercises in this lesson. Pair off in class. Partners may then take turns randomly selecting two or three sentences or phrases to fingerspell to each other while the instructor observes.

6. Write an English version of the glossed introductory paragraph.

Shopping for New Clothes

NEW CLOTHES BUY++

those=TWO JANE , LAWRENCE SOMETIMES GO-OUT WHAT-FOR , NEW CLOTHES
BUY++ . PLEASE=noun₂ those=TWO WINDOW SELL=noun+ LOOK-AT₂++>
UNDERSTAND+ HAPPEN MONEY BROKE . SHE=jane SEE DRESS+ NEW+ THROUGH
WINDOW , SOMETIMES **NEED** ENTER "TRY-ON"++ LET'S-SEE taste=AGREE BEST
WHICH . he=LAWRENCE LOOK-AT=her LET'S-SEE taste=AGREE , LIKE , MONEY
MANY₁ ∧ . . . #IF++ SEEM+ BUY **GOOD** , MAYBE PAY-CASH WHICH CHARGE-PLATE
NO-MATTER . OTHER TIME-PERIOD those=TWO "STRADDLE=back-and-forth" DROP NONE₂
BUY . SAME HE=lawrence NEW CLOTHES BUY+ WANT+ , SHE=jane PATIENT WAIT+
NEED ! EQUAL those=TWO . ONCE PAST+ SHE=jane "TRY-ON" NEW DRESS , **WRONG**
SMALL , **T-I-G-H-T** ! SEEM+ WEIGHT INCREASE+ EAT+ REDUCE CAREFUL SHAPE=body
NEED SHE ! HE=lawrence COMPLAIN+ NONE #IF++ SHE=jane WEIGHT INCREASE+
LITTLE-BIT , BUT **LUCKY** HE ! HERSELF=jane CONTINUE SHAPE=body PRETTY
WANT++ !

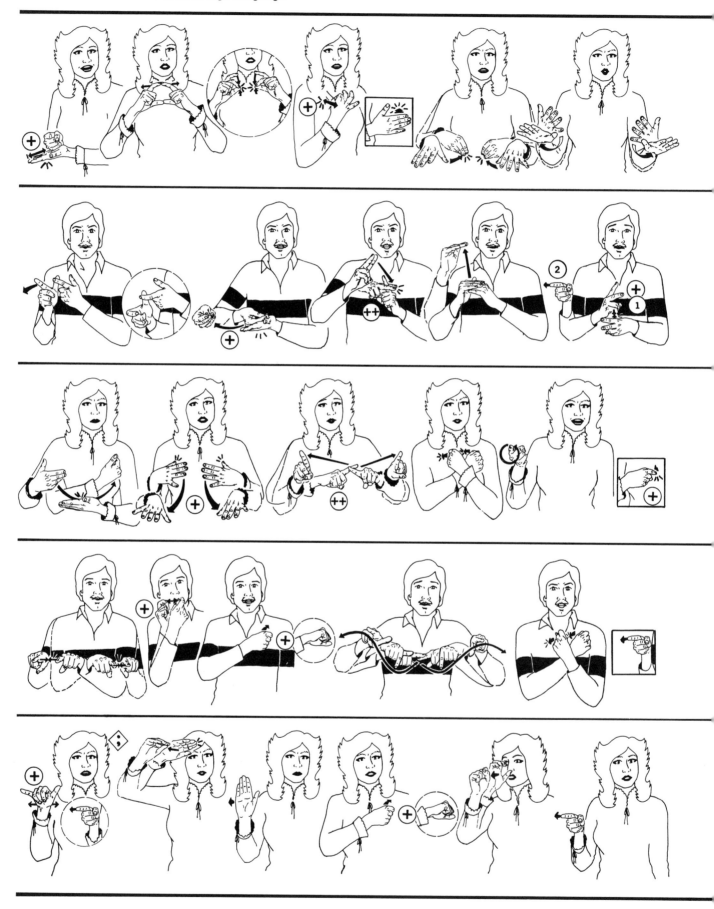

Glossed Sentences, Translations, and Grammatical Notes

1. CHARGE-PLATE CARD APPLY+ MY+ ACCEPT FINISH$_2$.

   My application for a credit card has been approved.

   APPLY can also mean "volunteer" or "become a candidate."

2. RUN BUY++ CHARGE=around TOO-MUCH CAREFUL YOU .

   Be careful you don't rush off shopping and overcharge.

3. NEW CLOTHES++ DIFFERENT++> LOVE ALWAYS ME .

   I always love to keep up with the latest clothing fashions.

4. ALSO LIPSTICK , PERFUME VARIOUS **LOVE** YOU .

   You also love a variety of cosmetics such as lipsticks and perfumes.

5. SAME‿YOU ; MAN HIS PERFUME ATTRACT-TO YOU .

   You are no different; you are attracted to men's colognes.

   The directional possessive sign (called HIS in this sentence) marks the preceding noun as possessive (equivalent to 's in English).

6. TRUE ! TOMORROW SELL REDUCE GO-OUT BUY++ we=TWO ?

That's true! Shall we go shopping tomorrow at the sale?

7. LOOK-AT=ahead₂+ NEXT SHOE MONEY REDUCE ; RUN ME !

I'm looking forward to the next shoe sale; I'm going to run to it!

Two-handed LOOK, moving forward, means "looking forward to" or "anticipating."

8. PREFER PATRONIZE FANCY_A SELL=noun+ YOU , CORRECT ?

You prefer to patronize the best stores, don't you?

PREFER might have derived from a combination of PLEASE and BEST. PATRONIZE means to repeatedly go to a person, place, or institution for something, but it can be used in quite general senses and is not limited to actions as a customer. The sign could refer to attending churches or to a teacher's habit of always questioning the same students. It *cannot* be used to mean "act in a condescending way." Various translations of FANCY include "finery," "quality" (in the sense of "best"), "high class," "formal," etc.

9. FANCY₁ SELL=noun+ BUY++ Q-U-A-L-I-T-Y **BEST** .

Well, you get the best quality shopping the best stores.

10. FORGET=not SATURDAY AGREE FINISH₁ we=TWO BUY++ .

Don't forget that we agreed to go shopping this Saturday.

In the sign FORGET=not, the "not" is shown with a headshake at the same time the sign is made.

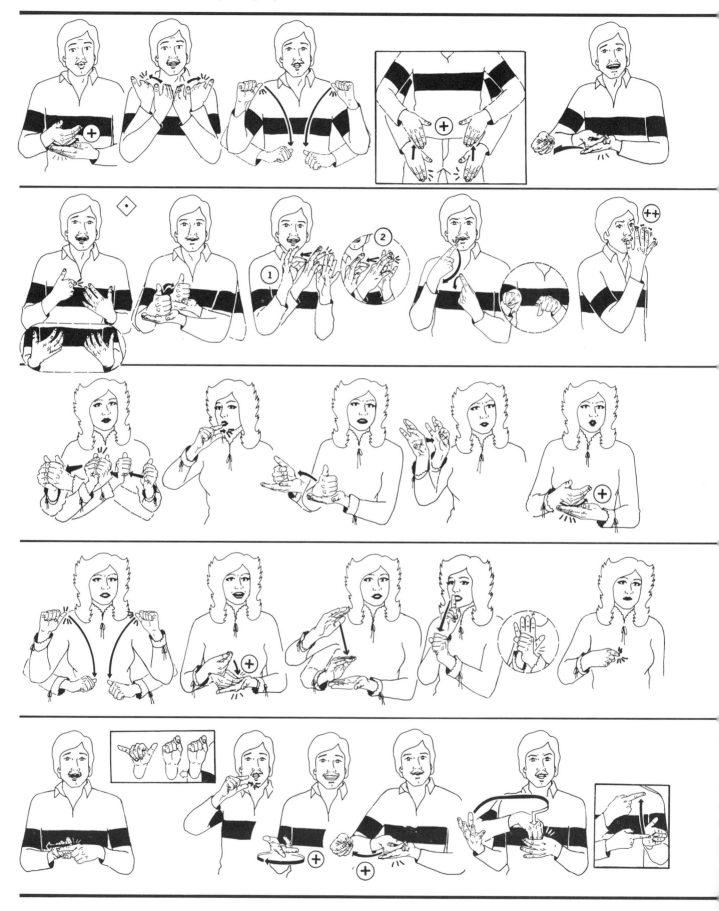

NEW+ "OPEN-NECK" COAT͡ PANTS BUY .

I want to buy a new casual suit.

COAT͡ PANTS is a compound of two signs that has the special meaning "suit."

WANT+ ME . you=WITH=me HELP=me CHOOSE taste=AGREE COLOR .

You come with me to help me pick the right color for me.

WITH in this sentence is a verb showing directional movement, incorporating "you," "me," and the direction both people take. taste=AGREE can also be translated as "becoming," "appropriate," "suitable."

11. WITH GLORIA HELP=her CHOOSE NEW+ COAT , PROMISE ME .

I promised to go with Gloria to help her pick out a new coat.

TELL=me SHE FIND NEW+ COAT MONEY‿REDUCE .

She told me that she found some new coats at a bargain price.

12. WIRE=her‿ T-T-Y GLORIA we=THREE BUY++ all=INCLUDE ONCE .

Call Gloria on the TTY and tell her we will all go shopping together.

all=INCLUDE ONCE means "all at once," "kill two birds with one stone," etc.

Vocabulary Review

Test your ability to produce the following signs or sign phrases.

ACCEPT	ENTER	PATRONIZE
taste = AGREE	EQUAL	PAY-CASH
APPLY	FANCY₁	PREFER
ATTRACT	FANCYₐ	PRETTY
BROKE	FORGET = not	PROMISE
BUY + +	HAPPEN	SAME‿YOU
CHARGE = around	all = INCLUDE	SEEM +
CHARGE-PLATE	INCREASE +	SHAPE = body
CHARGE-PLATE CARD	LIPSTICK	SHOE MONEY‿REDUCE
CHOOSE	LOOK-AT + +	SOMETIMES
CLOTHES	LOOK-AT = ahead₂ +	"STRADDLE = back-and-forth"
COAT‿PANTS	MAYBE	we = THREE
COLOR	NEW CLOTHES	THROUGH
COMPLAIN +	NO-MATTER	TIME-PERIOD
CONTINUE	OPEN-NECK COAT‿PANTS	TOMORROW
DRESS +	PAST +	"TRY-ON"
DROP	PATIENT	UNDERSTAND +

Notes

Translation Exercises—ASL to English

Translate the following glossed sentences into appropriate English equivalents.

1. SOMETIMES GO-OUT NEW+ CLOTHES BUY++ , HAPPEN FRIEND MEET , OFF-POINT CHAT++ ; BUY **NONE₂** !

2. SELL=noun+ GO , WINDOW LOOK-AT++> PLEASE=noun₂ YOU ?

3. we=TWO LOOK-AT₂+ ADVERTISE=noun , SEE SELL MONEY REDUCE , **RUN** BUY++ .

4. KNOW THAT JANE PREFER PATRONIZE "WHAT" , FANCY₁ SELL=noun+ .

5. PAST+ WIFE MY+ **LOVE** "WHAT" , GO SELL=noun+ DRESS+ "TRY-ON"++> .

6. PAST+ GO-OUT BUY++ NEW COAT PANTS , FIND LIKE **THAT=one** , **WRONG** MONEY ENOUGH=not , DROP BUY NONE₂ .

7. EAT+ FINISH₂ **FULL=eat** , RUN NEW+ CLOTHES BUY+ "NO-NO" , WHY++ CLOTHES **T-I-G-H-T** WILL .

8. SOMETIMES SELL=noun+ BUY++ FINISH , ARRIVE PAY=them GO-OUT , **LINE-UP** WAIT++ !

9. CORRECT ! OTHER PROBLEM : SOMETIMES "STUCK" BUY+ WHICH "STRADDLE=back-and-forth" .

10. FORGET=not TOMORROW NIGHT BUY++ we=TWO , AGREE FINISH PAST+ .

11. GO SELL=noun+ ALIKE H-E-C-H-T , ATTRACT YOU "WHAT" ?

12. BUY=around++ FINISH₂ GO PAY=them , SELL=noun+ WOMAN MAN alternate=TWO₂ ASK=you ALWAYS "WHAT" ; "PAY-CASH , CHARGE-PLATE WHICH ?"

Translation Exercises—English to ASL

Translate the following sentences from English into ASL equivalents.

1. When you shop for clothes, what stores do you patronize?
2. I like to shop at stores that offer variety at different prices.
3. The two of us like to shop for clothes during a sale.
4. Sometimes you're lucky enough to get a good buy for your money.
5. That's true, but sometimes you don't find the quality you want.
6. Window shopping is fun if you just want to see what the newest fashions are.
7. I saw an advertisement in the newspaper for a sale on fall suits.
8. I'm waiting for a shoe sale; I need to get some new shoes.
9. My old coat is wearing out; I need to look for a new one.
10. Why don't the three of us go shopping together this Saturday?
11. That's not a bad idea; we might find something on sale.
12. And maybe I can use my new credit card!

Mixed-Slot Substitution Drills

Practice signing the following target sentences, substituting the suggested vocabulary in each slot. If you have problems with any of the vocabulary, consult your instructor for help.

1. <u>TOMORROW</u> GO-OUT WHAT-FOR ,   <u>NEW CLOTHES</u> BUY + + .

   NOW⌒NIGHT   EAT = noun +

   DAY-AFTER-TOMORROW   NEW SHOES

   past = WEEK   NEW CAR

   WILL‿SATURDAY   NEW DRESS +

   past = NIGHT   NEW HAT

   TOMORROW   NEW CLOTHES

2. <u>CHARGE-PLATE CARD</u> APPLY +   MY + ,   <u>ACCEPT FINISH$_2$</u> .

   LOAN B-A-N-K   WAIT LET'S-SEE

   SELL = noun + CHARGE   TURN-DOWN

   CAR LOAN   JOT = list FINISH$_2$

   CHARGE-PLATE CARD   ACCEPT FINISH$_2$

3. NEXT <u>SHOE</u> MONEY‿REDUCE LOOK-AT = ahead$_2$ +   ME .

   　　　DRESS

   　　　COAT⌒PANTS

   　　　SHIRT

   　　　SHOE

4. <u>PERFUME SMELL</u> DIFFERENT + + > ATTRACT YOU ?

   LIPSTICK COLOR

   NAIL-POLISH

   SHAVE RUB = face$_2$

   SHAMPOO

   PERFUME SMELL

5. FORGET = not <u>T-H NIGHT</u> we = TWO BUY + + GO-OUT SEARCH = around COAT⌒PANTS .

   　　　　FRIDAY

   　　　　TOMORROW AFTERNOON

   　　　　TOMORROW‿MORNING

   　　　　SATURDAY

   　　　　WEEK = ahead

   　　　　T-H NIGHT

6. FIND   NEW   <u>COAT͡ PANTS</u>   LIKE ,   MAYBE   <u>CHARGE-PLATE</u> .

               SHOES   PAY-CASH

               COAT   SUSPEND   PUT$_2$

               GIRDLE   CHECK   WRITE

               COAT͡ PANTS   CHARGE-PLATE

7. you = WITH = me   HELP = me   CHOOSE   <u>COLOR</u>   agree = TASTE   MY + ?

                                      S-I-Z-E

                                      S-T-Y-LE

                                      COLOR

8. PAST +   WIFE   MY +   **LOVE**   BUY   "WHAT" ,   <u>NEW   DRESS</u> .

                                              COAT͡ PANTS

                                              GIRDLE

                                              SHIRT

                                              HAT

                                              STOCKING

                                              NEW   DRESS

9. PAST +   HUSBAND   MY +   **LOVE**   BUY   "WHAT" ,   <u>NEW   HAT</u> .

                                              TIE +

                                              SHIRT +

                                              WALK-SHORTS +

                                              SHOES

                                              SOCKS

                                              NEW   HAT

10. <u>PAST +</u>   GO-OUT   SELL = noun +   BUY = around + +   FINISH$_2$,   **WRONG**   <u>MONEY</u>   FORGET !

    PAST +   CHARGE-PLATE   CARD

    YESTERDAY   CHARGE-PLATE   CARD

    YESTERDAY   CHECK   "BOOK"

    PAST   SATURDAY   CHARGE-PLATE   CARD

    PAST +   MONEY

Suggested Activities

1. Act out the dialogue used in this lesson. Two persons may volunteer or be selected to role play each character. Give particular attention to emotions and facial expression.

2. Bring to class a large advertisement or two for some article(s) of clothing you would like to buy for yourself. Try "selling" someone else in the class on buying what you like by extolling the qualities or other virtues of the article(s) for that person.

3. Bring to class an advertisement or two for some personal item such as perfume, after-shave lotion, lipstick, deodorant, cologne, etc. Extoll the quality, color, guarantees, etc., of each item advertised to convince the class to "buy." (A genuine item may be used instead of an advertisement.)

4. Select a partner or pair off by drawing numbers. Each partner is to make a three-minute silent study of the other, noting physical features such as color of hair, eyes, skin, facial contour, height, weight, body build. Each partner then is to take turns recommending the type and color of clothing (e.g., suit, dress, or informal outfit) that would make the other person "best-dressed."

5. Practice expressive signing of the ASL to English translation exercises *before* translating them.

6. For fingerspelling practice, you may use some of the sentences or selected phrases from the sentences in the English to ASL translation exercises in this lesson. Pair off in class. Partners may then take turns randomly selecting two or three sentences or phrases to fingerspell to each other while the instructor observes.

7. Write an English version of the glossed introductory paragraph.

Sewing and Making New Clothes

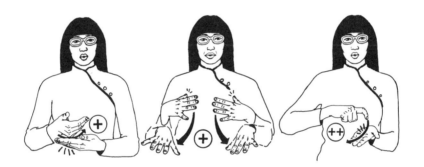

NEW+   CLOTHES   SEW+

GLORIA HERSELF LOVE "WHAT" ? SEW=hand+ , CROCHET+ , SEW MAKE CLOTHES HER+ . LONG-AGO+ INSTITUTION P-R-S-D HERSELF LEARN+ SEW+ HOW++ OLD MACHINE ITS PEDAL_A "KNOW_YOU" . KNACK PRETTY DRESS+ SEW+ SHE WHEW . BENNY those=TWO=gloria MARRY , MOTHER GIFT₁ SEW+ MACHINE ITS PEDAL_A . DAUGHTER BORN FINISH₂ two=YEAR=ahead GROW-UP LITTLE-BIT , GLORIA HERSELF MANY+ DRESS++ SMALL , **CUTE** SEW+ . DAUGHTER PRETTY DRESS+ ALWAYS WHEW ! MARRY FINISH₂ 15 YEAR PASS , HUSBAND HE GIFT=gloria₂ SURPRISE "WHAT" : SEW+   MACHINE **NEW** ITS ELECTRIC ! SHE=gloria PRIDE . . . LEARN++ ELECTRIC SEW+ WONDERFUL . HERSELF=gloria SEW+ NEW+ SHIRT+ SEVERAL₂ HIS=benny+ . KEE-KONG **THIRSTY** LEARN+ SEW+ WHY++ , HERSELF=kee-kong WANT+ MAKE DRESS+ HER+ . WHAT-FOR , MONEY **SAVE** ! SHE=gloria AGREE FINISH₁, TEACH UNDERSTAND+   SHE=kee-kong   COME=here+ .

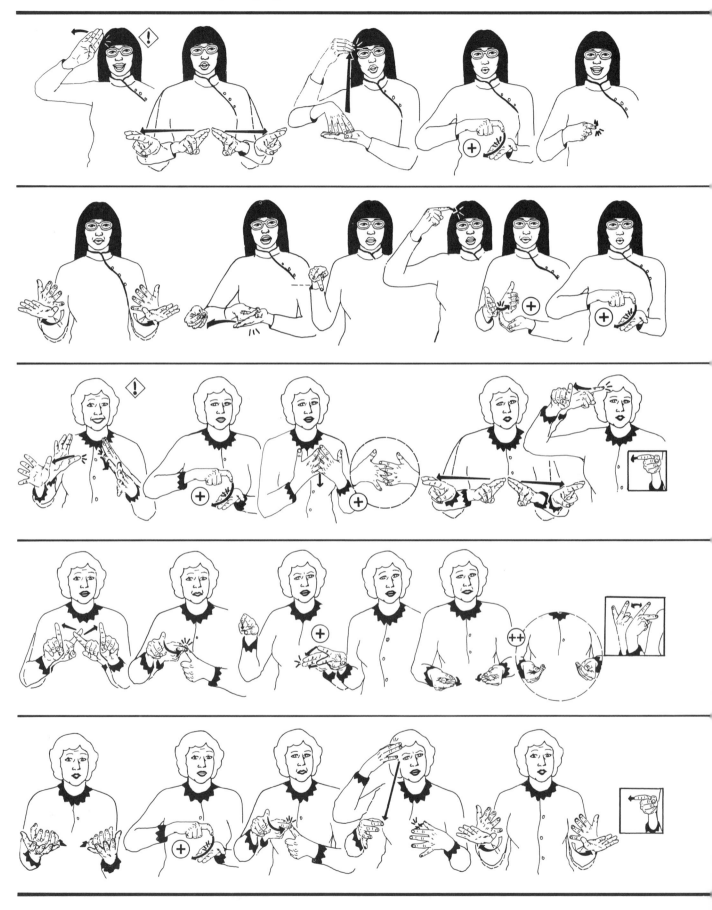

Glossed Sentences, Translations, and Grammatical Notes

1. HI ! READY LEARN SEW+ ME .

Hi, Gloria! I'm ready to learn about sewing.

The sign SEW means "to sew with a machine." Compare it with the sign SEW=hand in the Introductory Paragraph.

FINISH₂ BUY P-A-T-T-E-R-N THINK EASY SEW+ .

I've bought a pattern I think will be easy for me to sew.

THINK EASY may also be translated in certain contexts as "You think there's nothing to it?"

2. FINE₂ ! SEW MACHINE READY< > FOR YOU ;

That's fine! The sewing machine is ready for you to use;

BUT FIRST **NEED** scissors=CUT MATERIAL we=TWO .

but first, we have to cut out the material.

scissors=CUT mimes the cutting action of scissors.

WANT SEW+ FIRST , DECIDE FINISH₂ YOU ?

Have you decided what you want to sew first?

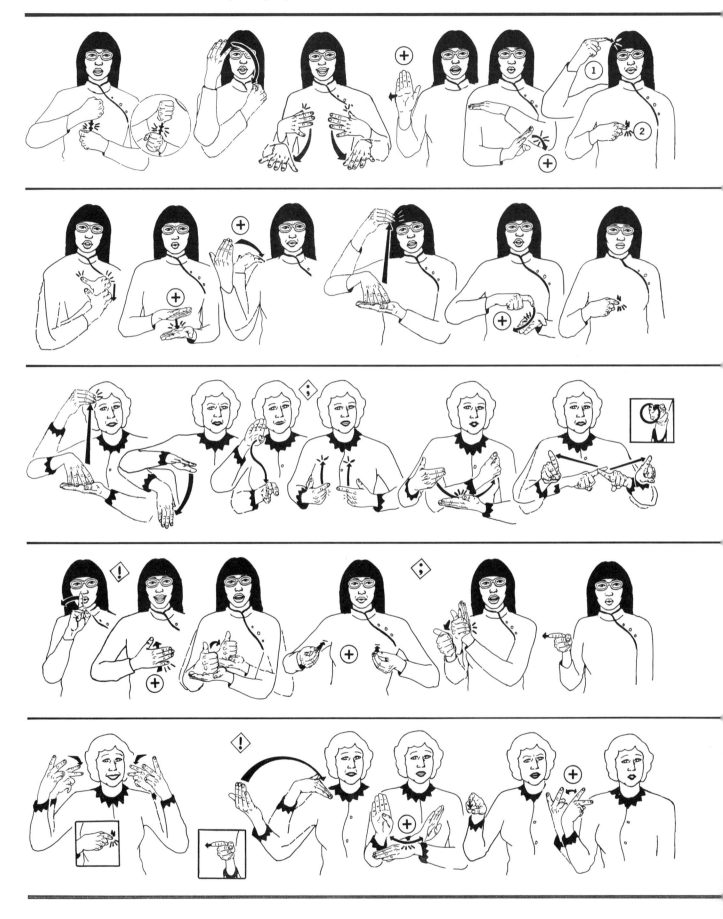

3. MAKE PRETTY DRESS ITS AUTUMN , THINK ME .

I thought I'd make a pretty new fall dress.

DRESS may have variable movements that help to portray different styles.

WISH SCHOOL PAST+ LEARN SEW+ ME .

I wish I had learned sewing in school before.

4. LEARN **LATE** NEVER ; LIFE NEW‿DIFFERENT ALWAYS .

It's never too late to learn; life is always changing.

The emphatic form of LATE means "too late." NEW‿DIFFERENT is a blend that means "changing" or "not remaining the same."

5. TRUE ! HAPPY you=HELP=me TEACH=me ; **SKILL** YOU !

That's true! I'm glad you can help teach me; you are very skilled!

HELP=me and TEACH=me are both directional signs incorporating the signer as the object of the action.

6. FLATTER ME YOU ! "COME-ON" BUSY **NEED** we=TWO !

You flatter me! Come on, we've got to get busy!

FLATTER is always made toward the signer even though it may refer to another person as the object. It may refer to "flattery" or to "personal vanity." The emphatic form **NEED** may be translated as "must," "got to," or "have to."

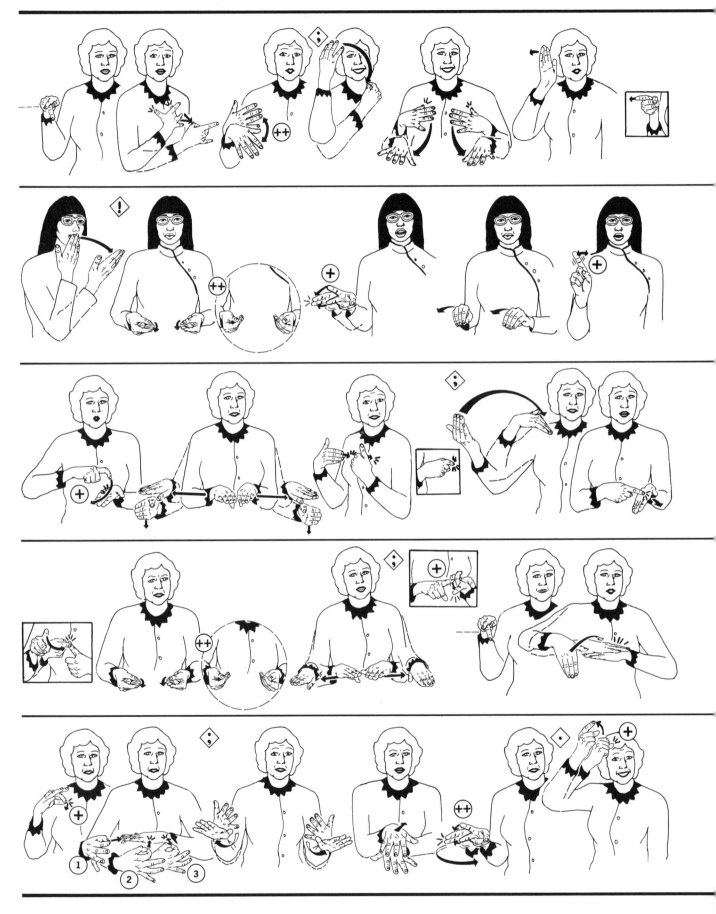

P-A-T-T-E-R-N **LIKE** WHEW ; PRETTY DRESS WILL YOU .

I really like that pattern; you will have a pretty dress.

7. THANK-YOU ! MATERIAL , scissors = CUT , PUT$_2$ WHERE ?

Thank you! Where can we put the material to cut it out?

8. SEW+ TABLE$_2$ HAVE ME ; "COME-ON" SHOW = you .

I have a sewing table; come and I will show you.

TABLE$_2$ means "a flat surface with sides." It is different from the sign TABLE used in Lesson 3, sentence 7. SHOW = you is another directional sign. Compare it with SHOW = me.

FIRST , MATERIAL FLAT$_2$; SECOND , P-A-T-T-E-R-N ON = top ,

First, lay the material flat; second, put the pattern on top and

PIN+ STICK = around ; FINISH$_2$ SLOW scissors = CUT . UNDERSTAND+ ?

pin it around the material; then slowly cut it out. Do you understand?

STICK = around in this sentence is a complex sign representing the action of putting or sticking in straight pins around material and a pattern, which are represented by the nondominant hand.

Vocabulary Review

Test your ability to produce the following signs or sign phrases.

BORN	LEARN + +	SECOND
BUSY	MANY +	SEVERAL₂
"COME-ON"	MARRY	SEW +
CROCHET +	MATERIAL	SEW = hand +
CUTE	MOTHER	SEW MACHINE
DAUGHTER	NEVER	SEW + TABLE
DRESS ITS AUTUMN	**NEW**	SHIRT +
ELECTRIC	NEW‿DIFFERENT	SHOW = you
FINE₂	PAPER ON = object	SKILL
FLAT₂	PEDALₐ	SLOW scissors = CUT
FLATTER ME	PIN + STICK = around	SMALL
GROW-UP	PRETTY DRESS	SURPRISE
HUSBAND	PRIDE	THANK-YOU
INSTITUTION	PUT₂	**THIRSTY**
KNACK	SAVE	WISH
"KNOW‿YOU"	SCHOOL	two = YEAR = ahead

Notes

Translation Exercises—ASL to English

Translate the following glossed sentences into appropriate English equivalents.

1. LONG-AGO+ MOTHER MY+ SEW+ HOW++ , OLD MACHINE PEDAL$_A$ SEW++ .

2. **WILL** YEAR++ MACHINE **NEW** ELECTRIC SEW+ "FINE" .

3. LONG-AGO+ MONEY POOR , CLOTHES SEW=hand , SEW+ #ALL ⊥ .

4. WIFE MY+ LONG-AGO SEW+ DRESS+ , BABY CLOTHES , SHIRT , DIFFERENT++> . **LOVE** SHE !

5. NOW+ WORK+ BUSY , TIME+ SEW+ NONE$_2$.

6. PAST+ INSTITUTION L-A. , HERSELF SEW+ WHAT-FOR , DRAMA DRESS$_A$+ .

7. ME+ SEW+ STUPID ;**ONE** KNOW "WHAT" SEW=hand+ BUTTON++ ∨ CAN ME .

8. LOOK-AT=past$_2$ REMEMBER WIFE PAST+ SEW+ SHIRT me=SAME=she , "OPEN-NECK" SHORT-SLEEVE$_2$.

9. SHIRT #DO++ , GIFT=me$_2$ SURPRISE ; WHAT-FOR CELEBRATE WEDDING FEW‿YEAR .

10. SEW=hand , SEW+ , CROCHET , KNIT , CAN YOU ?

11. me=**GIFT**=her$_2$ WIFE SEW+ MACHINE **NEW** ALL-INCLUDE FANCY, ME‿WANT .

12. me=GIFT=her$_2$ UNDERSTAND+ HERSELF #BACK SEW+ SHIRT me=SAME=she$_2$.

Translation Exercises—English to ASL

Translate the following sentences from English into ASL equivalents.

1. When I was growing up, my mother sewed most of our clothes.

2. For many years, she used a machine that operated by a foot pedal.

3. She made shirts, overalls, and dresses for the family.

4. She was also an expert at hand sewing and stitching.

5. Selecting the right pattern for what you want to sew is important.

6. The pattern tells you how much material you will need to buy.

7. Some patterns are more difficult to cut out than others.

8. Did you learn sewing in school before?

9. Do you know how to pin a pattern on material before cutting it out?

10. It's easier if you have a long sewing table, but you can use the floor.

11. I would like to learn how to crochet; will you teach me?

12. Yes, if you teach me how to sew my own clothes; I want to save money!

Single-Slot Substitution Drills

Practice signing the following target sentences, substituting the suggested vocabulary in each slot. If you have problems with any of the vocabulary, consult your instructor for help.

1. LEARN+ SEW+ WANT++ YOU ? FIRST , BUY <u>P-A-T-T-E-R-N</u> **NEED** YOU .

　　　　　　　　　　　　　　　　　　　　　　　　THREAD

　　　　　　　　　　　　　　　　　　　　　　　　MATERIAL

　　　　　　　　　　　　　　　　　　　　　　　　PIN++

　　　　　　　　　　　　　　　　　　　　　　　　SCISSORS

　　　　　　　　　　　　　　　　　　　　　　　　SEW+ MACHINE

　　　　　　　　　　　　　　　　　　　　　　　　P-A-T-T-E-R-N

2. LEARN+ <u>SEW+</u> ME WANT ; you=HELP=me TEACH=me YOU ?

　　　　　CROCHET

　　　　　SEW=hand

　　　　　STITCH

　　　　　SEW+

3. WIFE MY+ SEW+ SHIRT me=SAME=she she=GIFT=me$_2$ WHAT-FOR ,

　<u>BIRTHDAY MY+</u> .

　WEDDING CELEBRATE

　PLEASE=noun$_2$

　CHRISTMAS

　BIRTHDAY MY+

4. MATERIAL P-A-T-T-E-R-N PAPER-ON PIN+ STICK=around scissors=CUT <u>KNACK</u> YOU ?

　　　　　　　　　　　　　　　　　　　　　　　　　　　　　　　　　　　LEARN FINISH$_2$

　　　　　　　　　　　　　　　　　　　　　　　　　　　　　　　　　　　LEARN LATE+

　　　　　　　　　　　　　　　　　　　　　　　　　　　　　　　　　　　LEARN WANT++

　　　　　　　　　　　　　　　　　　　　　　　　　　　　　　　　　　　KNACK

5. BUTTON++ SEW=hand+ <u>KNACK</u> ME .

　　　　　　　　　　　STUPID

　　　　　　　　　　　NEED

　　　　　　　　　　　WANT

　　　　　　　　　　　HOW DON'T-KNOW

　　　　　　　　　　　KNACK

6. me=TEACH=you   SEW+   UNDERSTAND+   YOURSELF   BRING   <u>MATERIAL</u> .

        PIN+ ,   THREAD

        SEW+   MACHINE

        P-A-T-T-E-R-N

        SCISSORS

        MATERIAL

7. PAST+   MOTHER   MY+   KNACK   "WHAT"   <u>SEW=hand+</u> .

        SEW+

        CROCHET

        WEAVE

        KNIT

        EMBROIDER

        SEW=hand+

8. OLD   SEW   MACHINE   ITS   PEDAL$_A$ <u>SEW+   FINISH$_1$</u>   YOU ?

        SEE   FINISH$_1$

        EXPERIENCE   FINISH$_1$

        TRY   FINISH$_1$

        HAVE

        SEW+   FINISH$_1$

9. PAST+   WIFE   MY+   SEW+   <u>SHIRT</u>   me=SAME=she$_2$.

        ROBE

        COAT

        COAT‿PANTS

        PANTS

        SHIRT

10. NOW   DAY   PEOPLE   AGAIN   WANT   LEARN   <u>SEW=hand+</u>   SAME   LONG-AGO .

        KNIT

        CROCHET

        SPINNING

        EMBROIDER

        WEAVE

        SEW=hand+

Suggested Activities

1. Practice expressive signing of the ASL to English translation exercises *before* translating them.

2. Act out the dialogue used in this lesson. Since it involves only two females, it may help to pair off female class members to carry out the dialogue. Male members of the class can use the ASL to English translation exercises for similar practice in pairs.

3. Bring a simple pattern for a shirt, blouse, or coat to class and give sewing instructions in ASL.

4. Bring a slip cover or upholstery pattern to class and present the sewing instructions in ASL.

5. For fingerspelling practice, you may use some of the sentences or selected phrases from the sentences in the English to ASL translation exercises in this lesson. Pair off in class. Partners may then take turns randomly selecting two or three sentences or phrases to fingerspell to each other while the instructor observes.

6. Write an English version of the glossed introductory paragraph.

Lesson 8

Benny and Gloria's New Home

NEW HOME

BENNY , GLORIA HIMSELF HERSELF PAST+ PLAN+ DRAW₂ **NEW** HOUSE . FINISH₂
those=TWO BUILD BRICK++> . HOUSE **BEAUTIFUL** WHEW ! ONE FLOOR "L-SHAPE"
ELECTRIC all=INCLUDE . ENTER=noun+ FLOOR AROUND **ITALIAN** M-A-R-B-L-E
BLUE *GREEN* BLACK MIX , BEAUTIFUL TRUE ! FORMAL ROOM LARGE , EAT_A ROOM
FORMAL , FAMILY ROOM COMFORTABLE , KITCHEN COLOR₂ BRIGHT PLUS DOOR+
SHELF++∨ EAT=noun+ PUT=shelf₂++∨ . BED ROOM THREE , BATH TWO PLUS
SMALL TOILET . BASEMENT INCLUDE R-E-C ROOM , WASH=clothes ROOM , WORK
ROOM THAT=there BENNY PUT_A ALL CARPENTER THING++ . TWO FIRE
MANTEL . . . ONE WHERE ? FAMILY ROOM ; OTHER WHERE ? R-E-C ROOM . FORMAL
ROOM GLASS SLIDE=door₂ OUT AROUND PRIVATE BRICK++> WALL P-A-T-I-O WITH
BRICK+ B-B-Q . those=TWO=benny=gloria PLEASE=noun₂ **NEW** HOUSE . DRINK_A BAR
GO=down R-E-C ROOM HAVE . FRIEND THEIR COME=here PLAY-POOL , PING-PONG
VARIOUS .

Glossed Sentences, Translations, and Grammatical Notes

GLORIA HOUSE **NEW** ELECTRIC all = INCLUDE , **LOVE** SHE .

Gloria loves her brand new, all-electric house.

Emphatic sign **NEW** means "brand new." all = INCLUDE means "everything included."

PROBLEM : SUPPOSE ELECTRIC OFF ; COOK , VACUUM CAN'T SHE !

There's one problem: if the electricity goes off, she can't cook or vacuum!

The noun KITCHEN has hands touching and a single movement, while for the verb COOK, the hands do not touch and multiple movements may occur.

---

2. **ONCE-IN-A-WHILE** ELECTRIC OFF WHY+ + , STORM‿LIGHTNING .

The electricity only goes off once in a great while because of an electrical storm.

The emphatic sign **ONCE-IN-A-WHILE** is executed slowly and with larger circular movements than in its regular form. It can mean "seldom," "almost never," and "rarely."

SUPPOSE ELECTRIC $NONE_2$, we = TWO FIX COLD+   EAT = noun+ .

If there's no electricity, we fix ourselves a cold meal.

NONE can be made with either one or two hands: $NONE_1$ or $NONE_2$. FIX and MAKE are similar, but the fists remain touching in FIX; for MAKE, the fists must separate between twists.

---

3. GOOD THING FIRE‿MANTEL OUR HOME HAVE .

It's a good thing we have a fireplace in our home.

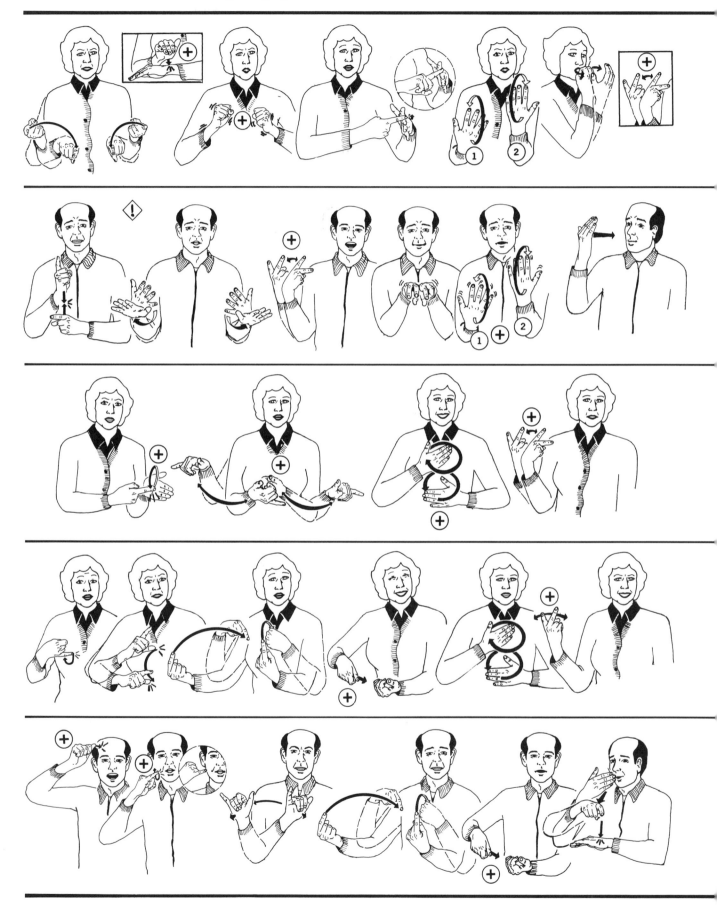

4. HAPPEN EVENING CHILLY , START FIRE **WARM** we = TWO .

If evenings are chilly, we make ourselves a cozy fire.

Raising the eyebrows while signing EVENING CHILLY also supports the conditional meaning: *"If* the evening is chilly. . . ."

5. CORRECT ! FINISH$_2$ we = TWO "SNUGGLE-UP" FIRE CLOSE-UP .

That's right! And then we snuggle up close to the fire.

FINISH here is made with a firm, single movement. "SNUGGLE-UP" is a variant of the sign SIT-TOGETHER: the index fingers rub lightly against each other.

6. ONCE-IN-A-WHILE PARTY PLEASE = noun$_2$ we = TWO .

Benny and I enjoy an occasional party.

PLEASE = noun$_2$ can be translated as "pleasure," "pleasing," and "enjoy."

JANE , LAWRENCE COME = here PLAY-POOL PLEASE = noun$_2$ those = TWO .

Jane and Lawrence enjoy coming over to play pool.

PLAY-POOL is a mime sign depicting the act of moving a cue stick.

7. ALEXANDER , JENNIFER those-two = SAME = them COME = here PLAY-POOL GOOD TIME .

Alexander and Jennifer also come over to play pool and have a good time.

The movement of SAME + must connect the spatial locations established for the two couples.

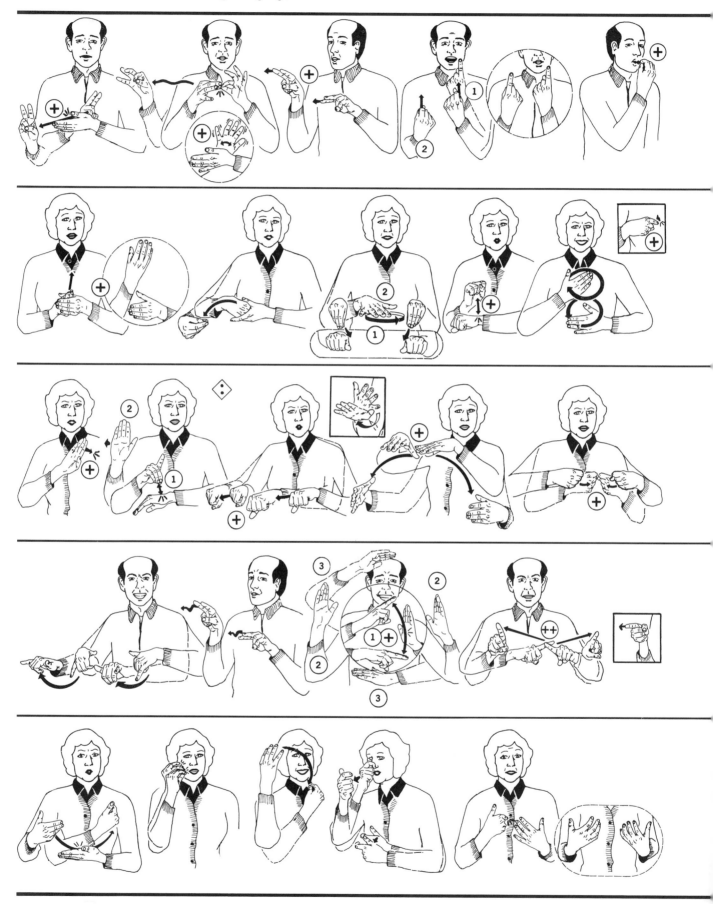

two = WEEK + +   CAPTION   MOVIE   LOOK-AT$_2$,   POPCORN   EAT + .

We all watch a captioned film and eat popcorn every other week.

Time signs like two = WEEK + + are frequently placed at the beginning of the sentence to establish a time frame for the activities to follow.

8. GROW = noun +   OUT   SOW-SEED AROUND   WORK   PLEASE = noun$_2$ ME + .

In the springtime, I really enjoy working outside in the garden.

BENNY   DUTY HIS :   MOW +   FINISH$_1$,   HEAP$_2$ +   TRIM + > .

It is Benny's job to mow the lawn and then to trim the bushes.

The movement of TRIM should follow the shape of HEAP$_2$ +.

9. STILL$_2$ LOOK-AT = around$_2$ PAINTING +   DIFFERENT + + >   SHE = gloria .

Gloria is still looking around at many different paintings.

PAINTING here involves a repeated stroking action; the size of the strokes indicates the approximate sizes of several paintings.

10. **NEW**   HOME   PRETTY ,   INTEREST   ME WANT .

I want my new home to be attractive and interesting.

ME is blended so well into the next sign, WANT, that a separate handshape with the index finger pointing toward the subject is not really visible.

Vocabulary Review

Test your ability to produce the following signs or sign phrases.

BAR

BASEMENT

BATH ROOM

BEAUTIFUL

BED ROOM

BLUE

BRICK + + >

BRIGHT

BUILD

CAPTION MOVIE

"CLOSE-UP"

COLD EAT = noun +

COOK

clipper = CUT

DIFFERENT + + >

DUTY HIS

ELECTRIC all = INCLUDE

ELECTRIC OFF

EVENING CHILLY

FIRE MANTEL

FIRE **WARM**

FIX

GO = down

GOOD THING

GROW = noun +

HEAP$_2$ +

HOME

INTEREST

MOW = grass

ONCE-IN-A-WHILE

OUT +

PAINTING

PLAY-POOL

POPCORN

PROBLEM

those-two = SAME = them

SHELF + + ∨

SLIDE = door$_2$

"SNUGGLE-UP"

SOW-SEED AROUND

STILL$_2$

STORM LIGHTNING

THAT = there

TOILET

VACUUM

WALL

WASH = clothes

WATCH

two = WEEK + +

Notes

Translation Exercises—ASL to English

Translate the following glossed sentences into appropriate English equivalents.

1. DAUGHTER MY+ DUTY HER "WHAT" , VACUUM HOUSE #ALL=around .

2. FRIEND MY+ those=FOUR COME=here₂ WHAT-FOR , play=CARDS .

3. SON YOUR+ MOW+ LIKE HE ? PAY ONE-DOLLAR one=HOUR WILL ME .

4. WIFE we=TWO INTEREST₂ "WHAT" , LOOK-AT=around OLD PAINTING+ .

5. PAST+ SUMMER OUT SOW-SEED AROUND MY+ GROW TOMATO **BIG=tomato** .

6. long=PAST+ GIRL SWEETHEART we=TWO PLEASE=noun "SNUGGLE-UP" FIRE CLOSE-UP .

7. WIFE we=TWO GO+ FRIEND HOUSE WHAT-FOR , PLAY-POOL PLEASE=noun we=TWO .

8. ONCE-IN-A-WHILE ELECTRIC OFF WHY++ BAD STORM LIGHTNING !

9. PLEASE=noun COOK EAT=noun+ DIFFERENT++> YOU ?

10. FIRE_MANTEL CLEAN+ CHIMNEY UP=inside , HATE ME !

11. HOUSE YOUR+ FIRE_MANTEL ONE , TWO HAVE YOU ?

12. HAPPEN EVENING CHILLY , #DO+ you=TWO?

Translation Exercises—English to ASL

Translate the following sentences from English into ASL equivalents.

1. Does your house have sliding glass doors to a patio?

2. How often does your family make and eat popcorn?

3. My new house has one fireplace.

4. How many fireplaces do you have in your new house?

5. Do you have an all-electric home?

6. Have you ever experienced a sudden loss of electrical power while vacuuming your carpets?

7. Do you have a garden at home?

8. I want to start a new garden next spring.

9. Who mows the grass and prunes the bushes around your home?

10. We want to finish the basement in our house next winter.

11. What do you like to do on chilly evenings?

12. Do you have any large paintings in your house?

Single-Slot Substitution Drills

Practice signing the following target sentences, substituting the suggested vocabulary in each slot. If you have problems with any of the vocabulary, consult your instructor for help.

1. FRIEND INVITE <u>we = TWO</u> GO = there .
                we = THREE
                we = FOUR
                we = FIVE
                we = TWO

2. we = TWO INTEREST "WHAT" ? <u>PLAY-POOL</u> .
                                    SWIM +
                                    PAINTING
                                    BICYCLE +
                                    RUN +
                                    TENNIS
                                    PLAY-POOL

3. SEARCH NEW + <u>PAINTING +</u> .
                    CLOTHES
                    CAR
                    RESTAURANT
                    WORK +
                    PAINTING +

4. SOW-SEED AROUND MY + GROW <u>FLOWER +</u> .
                                        LETTUCE
                                          TOMATO
                                        ONION
                                        GREEN P-E-P-P-E-R-S
                                        FLOWER +

5. ME WANT SEE <u>CAPTION MOVIE</u> YOUR + .
                        PAINTING +
                        NEW HOUSE
                        NEW FIRE MANTEL
                        SOW-SEED AROUND
                        CAPTION MOVIE

6. NOW‿WEEK   MOW = grass +   DUTY   WHO ?   <u>HIS +</u> .

                                                            those = TWO

                                                            WIFE

                                                            MY +

                                                            BOY +

                                                            we = TWO

                                                            HIS +

7. WEEK = next   COME   HOUSE   MY + ,   we = TWO   <u>CHAT + +</u> .

                                                            PLAY-POOL

                                                            DANCE

                                                            SING

                                                            PAINT +

                                                            COOK +

                                                            CHAT + +

8. ELECTRIC   OFF   WHY + +   <u>LIGHTNING</u> .

                                        DISCONNECT

                                          BROKE

                                          BURN

                                          FIX

                                          LIGHTNING

9. **NEW**   HOUSE   YOUR +   <u>**BEAUTIFUL**</u>   WHEW !

                                        LARGE

                                        FANCY_A

                                        "MONEY-WHEW"

                                        "FINE"

                                        BEAUTIFUL

10. **NEW**   HOUSE   YOUR +   <u>BED   ROOM</u>   MANY₂ ∧ ?

                                        BATH

                                          ROOM +

                                          FLOOR +

                                          DOOR +

                                          FIRE‿MANTEL

                                        BED   ROOM

Suggested Activities

1. Describe your home to your class, using as much of the Sign review vocabulary from this lesson as you can.

2. Cut out some descriptions used in advertising homes for sale, both new and old. Bring them to class for possible translation material. You might try to describe a house that really appeals to you.

3. Obtain the floor plan for a new house and bring it to class. Try describing a set of floor plans using principles of positioning, directionality, sizing, etc., that you have learned in your Sign Language training.

4. Find out about captioned films for the deaf and whether you might possibly be able to see one with deaf friends so that you will appreciate the value of such media for deaf or hearing-impaired persons.

5. Visit the home of a deaf friend who has a closed captioned decoder so you can see how such devices are helpful and necessary for deaf people to understand more fully TV programs and entertainment.

6. If you visit the home of deaf friends, learn additional ASL signs they may use to describe things around their house or apartment.

7. Act out the dialogue used in this lesson. Two people may volunteer or be selected from the group to portray each character.

8. For fingerspelling practice, you may use some of the sentences or selected phrases from the sentences in the English to ASL translation exercises in this lesson. Pair off in class. Partners may then take turns randomly selecting two or three sentences or phrases to fingerspell to each other while the instructor observes.

9. Write an English version of the glossed introductory paragraph.

At the Dentist

DENTIST GO+

APPEAR tooth=PAIN++ BAD DENTIST GO **NEED** KNOW+ YOU . IMPORTANT DENTIST
GO ATTEMPT one=YEAR=ahead++ REGULAR WHY++ , EXAMINE₂ TOOTH=plural
LET'S-SEE GOOD #OR APPEAR PROBLEM . REPAIR QUICK BEFORE WORSE+ .
SOMETIMES DENTIST GO WHY++ , C-A-V-I-T-Y . DENTIST LOOK-AT=*around-mouth* . #IF++
C-A-V-I-T-Y BAD , tooth=DRILL **NEED** . WHAT-FOR , BLACK WEAR-OUT IN TOOTH REMOVE
BEFORE IN+ NEW+ . DENTIST FEW POINT++∨ : FIRST , SHOOT=cheek SHOOT=gum
MEDICINE FINGERSPELL...N-O-V-O-C-A-I-N . THAT G-U-M FREEZE , MAYBE CHEEK FEEL
NONE . FINISH₂ DENTIST PROCEED WORK++ tooth=DRILL . HELP tooth=PAIN REDUCE
FINE , BUT LATER FACE FEEL HALF MISSING ! ALWAYS PEOPLE STORY-TALK GO
DENTIST NOT PLEASE=noun₂ , BUT #IF++ GO++ REGULAR PROBLEM REDUCE !
ALSO DENTIST tooth=BRUSH ELECTRIC MAKE TOOTH=plural WHITE , SHINY=tooth₂ ,
FEEL GOOD !

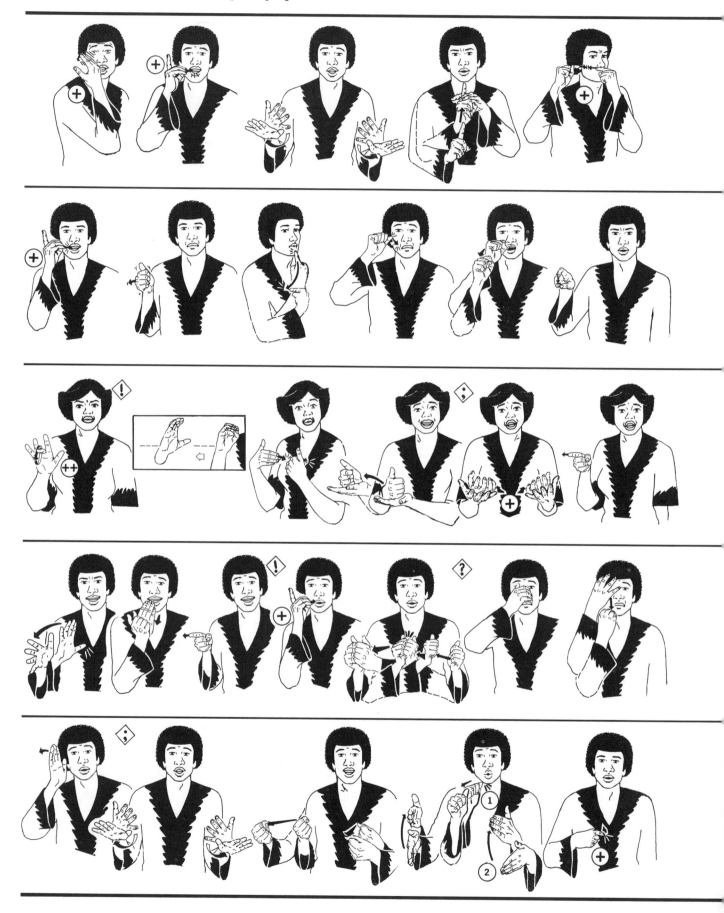

Glossed Sentences, Translations, and Grammatical Notes

1. near=PAST DENTIST FINISH₂ ,   APPEAR   tooth=PAIN+ .

I just recently went to the dentist; now I have a bad toothache.

In near=PAST as in near=RECENT (see Lesson 2, sentence 1), the hand is positioned very close to the face. Note the difference in handshapes but the similarity of movements. APPEAR is translatable as "appear," "pop up," "come up," "crop up," etc. PAIN made close to the teeth means "toothache."

DENTIST HIMSELF TELL=me OPERATE=mouth tooth=PULL **NEED** !

The dentist told me I have to have that tooth removed by surgery!

DENTIST here is a modified "D" form of the traditional sign meaning "dentist." OPERATE, like PAIN, takes on a different meaning with different body locations; made next to the mouth or teeth, it means "oral surgery."

2. PITY++ ! O-I-L C-L-O-V-E HAVE , it=HELP=you ; WANT+ YOU ?

You poor thing! I have some oil of cloves that will help you; do you want some?

3. FINE , SWEET‿YOU ! DENTIST you=WITH=me ? MASK=nose SLEEP

That's fine; you're sweet! Will you go to the dentist with me? I'll be put to sleep

WITH in this sentence is a verb showing directional movement. (See Lesson 6, sentence 10.) It can also be translated as "accompany." The sign MASK=nose here means being given "gas" or "ether." It could also be used to mean any kind of mask worn over the nose for protection from dust, germs, etc.

WILL ; FINISH₂ DRIVE NOT‿ALLOW ME+ .

with ether; when it's finished, I won't be allowed to drive.

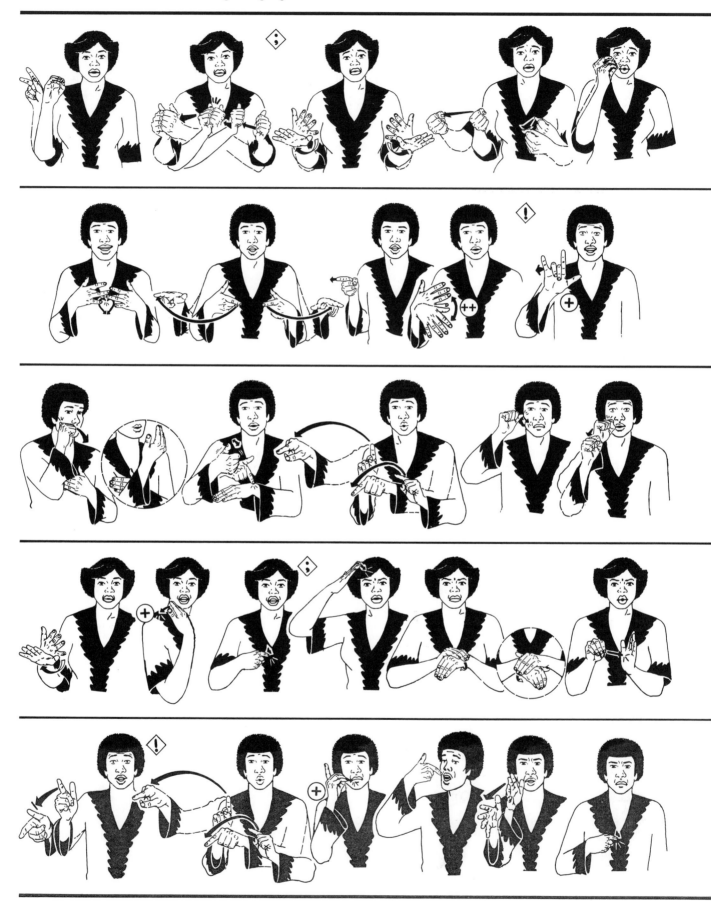

4. O-K   me = WITH = you ;   FINISH₂   DRIVE   HOME .

OK, I'll go with you and drive you back home when you're finished.

5. HEART‿LARGE   YOU   WHEW !   "I-LOVE-YOU" + !

You really have a big heart, and I just love you for it!

HEART‿LARGE is a blend, equivalent to the figurative expression, "You have a big heart." It could also be used to literally indicate an "enlarged or oversized heart." "I-LOVE-YOU" is a sign made with the superimposed fingerspelled letters I, L, and Y. It can have either a casual meaning or an intimate meaning.

TOMORROW‿MORNING   TIME   TEN   GO   OPERATE = mouth   tooth = PULL .

I go to have that tooth removed by surgery at ten o'clock tomorrow morning.

6. FINISH₁   PAST +   ME ;   KNOW   COMFORTABLE   **NONE** .

I've been through that before; I know it's not comfortable at all.

NONE is made with the "zero" handshape striking the other palm. It means "not at all!" In other contexts, it may mean "absolutely none!" or "absolutely nothing!"

7. **SECOND = you** !   GO   DENTIST   tooth = DRILL   "VOMIT"   ME !

I agree with you 100%! I hate going to the dentist to have a tooth drilled!

In DRILL, here, the index finger is positioned near the tooth where drilling took place. Movement is simulated. "VOMIT" may mean "hate," "detest," or "grossly dislike." Your instructor can demonstrate its difference from VOMIT, meaning "to throw up."

8. ALWAYS BAD NOT ; DENTIST TOOTH = plural CLEAN + FEEL͜ GOOD .

It's not always bad; when the dentist cleans your teeth, it feels good.

In the sign TOOTH = plural, the index finger arcs in front of the upper jaw, indicating "a set of teeth."

9. TRUE + + . TOOTH = plural **CLEAN** LIKE BEST ME + .

That's true. I like real clean teeth the best.

NOW O-I-L C-L-O-V-E tooth = MASSAGE PLEASE + tooth = PAIN REDUCE .

Now please rub some oil of cloves on my tooth to reduce the pain.

10. O-K₂ , DENTIST ASSISTANT **GOOD** ME + .

OK. I'm a good dental assistant.

11. MAYBE , LET'S-SEE ; WHEW , tooth = PAIN **TOO-MUCH** !

Maybe, we'll see; oh, that tooth hurts so much!

Vocabulary Review

Test your ability to produce the following signs or sign phrases.

APPEAR	LOOK-AT = *around-mouth*	REMOVE
ASSISTANT	MASK = nose	REPAIR
ATTEMPT	tooth = MASSAGE	**SECOND = you**
BAD NOT	MAYBE	SHINY = tooth₂
tooth = BRUSH	MEDICINE	SHOOT = cheek
CLEAN	MISSING	SHOOT = gum
CLEAN +	**NONE**	SLEEP
COMFORTABLE	NOT͜ ALLOW	SWEET͜ YOU
DENTIST	OPERATE = mouth	TIME͜ TEN
tooth = DRILL	tooth = PAIN + +	TOMORROW͜ MORNING
DRIVE	near = PAST	TOOTH = plural
HEART͜ LARGE	PEOPLE	"VOMIT"
it = HELP = you	PITY + +	WEAR-OUT
"I-LOVE-YOU" +	POINT + +	WHITE
IN +	tooth = PULL	WORSE +
LATER	REGULAR	one = YEAR = ahead + +

Notes

Translation Exercises—ASL to English

Translate the following glossed sentences into appropriate English equivalents.

1. APPEAR   tooth = PAIN + + ,   #DO$_2$ YOU ?

2. PAST +   DENTIST   OPERATE = mouth   tooth = PULL ,   FINISH$_1$ YOU ?

3. PAST +   OPERATE = mouth   tooth = PULL ,   REMEMBER +   DENTIST   #WHAT   MASK = nose   SLEEP   QUICK   ME .

4. DENTIST   LOOK-AT = *around-mouth* = your   FIND   C-A-V-I-T-Y ,   tooth = DRILL   **NEED**   YOU !

5. FIRST ,   MEDICINE   N-O-V-O-C-A-I-N   SHOOT = cheek   SHOOT = gum ;   FINISH$_2$,   AFTER-WHILE   PROCEED   tooth = DRILL .

6. MEDICINE   N-O-V-O-C-A-I-N   SHOOT = cheek   SHOOT = gum   "VOMIT"$_2$ ME !

7. DENTIST   OLD +   BLACK   IN = tooth +   YOUR +   SUBTRACT = tooth +   FINISH$_1$,   SHOOT = water = around = mouth   CLEAN ,   NEW +   IN = tooth +   FINISH$_1$,   FEEL   BETTER !

8. PAST +   tooth = PAIN +   YOU ,   O-I-L   C-L-O-V-E   tooth = MASSAGE   FINISH$_2$?   **HELP** = you ?

9. TOOTH = plural   YOUR +   **WHITE** ,   SHINY = tooth$_2$;   LUCKY   YOU   WHEW !

10. WEEK + past   GO-OUT   DENTIST   ME ;   TOOTH = plural   CLEAN +   FINISH$_2$ ME .

11. APPOINTMENT   DENTIST   MY +   WEEK = ahead   ME .

12. GO +   DENTIST   REGULAR   TOOTH = plural   PROBLEM   **REDUCE**   WILL   YOU !

Translation Exercises—English to ASL

Translate the following sentences from English into ASL equivalents.

1. Do you go to your dentist regularly once a year?

2. I've had tooth extractions both by my dentist and by dental surgery.

3. Someone must drive you home after dental surgery.

4. A toothache may be caused by a cavity in your tooth.

5. Oil of cloves sometimes helps reduce the pain temporarily.

6. My dentist sometimes gives me a shot of novocain before drilling.

7. It takes a long time for the novocain effects to wear off.

8. That's right! You may feel that part of your face is missing!

9. Your mouth feels very good after the dentist cleans your teeth.

10. A good dentist is like a good friend in time of need.

11. You've got to find the right one; then you're in good hands.

12. If you brush your teeth regularly, you should have fewer problems.

Mixed-Slot Substitution Drills

Practice signing the following target sentences, substituting the suggested vocabulary in each slot. If you have problems with any of the vocabulary, consult your instructor for help.

1. TOMORROW MORNING TIME 11:00 GO OPERATE = mouth tooth = PULL WILL ME.
 YESTERDAY   TIME 9:30   FINISH$_1$
 two = WEEK = past   TUESDAY   FINISH$_1$
 TOMORROW AFTERNOON TIME 4:00   WILL
 WILL TUESDAY   TIME 10:00   FOUR
 TOMORROW MORNING   TIME 11:00   WILL

2. WEEK = past GO-OUT DENTIST ME ; TOOTH = plural CLEAN + FINISH$_2$ ME .
                 tooth = DRILL TWO
                 NEW + IN = tooth +
                 TOOTH = plural INVESTIGATE
                 TOOTH BREAK REPAIR
                 TOOTH = plural PULL + +
                 TOOTH = plural CLEAN +

3. TOMORROW MORNING DENTIST APPOINTMENT
      ME ; you = WITH = me WILL YOU ?
     YOU ; me = WITH = you   ME
   we = TWO ; you = WITH = us   YOU
   you = TWO ; me = WITH = you   ME
      ME ; you = WITH = me   YOU

4. GO DENTIST tooth = BRUSH + ELECTRIC EXPERIENCE FINISH$_1$ YOU ?
       tooth = DRILL ∧
       SHOOT = gum N-O-V-O-C-A-I-N
       X SNAPSHOT = tooth
       tooth = PULL +
       NEW IN = tooth + ∧
       tooth = BRUSH ELECTRIC

5. APPEAR **tooth = PAIN +** #DO YOU , MAYBE O-I-L C-L-O-V-E tooth = MASSAGE .
                   TAKE-PILL + A-S-P-I-R-I-N
                   TELEPHONE DENTIST
                   GO DENTIST EMERGENCY
                   O-I-L C-L-O-V-E tooth = MASSAGE

6. <u>FIRST TIME</u> APPEAR TOOTH = plural C-A-V-I-T-Y , <u>ME +</u> <u>OLD 21</u> .
     AFTER ⊥   ONCE-IN-A-WHILE
     SOMETIMES   ONE , TWO
     SOMETIMES   **NONE**$_2$
     FIRST TIME   ME + OLD 21

7. GO DENTIST <u>tooth</u> = DRILL C-A-V-I-T-Y **"VOMIT"** ME !
                   SHOOT = gum N-O-V-O-C-A-I-N
                   right-tooth = PULL ,   left-tooth = PULL
                   tooth = DRILL R-O-O-T C-A-N-A-L
                   OPERATE = mouth
                   tooth = DRILL C-A-V-I-T-Y

8. near = PAST GO DENTIST ME WHY + + , <u>IN = *tooth* +</u> <u>FALL-OUT</u> .
                                       IN = *tooth* +   BREAK
                                       tooth = PAIN BAD
                                       TOOTH = plural INVESTIGATE
                                       C-A-V-I-T-Y NEW + APPEAR
                                       IN = *tooth* + FALL-OUT

9. GO + DENTIST REGULAR TOOTH = plural <u>PROBLEM **REDUCE**</u> WILL YOU .
                                   SHINY$_2$, **WHITE**
                                     C-A-V-I-T-Y **NONE**$_2$
                                     CLEAN
                                     PROBLEM **REDUCE**

10. TOMORROW GO DENTIST OPERATE = mouth , tooth = PULL you = WITH = me ,
     <u>SWEET YOU</u> .
     HEART LARGE YOU
     I-LOVE-YOU
     PAY = you ME
     EXCHANGE WILL ME
     SWEET YOU

Suggested Activities

1. Act out the dialogue used in this lesson by pairing off one male and one female, if possible, to role play the characters. Give special attention to emotions and facial expression.

2. Practice signing the ASL to English translation exercises *before* translating the sentences. Watch facial expression needed for each sentence.

3. Relate to the class a dental experience you will never forget.

4. Set up a role-playing situation whereby one person is the "dentist" and the others are the dental patients. Use your experiences or your imagination in creating various patient types and see how the "dentist" reacts. Switch the dental role occasionally.

5. For fingerspelling practice, you may use some of the sentences or selected phrases from the sentences in the English to ASL translation exercises in this lesson. Pair off in class. Partners may then take turns randomly selecting two or three sentences or phrases to fingerspell to each other while the instructor observes.

6. Write an English version of the glossed introductory paragraph.

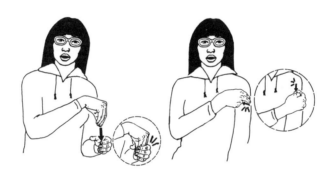

IN HOSPITAL

WEEK=past those=TWO LAWRENCE , JANE GO-OUT EAT$_A$, DANCE , GOOD TIME
PLEASE=noun$_2$! HAPPEN QUICK APPEAR SHE+jane stomach=PAIN+ . HE=lawrence BRING
HOME HER=jane BUT stomach=PAIN+ WORSE++ . HERSELF=jane FACE CHANGE
WHITE COVER=face **SICK** WHEW ! BEG+ GO DOCTOR NOW ! HE=lawrence QUICK
BRING HER=jane PUT$_2$ CAR , DRIVE⊥ HOSPITAL EMERGENCY ROOM . SHE=jane
stomach=PAIN++ PATIENT=verb **CAN'T** ! DOCTOR CAREFUL EXAMINE$_2$ FINISH$_2$ SUSPECT
A-P-P-E-N-D-I-X , PROCEED OPERATE=right-side NOW DECIDE HE=doctor ! HE=lawrence
PRAY+ SHE=jane ALL-RIGHT WILL . OPERATE=right-side FINISH$_2$, DOCTOR HIMSELF
WRITE=note GIVE=him=lawrence , INFORM=him SHE=jane ALL-RIGHT WILL .
HIMSELF=lawrence RELIEVED . DOCTOR TELL=him=lawrence GO ROOM CAN #IF++
WANT++ , STAY WITH HER=jane. HE=lawrence THANK-YOU=him=doctor . HOUR AROUND
SHE=jane WAKE-UP SLOW , SMILE , CHAT LITTLE-BIT **SLEEP-HARD** AGAIN !

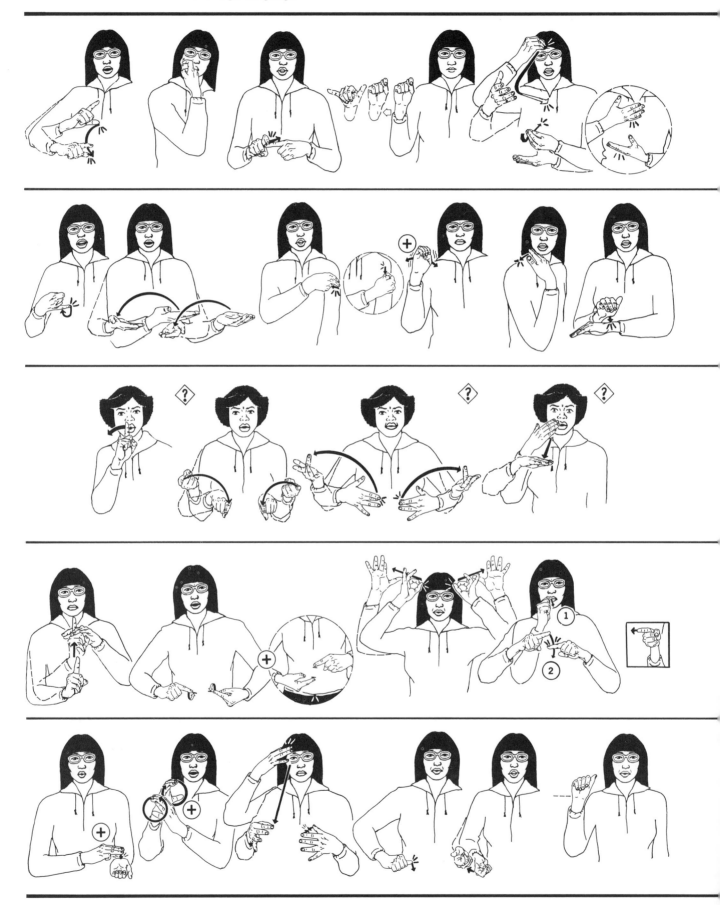

Glossed Sentences, Translations, and Grammatical Notes

1. LAWRENCE near=RECENT WIRE=me T-T-Y INFORM=me

Lawrence just informed me over the TTY that

JANE BRING ⊥ HOSPITAL EMERGENCY LAST NIGHT !

Jane was taken to the hospital emergency room last night!

BRING moves forward, which establishes a "location" for the hospital directly in front of the signer.

2. **TRUE ? HAPPEN WHAT'S-UP ? BAD ?**

Really? What happened? Is it anything serious?

3. APPEAR stomach=PAIN TERRIBLE , PATIENT=verb **CAN'T** SHE=jane .

Jane couldn't tolerate the terrible abdominal pain she had.

Compare stomach=PAIN with tooth=PAIN in Lesson 9, sentence 1. PATIENT can be translated as "tolerate," "abide," or "bear" (as in "to bear a burden").

DOCTOR EXAMINE , DECIDE OPERATE=right-side ELIMINATE=right-side A-P-P-E-N-D-I-X .

The doctor examined her and decided to perform an appendectomy.

Compare OPERATE here with the way it is made in Lesson 9, sentence 1. Note that ELIMINATE is made in the same location as OPERATE.

NOW+ O-K SEEM+ , LAWRENCE RELIEVED FINISH₁ !

Now it seems Jane is OK, and Lawrence is relieved!

4. NOW NIGHT GO VISIT **NEED** we=TWO .

We must go to the hospital to visit her tonight.

5. VISIT TIME ANY BETWEEN FOUR>EIGHT CAN .

We can visit her any time between four and eight o'clock.

In FOUR > EIGHT, the hand moves to the right as it changes from one number to the other; this indicates the range of the time interval.

6. YOU IN HOSPITAL , BELIEVE **CAN'T** !

I can't believe you're in the hospital!

HAPPY SEE=you ; FACE FINE ! FEEL YOU ?

We are happy to see you; you look fine! How do you feel?

The sign FACE relates to physical appearance ("visage" and "resemblance") as well as to the face as a body part.

7. FINE ! HAPPY COME SEE͜ME you=TWO .

Just fine! I'm very happy the two of you came to see me.

SEE͜ME has a short movement—in towards the signer's face and chest.

NURSE SHOOT=arm HELP=me PAIN+ REDUCE .

The nurse gave me a shot to help reduce the pain.

SHOOT, like PAIN and OPERATE, can of course be made next to many parts of the body.

8. DOCTOR OPERATE=right-side FINISH$_2$, SEW=hand=right-side MANY$_2$?

After the doctor operated on you, how many stitches did you get?

In this sentence, SEW=hand is modified to show the location of the object being sewn. Because the context is "surgery," the sign translates as "stitches."

9. ALMOST-NOTHING . DOCTOR **THIRSTY** NOT ! OPERATE=right-side SMALL-MEASURE .

Hardly any. The doctor wasn't anxious to cut me wide open! He just made a small incision, less than two inches.

ALMOST-NOTHING can mean "hardly any," "very little," or "next to none." The emphatic **THIRSTY** is used here figuratively to mean "crave" or "strongly desire." In a negative context, however, a colloquial translation is "wasn't anxious to." SMALL-MEASURE can vary in location with the thing being measured; here, the "scar."

WELL QUICK WILL ME , UNDERSTAND+ TAKE-PILL+ REGULAR .

I will heal fast provided I take my medicine regularly.

A repeated form, UNDERSTAND+, is used here in an idiomatic sense of "provided" or "if."

Vocabulary Review

Test your ability to produce the following signs or sign phrases.

AGAIN	FACE FINE	SLEEP-HARD
ALL-RIGHT	FEEL YOU	SMALL-MEASURE
ALMOST-NOTHING	GOOD TIME	SMILE
ANY	HAPPEN	STAY
BAD	HOSPITAL	SUSPECT
BEG+	INFORM = me	TAKE-PILL+
BELIEVE	NOW	TELL = you/him/her
BETWEEN FOUR>EIGHT	NURSE	TERRIBLE
CAN'T	OPERATE = right-side	TRUE
CAR	stomach = PAIN	VISIT
CAREFUL	PAST NIGHT	WAKE-UP
DOCTOR	PATIENT = verb	WEEK = past
EITHER	PRAY	WELL QUICK
ELIMINATE = right-side	SEW = hand = right-side	WHITE COVER = face
EMERGENCY	SHOOT = arm	WIRE = me T-T-Y
EXAMINE	SICK	WRITE = note

Notes

Translation Exercises—ASL to English

Translate the following glossed sentences into appropriate English equivalents.

1. PAST+ GO HOSPITAL OPERATE=right-side ELIMINATE=right-side FINISH₂ YOU ?

2. GO HOSPITAL OPERATE=right-side ELIMINATE=right-side NEVER ME .

3. PAST+ APPROXIMATE TEN YEAR GO HOSPITAL OPERATE=right-side OTHER #WHAT , H-E-R-N-I-A .

4. MANY₂+ TIME-PERIOD GO++ HOSPITAL EMERGENCY , REASON+ DIFFERENT++> .

5. **PAST** SEVERAL YEAR ME GO HOSPITAL EMERGENCY WHY++ , BREAK H-E-E-L .

6. DOCTOR EXAMINE₂ CAREFUL FINISH₂ , he=SEND=me X͡ SNAPSHOT ROOM .

7. X͡ SNAPSHOT FINISH₂ , FIND **TRUE** BREAK H-E-E-L , **NEED** right=foot=leg=COVER .

8. **HAPPEN** BOY **YOUNG** OLD TWELVE THIRTEEN BETWEEN BRING=into EMERGENCY ; KNEE HIS+ **WEAR-OUT** , BLOOD WHEW !

9. HOW HAPPEN ? **BAD** HIMSELF FALL=continuous HIT=object ROCK , KNEE **WEAR-OUT** FINISH₂ !

10. DOCTOR #DO , PAY-ATTENTION=boy FIRST , IGNORE=me ; ME+ WAIT++ two=**HOUR** , NEVER FORGET !

11. WILL right=foot=leg=COVER FINISH₂ AT-LAST , ME GO-OUT HOME : CRUTCH₂ USE THREE **MONTH** **NEED** ME !

12. LOOK-AT=past REMEMBER STAY₁+ HOSPITAL SIX DAY ; AT-LAST PARDON , GO-OUT HOME !

Translation Exercises—English to ASL

Translate the following sentences from English into ASL equivalents.

1. Have you ever had an operation before?

2. Operating procedures now are different than they used to be.

3. A hospital emergency room can be very busy at times.

4. You may have to wait a long time for attention.

5. Some hospitals have liberal visiting hours.

6. Other hospitals have restricted visiting hours, maybe between four and eight in the evening.

7. I cut my leg just above my foot on broken glass; it took six stitches to close the cut.

8. How many stitches did you have after your surgery?

9. Have you visited any relatives or friends in the hospital?

10. No one enjoys staying in a hospital, but sometimes it's necessary.

11. A friendly, pleasant nurse can help you recover quickly.

12. Would you like to work in a hospital ward or emergency room?

Mixed-Slot Substitution Drills

Practice signing the following target sentences, substituting the suggested vocabulary in each slot. If you have problems with any of the vocabulary, consult your instructor for help.

1. PEOPLE "SLEEP-IN" HOSPITAL WHAT-FOR , REASON DIFFERENT++ > , MAYBE
   <u>APPEAR **SICK**</u> .
   OPERATE SOMETHING
   HEART⌒HIT
   CAR COLLIDE , HURT **BAD**
   APPEAR **SICK**

2. <u>LONG-AGO OPERATE FINISH₂ ME #WHAT</u> , <u>TONSILS = remove</u> .

PAST+	W-A-R-T ELIMINATE = left-elbow
near = RECENT	K-N-E-E BREAK , FIX
SEVERAL YEAR PAST	H-E-R-N-I-A
YEAR = past+	LUMP GROW ELIMINATE = right-neck
LONG-AGO	TONSILS = remove

3. PAST+ HOSPITAL EMERGENCY FINISH₁ ME WHAT-FOR , <u>right = LEG GLASS CUT</u> .
   right = HEEL BREAK
   stomach = PAIN+ **TERRIBLE**
   right-foot = PUNCTURE N-A-I-L
   left = ARM SPRAIN
   right = LEG GLASS CUT

4. DOCTOR <u>OPERATE = right-side</u> FINISH₂ SEW = hand = right-side MANY₂ ?
   OPERATE = neck = right-side
   OPERATE = left-arm
   OPERATE = chest = center
   OPERATE = right-side

5. PAST+ OPERATE FINISH₂ , PAIN+ REDUCE HOW++ ,
   <u>TAKE-PILL+ SIX-HOUR+</u> .
   NURSE SHOOT = arm EVERY-MORNING
   SLEEP NOW-AND-THEN
   CHAT+ FRIEND , FORGET SELF
   THINK POSITIVE
   TAKE-PILL+ SIX-HOUR+

6. VISIT HOSPITAL SEE FRIEND WANT+ YOU , LIMIT THE TIME BETWEEN
   <u>FOUR>EIGHT</u> .
   TWO>EIGHT THIRTY
   TWELVE>EIGHT
   ONE>EIGHT
   TEN>FOUR , SIX>EIGHT THIRTY
   FOUR>EIGHT

7. FRIEND MY+ OPERATE=right-side , ELIMINATE=right-side A-P-P-E-N-D-I-X
   FINISH , <u>FACE **FINE**</u> .
           SICK WHEW
           WHITE **COVER**=**face**
           WEAK WHEW
           FACE **FINE**

8. PAST+ <u>**DIZZY+**</u> SAME=continuous$_2$+ GO HOSPITAL INVESTIGATE , **WRONG** , VANISH .
      chest=PAIN+
      right-hip=PAIN+
      head=PAIN+
      stomach=PAIN+
      DIZZY+

9. WIFE MY+ "SLEEP-IN" HOSPITAL WHY++ , DOCTOR ORDER
   <u>X SNAPSHOT #ALL=body</u> .
   BODY INVESTIGATE
   TEST++ DIFFERENT++>
   REST , LET'S-SEE **IMPROVE**
   MAYBE OPERATE=stomach
   X SNAPSHOT #ALL=body

10. HOSPITAL PARDON FINISH$_2$ GO-OUT HOME , HERSELF=wife IMPROVE WILL ,
    UNDERSTAND++ <u>TAKE-PILL++ REGULAR</u> .
           EXERCISE LITTLE-BIT++
           REST NOW-AND-THEN
           OFF-WORK+ FOUR=week
           SEE DOCTOR TWO=week++ ∨
           TAKE-PILL++ REGULAR

Suggested Activities

1. Relate to the class a hospital experience you have had, whether it be one of your own or that of a family member or close associate.

2. Act out the dialogue used in this lesson. Three persons may volunteer or be selected from the group to portray the characters.

3. Practice signing the ASL to English translation exercises *before* translating the sentences. Watch facial expression needed for each sentence.

4. For fingerspelling practice, you may use some of the sentences or selected phrases from the sentences in the English to ASL translation exercises in this lesson. Pair off in class. Partners may then take turns randomly selecting two or three sentences or phrases to fingerspell to each other while the instructor observes.

5. Write an English version of the glossed introductory paragraph.

At the Doctor's Office

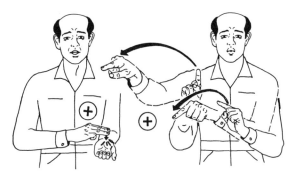

GO   DOCTOR

GO DOCTOR WHAT-FOR ? REASON DIFFERENT + + > : MAYBE SICK + , BLOW-NOSE ,

COUGH BAD , MEDICINE NEED + ; MAYBE stomach = OPERATE stomach = SEW = hand +

FINISH₂ GO DOCTOR INVESTIGATE LET'S-SEE ALL-RIGHT ; MAYBE TIME INVESTIGATE

YEAR = ahead + YOUR + ; MAYBE FALL left = FOREARM BREAK , GO DOCTOR PUT

left = forearm = COVER **NEED** ! MOST TIME GO DOCTOR SICK SOMETHING , WILL DOCTOR

FIRST PUT THERMOMETER = mouth LET'S-SEE TEMPERATURE FINISH₁ , SECOND

STETHOSCOPE = around INVESTIGATE HEART , CHEST = around . WILL DOCTOR ASK = you +

LET'S-SEE FIND PROBLEM . THIRD , MAYBE WRITE R-X MEDICINE GIVE = you₁ . #IF + +

GO DOCTOR INVESTIGATE YEAR = ahead + YOUR + , WILL DOCTOR BLOOD DRAIN = arm ,

ASK = you GIVE = him SMALL-MEASURE U-R-I-N-E WHAT-FOR , INVESTIGATE ANALYSIS LET'S-

SEE FIND PROBLEM ANY . ONCE-IN-A-WHILE DOCTOR SEND = you HOSPITAL . MAYBE

TELL = you X͡ SNAPSHOT O-R OTHER INVESTIGATE .

Glossed Sentences, Translations, and Grammatical Notes

1. NOW‿AFTERNOON APPOINTMENT DOCTOR TIME‿THREE , YOU .

   You have an appointment with the doctor at three this afternoon.

   NOW‿AFTERNOON means "this afternoon." APPOINTMENT is a modified form of RESERVATION; it is made with "A" handshapes, whereas RESERVATION is made with fist handshapes. The movement is the same for both. TIME‿THREE may be translated as "at three" or "at three o'clock."

2. WORK FINISH₁ EARLY WILL ME ,

   I'll finish work early and

   HOME COME = here₂ AROUND‿TWO = approximate ; we = TWO GO-OUT .

   come home around two o'clock; then we can go.

   AROUND (here meaning "approximately") is not made horizontally (as in Lesson 8), but vertically, in the same plane as a clockface. TWO = approximate is made with a slight side-to-side shaking movement, so by itself it means "approximately two." As in English, "time" or "o'clock" is deduced from the context.

3. PAST+ DOCTOR BLOOD DRAIN = arm+ , U-R-I-N-E , CHEST ,

   Before, the doctor took your blood sample and checked your urine, chest,

   DRAIN = arm is a sign miming a suction action in taking blood from the arm.

   WEIGHT INVESTIGATE FINISH₁ ; NOW‿AFTERNOON WHAT ?

   and weight. What will he do this afternoon?

   INVESTIGATE may also be translated as "check" or "explore."

4. TEST+ ANALYSIS FINISH₂ , DOCTOR SATISFIED **NOT** .

After the tests' analyses, the doctor was not satisfied.

MORE+ INVESTIGATE WANT+ . HOSPITAL SEND-TO ;

He wants to do more checking so he's sending me to the hospital

In the phrase HOSPITAL SEND-TO, the object "me" is understood from the context.

WHAT-FOR , X SNAPSHOT , HEART NEEDLE-WRITE , VARIOUS .

for X rays, an EKG, and so forth.

HEART NEEDLE-WRITE depicts the graphic movements of an EKG needle or an electrocardiogram.

5. BODY YOUR+ OLD INCREASE+ CAREFUL INVESTIGATE **NEED** .

The older you are, the more carefully you must check your health.

6. TRUE , BUT HOSPITAL PLACE-IN=me **don't=WANT** !

That's true, but I don't want the doctor to put me in the hospital!

The sign PLACE-IN represents the grasping of a person or an object and placing or putting that person or object in a certain location; in this case it starts at the signer's body and moves toward the location established for the hospital. In **don't=WANT**, the negation of WANT is shown by outward twisting of the hands.

7. MAYBE DOCTOR R-X MEDICINE WRITE GIVE=you .

Maybe the doctor will give you a prescription.

PROBLEM APPEAR ANY , DOCTOR WRITE=between INFORM=you+ ;

If any problem appears, the doctor will inform you by writing notes;

WRITE=between is a directional sign in which both hands move simultaneously between two locations, representing the two writers.

ANXIOUS **DON'T+** , DOCTOR GOOD !

don't worry, the doctor is good!

ANXIOUS here denotes an emotional concern, rather than a mental concern as in WORRY—which could also be translated as "anxious."

---

8. PAST+ DOCTOR STETHOSCOPE HEARTBEAT MY FINISH$_2$

Before, the doctor checked my heartbeat with a stethoscope

STETHOSCOPE here means "use a stethoscope to check."

O-K$_2$ SEEM+ ; FIND NONE$_1$. NOW LET'S-SEE !

and it seemed OK; he found nothing wrong. Now we'll see!

Vocabulary Review

Test your ability to produce the following signs or sign phrases.

ANALYSIS

ANXIOUS

APPOINTMENT

AROUND TWO = approximate

ASK = you/him/her

BLOOD

BLOW-NOSE

BODY

BREAK

CHANGE

CHEST

CHEST = around

COME = here$_2$

COUGH

left-forearm = COVER

DON'T

DRAIN = arm

FALL

FIND

left = FOREARM

GIVE = you/him/her

HEART

HEARTBEAT

HEART NEEDLE-WRITE

HOSPITAL

INFORM = you +

INVESTIGATE FINISH$_1$

MORE

MOST

NOW AFTERNOON

OLD INCREASE +

stomach = OPERATE

OTHER

PLACE-IN = me

REASON

R-X

SATISFIED

SEND-TO

stomach = SEW = hand +

STETHOSCOPE = around

TEMPERATURE

TEST +

THERMOMETER = mouth

TIME THREE

WEIGHT

WRITE = between

X SNAPSHOT

YEAR = ahead +

Notes

Translation Exercises—ASL to English

Translate the following glossed sentences into appropriate English equivalents.

1. REMEMBER DOCTOR TELL=you WEIGHT DECREASE+ **NEED** YOU !

2. KNOW+ ME ; WEIGHT INCREASE+ TOO-MUCH , **BAD** !

3. EAT+ LIMIT **NEED** ME , WHY++ WEIGHT INCREASE **EASY** !

4. past=WEEK ME+ GO DOCTOR WHAT-FOR , BODY INVESTIGATE **FULL** .

5. DOCTOR FIND WRONG+ ME NONE₂ , BUT REQUIRE HEART NEEDLE-WRITE , X SNAPSHOT , PLUS TEST+∨ VARIOUS .

6. NURSE BLOOD DRAIN=arm+ MY+ LOOK-AT=arm+ LIKE ME , INTEREST=arm₁ .

7. ALIKE HEART NEEDLE-WRITE TEST+ LOOK-AT=machine₂ INTEREST₂ .

8. PAST+ ME+ GO DOCTOR WHY++ , SICK=continuous+ COLD+ , COUGH+ **BAD** CONTINUE STUBBORN .

9. AFRAID+ MAYBE APPEAR PNEUMONIA ; EXPERIENCE PAST+ FINISH₂ ME , FUNNY **NONE₁** .

10. DOCTOR INVESTIGATE FINISH₂ TELL=me WORRY NOT **NEED** , WILL ALL-RIGHT .

11. DOCTOR WRITE GIVE=me R-X MEDICINE **STRONG** ; he=TELL=me one=WEEK COLD , COUGH VANISH .

12. long=PAST DOCTOR OPERATE left=ELBOW ELIMINATE=left=elbow W-A-R-T MY+ , FINISH₂ hand=SEW=left=elbow **SIX** .

Translation Exercises—English to ASL

Translate the following sentences from English into ASL equivalents.

1. What time is your appointment with the doctor?
2. The doctor will give me a complete physical checkup.
3. I once had a very bad chest cold with a stubborn hacking cough.
4. The doctor sent me to the hospital for chest X rays.
5. Have you ever had an EKG while walking a treadmill?
6. When was the last time you saw your doctor?
7. When I broke my heel, I had to wear a cast on my leg for three months!
8. How many stitches were required after your stomach operation?
9. I like to watch a nurse draw blood samples from my arm.
10. Communication between a doctor and a deaf patient takes patience and time.
11. The doctor and the patient may have to write notes back and forth.
12. Prescriptions can be costly; sometimes you save money by buying generics.

Double-Slot Substitution Drills

Practice signing the following target sentences, substituting the suggested vocabulary in each slot. If you have problems with any of the vocabulary, consult your instructor for help.

1. <u>TOMORROW MORNING</u> APPOINTMENT DOCTOR TIME <u>TEN</u> ME .

   WILL WEDNESDAY   TEN THIRTY

   WILL WEDNESDAY   ELEVEN FIFTEEN

   WILL FRIDAY   NINE FORTY FIVE

   WILL FRIDAY   ELEVEN THIRTY

   TOMORROW MORNING   TEN

2. HAPPEN FALL YOU , left=<u>FOREARM</u> BREAK <u>X SNAPSHOT</u> **NEED** YOU .

                   right=LEG   X SNAPSHOT

                   right=LEG   right-leg=COVER

                   left=WRIST   left-wrist=COVER

                   left=FOREARM   X SNAPSHOT

3. GO DOCTOR BODY EXAMINE YOU , <u>FIRST</u> #DO$_1$, <u>BODY WEIGHT</u> .

                                           SECOND   THERMOMETER=mouth

                                           THIRD   BLOOD DRAIN=arm+

                                           FOURTH   GIVE=doctor SMALL-
                                                                 MEASURE U-R-I-N-E

                                           FIFTH   DOCTOR STETHOSCOPE=
                                                                 around

                                           FIRST   BODY WEIGHT

4. PAST+ GO DOCTOR EXAMINE FINISH$_2$, HOSPITAL SEND-TO
   <u>HOW HAPPEN</u> , X SNAPSHOT=right-leg NEED+ ME .

   WHY++ ,   BLOOD ANALYSIS

   WHAT-FOR ,   HEART NEEDLE-WRITE

   WHY++ ,   STOMACH TEST+

   HOW HAPPEN , X SNAPSHOT=right-leg

5. NURSE , DOCTOR <u>BLOOD DRAIN=left-arm</u> MY+ <u>LOOK-AT=left-arm</u> INTEREST$_1$ ME .

                       HEART NEEDLE-WRITE   LOOK-AT=machine$_2$

                       WRAP=left-arm , SQUEEZE+   LOOK-AT=left-arm

                       SEW=hand CUT=elbow   LOOK-AT SEW=hand

                       SHOOT=arm SOMETHING   LOOK-AT SHOOT=arm

                       BLOOD DRAIN=left-arm   LOOK-AT=left-arm

6. LONG-AGO **SICK** ME , WHEW ; SOMEONE BECKON DOCTOR EXAMINE , FIND

#WHAT <u>STRIKE-CHANCE</u> <u>PNEUMONIA</u> ME .

    APPEAR   S-C-A-R-L-E-T-I-N-A

    STRIKE-CHANCE HOT S-T-R-O-K-E

    HAPPEN   F-L-U BAD

    APPEAR   U-L-C-E-R STOMACH

    STRIKE-CHANCE PNEUMONIA

7. PAST+ me=PLACE-IN HOSPITAL <u>ONCE</u> ME WHAT-FOR , <u>OPERATE=lower=right-side</u> .

    TWICE   OPERATE SMALL

    ONCE   LOOK-AT=around

    FEW TIME-PERIOD   REASON DIFFERENT++

    WILL MONTH=ahead   MAYBE OPERATE

    ONCE   OPERATE=lower=right-side

8. LONG-AGO+ <u>SMOKE+ HEAVY</u> ME ; DOCTOR <u>TELL=me STOP</u> .

    COUGH BAD   GIVE=me MEDICINE

    STOMACH UPSET   BLAME=it WORK

    WEIGHT TOO-MUCH   ORDER₁ D-I-E-T STRICT

    SMOKE+ HEAVY   TELL=me STOP

9. <u>SMOKE+ STOP</u> FINISH₂ ME , **WRONG** <u>WEIGHT INCREASE++</u> .

  MEDICINE TAKE-PILL+   SLEEP++

  MEDICINE TAKE=spoon   BODY RASH=all-over

  COUGH++ REDUCE   NOSE-RUN₂++

  MEDICINE TAKE-PILL+   NERVOUS

  SMOKE+ STOP   WEIGHT INCREASE++

10. SUPPOSE+ <u>right=HEEL</u> BREAK YOU ; <u>right=HEEL</u> COVER REQUIRE YOU !

    left=FOREARM   left=FOREARM

    right=LEG   right=LEG

    right=FOREARM   *right=FOREARM*

    left=LEG   left=LEG

    right=HEEL   right=HEEL

Suggested Activities

1. Act out the dialogue used in this lesson by pairing off one male and one female, if possible, to role play the characters. Give special attention to emotions and to facial expression.

2. Practice signing the ASL to English translation exercises *before* translating the sentences. Watch facial expression needed for each sentence.

3. Relate to the class a medical experience you will never forget.

4. Set up a role-playing situation whereby one person is the "doctor" and the others are the medical patients. Use your experiences or your imagination in creating various patient types and see how the "doctor" reacts. Switch the doctor role occasionally.

5. For fingerspelling practice, you may use some of the sentences or selected phrases from the sentences in the English to ASL translation exercises in this lesson. Pair off in class. Partners may then take turns randomly selecting two or three sentences or phrases to fingerspell to each other while the instructor observes.

6. Write an English version of the glossed introductory paragraph.

Spring Cleaning

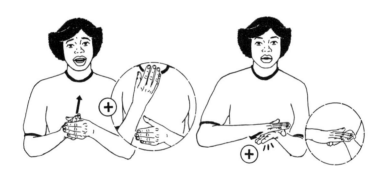

GROW = noun +   CLEAN +

YEAR = ahead + +   AROUND M-A-R-C-H ,   TIME THINK HOUSE CLEAN = around + + ,   WHY + +
GROW = noun +   TIME-PERIOD NOW . CLOTHES CLOSET-RACK +   CLEAN +   **NEED** . OLD +
CLOTHES don't = WANT ,   SAVE don't = WANT ,   PUT-IN$_A$ BOX WHAT-FOR ,   GIFT$_2$ POOR
PEOPLE . WINDOW +   IN + ,   OUT WASH = object **CLEAN** SHINY$_2$. WALL +   WASH = object$_A$
CLEAN FINISH , MAYBE DECIDE PAINT WHICH PAPER on = WALL . DRAPE +   TAKE-DOWN
PUT$_2$ DRY CLEAN + . ALSO CURTAIN +   PUT-IN$_2$ WASHING-MACHINE FINISH IRON LATER .
GARAGE ALSO EVERY THING PUT-OUT$_2$ FINISH$_2$ CLEAN = around + + . LAST DECIDE
OLD +   THING , J-U-N-K , VARIOUS SAVE don't = WANT , EITHER THROW-AWAY WHICH
MAYBE SELL + . KITCHEN CABINET +   IN +   TAKE-DOWN , CLEAN + +   FINISH , PUT$_A$
#BACK . LAST FLOOR CLEAN = around + +   MAYBE T-I-L-E RUB-ON = floor SHINY$_2$. MUCH
WORK = continuously , WHEW ! BUT FINISH , HOUSE **CLEAN** SMELL ! WORTH , TRUE !

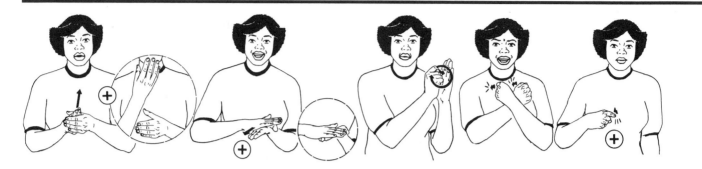

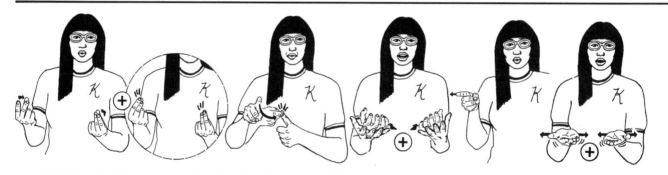

Glossed Sentences, Translations, and Grammatical Notes

1. GROW = noun +   CLEAN +   TIME-PERIOD ,   **LOVE**   ME !

I just love spring cleaning time!

The sign GROW with short, repeated movements may be used as a noun, meaning "spring" or "springtime" ("the time of growth"). Note the difference between the signs TIME-PERIOD and TIME (Lesson 11, sentence 1).

2. you = SAME = me .   CLEAN = around + +   FINISH$_2$,   FEEL BETTER .

Me, too. I feel better when all the cleaning is done.

you = SAME = me may be translated as "me, too," "the same here," or "the same with me." The sign CLEAN is repeated and moves in an arc to signify "cleaning in many places around the house."

KEE-KONG   you = TWO = jennifer   COME = here   HELP = me ,   HAPPY   ME .

I'm glad you and Kee Kong could come to help me.

3. #DO +   FIRST   WANT +   YOU ,   "WHAT" ?

What do you want me to do first?

"WHAT," with upturned palm(s) shaking slightly side-to-side, is a general interrogatory sign that is found usually at the end of sentences.

4. CURTAIN + ,   DRAPE +   TAKE-DOWN   PLEASE .   DRAPE +

Please take down the curtains and the drapes. The drapes

The downward execution of CURTAIN is a wiggling movement whereas for DRAPE, it is straight. TAKE-DOWN should start from the same location as the object(s) being removed.

PUT-IN+   DRY ROLL₁+   REMOVE   DIRTY ;

are to be put through the dryer to remove the dirt and dust.

ROLL₁ is a one-handed sign representing the movement inside a clothes dryer.

CURTAIN+   PUT-IN+   WASHING-MACHINE ,   LATER   IRON .

Put the curtains in the washing machine and later iron them.

5.   GIVE=me   WINDOW   SPRAY-CONTAINER ;   WASH$_A$ WINDOW+

Give me some window spray cleaner; I'll wash the windows

SPRAY-CONTAINER can refer to any aerosol or pump-action bottle or can. This two-handed alternating form of WASH moves in the same vertical plane as WINDOW+. The orientation of WASH or WASH$_A$ will vary according to the orientation and location of the object being washed.

OUT   IN+ ,   FINISH₁ ,   SHINY₂   WILL .

on the outside and inside, and they will be sparkling when I'm finished.

6.   FINE₂ !   ME   WANT   WASH=wall$_A$+ + ,   WHY+ + ,

Fine! I want to wash the walls because

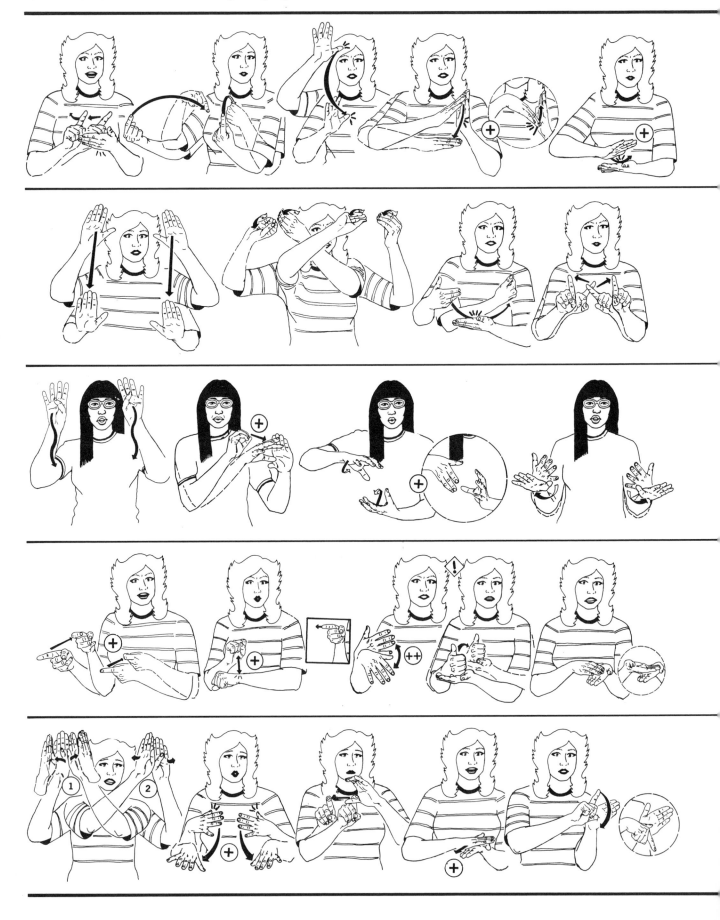

WEEK = ahead   COME = here   MAN   PAINT ,   PAPER

next week a man will come to paint and wallpaper

WEEK = ahead means "next week" or "in a week." The forward movement (shown by " = ahead") represents time in the future.

WALL   DECORATE   NEW‿DIFFERENT .

and redecorate.

There is no verbal prefix in ASL that means "re-," although this concept can be expressed with the sign AGAIN. Here, the signer expresses "redecorate" by focusing on the "changing nature" of NEW‿DIFFERENT (see also Lesson 7, sentence 4).

7. CURTAIN +   PUT-IN +   WASHING-MACHINE   FINISH$_2$.

I've put the curtains in the wash.

8. **SPEED**   WORK   YOU   WHEW !   HELP = me   KITCHEN

You are a very fast worker! You can help me clean

CABINET + > ,   CLOTHES   CLOSET-RACK   CLEAN +   LATER + + .

the kitchen cabinets and the clothes closets after a while.

The sign CABINET + depicts a series of doors at eye level or above. CLOSET-RACK depicts a rod on which one hangs clothes. LATER, repeated, is usually translated as "after a while."

Vocabulary Review

Test your ability to produce the following signs or sign phrases.

#BACK

BOX

BUT

CABINET +

CLEAN = around + +

CLOTHES‿CLOSET-RACK

CURTAIN +

DECORATE

DIRTY

DRAPE +

DRY‿CLEAN +

DRY‿ROLL$_1$ +

EITHER

FAST

FEEL‿BETTER

FINE$_2$

FLOOR

GARAGE

GIVE = me

HOUSE

IRON

KITCHEN

LAST

LATER + +

MAN = informal

MUCH

OLD +

PAINT

PAPER‿on = WALL

PLEASE

POOR‿PEOPLE

PUT-IN$_A$

PUT-IN$_2$‿DRY‿ROLL$_1$ +

PUT-OUT$_2$ +

RUB-ON = floor‿SHINY$_2$

SHINY$_2$

SPRAY-CONTAINER

TAKE-DOWN = object

THROW-AWAY

don't = WANT

WANT +‿YOU

WASH = object = wall$_A$ +

WASH$_1$‿WINDOW

WASHING-MACHINE

WEEK = ahead

WHICH

WINDOW

WORK = continuously

YEAR = ahead + +

Notes

Translation Exercises—ASL to English

Translate the following glossed sentences into appropriate English equivalents.

1. GROW=noun+ CLEAN+ TIME-PERIOD BUSY ALWAYS we=TWO , WHY++ , #DO=around++ **MANY₂** !

2. WINDOW+ IN+ , OUT WASH=object CLEAN , SHINY₂ **NEED** .

3. CURTAIN+ TAKE-DOWN PUT-IN_A WASHING-MACHINE FINISH , LATER IRON CLEAN .

4. DRAPE+ TAKE-DOWN MAYBE PUT₂ DRY CLEAN+ WHICH PUT-IN₂ DRY ROLL₁+ WHAT-FOR REMOVE DIRTY .

5. WORK+ OTHER "WHAT" , WALL++ WASH=object **CLEAN** .

6. MAYBE DECIDE PAINT=object=wall COLOR DIFFERENT CHANGE .

7. KITCHEN CABINET+ IN+ TAKE-DOWN++ , CLEAN=object=cabinet FINISH₂ , PUT_A #BACK .

8. GARAGE EVERY THING PUT-OUT₂++ , DECIDE SAVE #WHAT , CLEAN=around= garage FINISH₂ , PUT_A #BACK.

9. GARAGE PUT_A #BACK FINISH , OTHER+ LEFT , DECIDE THROW-AWAY O-R MAYBE SELL+ .

10. CLOTHES CLOSET-RACK CLEAN+ , MAYBE DECIDE OLD++ CLOTHES GIFT=them₂ POOR PEOPLE .

11. LAST FLOOR CLEAN+ ; #IF T-I-L-E , SWEEP , MOP , W-A-X RUB-ON=floor SHINY₂ .

12. HOUSE **CLEAN** THROUGH⊥ THROUGH⊤ FINISH₂ , FEEL **GOOD** !

Translation Exercises—English to ASL

Translate the following sentences from English into ASL equivalents.

1. Do you like spring cleaning time?

2. Spring cleaning requires a lot of work and a lot of time.

3. There are drapes to be cleaned and curtains to wash and iron.

4. All of the windows need to be washed inside and out.

5. Walls must be washed and some painting or redecorating may be needed.

6. Closets have to be cleaned out and winter clothes put in storage.

7. Spring cleaning also means time to clean out the garage or basement.

8. You might find old clothes to give away or used articles to sell.

9. You will also find some junk to throw away.

10. It is a good idea to clean out the kitchen cabinets and perhaps wax them.

11. Another job is cleaning all your pictures and paintings on the walls.

12. If you have a fireplace, you will have to give it a thorough cleaning, too.

Mixed-Slot Substitution Drills

Practice signing the following target sentences, substituting the suggested vocabulary in each slot. If you have problems with any of the vocabulary, consult your instructor for help.

1. YEAR = ahead + + GROW = noun + TIME-PERIOD CLEAN = around **NEED** #WHAT ,

   <u>WALL WASH = object = wall$_A$</u> .

   CURTAIN WASHING-MACHINE

   CURTAIN DRY ROLL + PUT-IN = dryer

   CURTAIN + IRON

   WALL WASH = object = wall$_A$

2. YEAR = past GROW + = noun CLEAN + TIME-PERIOD , WIFE we = TWO DECIDE

   DECORATE + <u>BED ROOM</u> NEW⌣DIFFERENT .

                EAT + ROOM

                KITCHEN

                BATH ROOM

                BED ROOM

3. BEFORE PAINT = object = wall , PAPER on = WALL

   <u>PICTURE + TAKE-DOWN = object</u> **NEED** .

   DRAPE + TAKE-DOWN = object

   W-A-L-L WASH = object = wall$_1$

   WINDOW + WASH = object = window$_1$

   PICTURE + TAKE-DOWN = object

4. <u>EAT + ROOM</u> DECORATE + #WHAT , <u>PAPER *on = WALL*</u> .

   BED ROOM   PAINT = object = wall

   FAMILY ROOM   P-A-N-E-L PUT-ON = *wall* +

   KITCHEN   PAINT = object = wall

   EAT + ROOM   PAPER *on = WALL*

5. GARAGE CLEAN + EVERY⌣THING PUT-OUT$_2$ FINISH$_2$, DECIDE

   <u>THROW-AWAY</u> #WHAT .

   don't = WANT

   GIFT$_2$ FRIEND

   MAYBE Y-A-R-D SELL +

   SAVE FUTURE

   THROW AWAY

6. GROW = noun +   CLEAN +   TIME-PERIOD

<u>KITCHEN CABINET</u> +   IN +   <u>TAKE-DOWN</u> + ,   CLEAN + .

CLOTHES CLOSET-RACK +   PUT-OUT$_2$

CLOTHES DRAWERS   LIFT-OUT

DOOR SHELF +   PUT-OUT$_2$

KITCHEN CABINET +   TAKE-DOWN +

7. <u>KITCHEN CABINET</u> +   IN +   <u>TAKE-DOWN</u> + ,   CLEAN +   FINISH$_2$,   PUT$_A$ #BACK .

CLOTHES CLOSET-RACK   PUT-OUT$_2$

CLOTHES DRAWERS   LIFT-OUT

DOOR SHELF +   PUT-OUT$_2$

KITCHEN CABINET +   TAKE-DOWN +

8. TOMORROW MORNING GO-OUT BUY + +   ME WHAT-FOR ,

<u>PAINT DIFFERENT</u> .

WALL$_2$ PAPER

SPRAY-CONTAINER CLEAN +

WASHING-MACHINE SOAP

W-A-X ITS FLOOR

PAINT DIFFERENT

9. GROW = noun +   CLEAN +   FINISH$_2$ YOU ,   MAYBE HAVE OLD CLOTHES HEAP$_2$;

DECIDE   alternate = TWO$_2$:   <u>GIFT$_2$ POOR PEOPLE ,   SELL = object +</u> .

SELL + object + ,   GIFT CHURCH

SAVE + ,   CUT-UP = object +

CUT-UP = object ,   SEW = hand +

THROW-AWAY ,   SAVE +

GIFT$_2$ POOR PEOPLE ,   SELL = object +

10. HOUSE **CLEAN** THROUGH⊥ THROUGH⊤ FINISH$_2$,   <u>FEEL **GOOD**</u> ME !

OFF-WORK + +

GO-OUT OFF-WORK +

GO-OUT GOOD TIME

REST one = WEEK

FEEL **GOOD**

Suggested Activities

1. Act out the dialogue used in this lesson. Three persons may volunteer or be selected from the group to portray each character. Give special attention to facial expression.

2. Practice signing the ASL to English translation exercises *before* translating the sentences.

3. Share with the class an unforgettable incident or experience you've had related to spring cleaning.

4. Bring to class a picture related to spring cleaning or redecorating. Be prepared to describe this activity to the class *before* allowing class members to see the picture you have.

5. For fingerspelling practice, you may use some of the sentences or selected phrases from the sentences in the English to ASL translation exercises in this lesson. Pair off in class. Partners may then take turns randomly selecting two or three sentences or phrases to fingerspell to each other while the instructor observes.

6. Write an English version of the glossed introductory paragraph.

Yard Cleanup

OUT   AROUND   CLEAN = around +

AUTUMN ,   GROW = noun +   TIME-PERIOD   HOUSE   OUT   AROUND   CLEAN = around +   **NEED** !
GROW = noun +   TIME-PERIOD   BEFORE +   GRASS ,   FLOWER +   GROW + ,   RAKE = around   ALL-
OVER   **NEED** ,   WHY + + ,   COLD +   TIME-PERIOD   WIND   STRONG ,   BLOW = around$_2$ PAPER ,
T-R-A-S-H ,   LEAF + + ,   VARIOUS   SAME   *TREE* limb = FALL   ALL-OVER .   #IF   LEAVE +   MAYBE
FLOWER + ,   GASS   GROW +   GOOD   NOT ,   LOUSY !   ALSO   ALL-OVER   PRETTY   NOT !   #IF
PRIDE ,   LIKE   HOUSE   **CLEAN**   OUT   AROUND   ALIKE   IN + !   #DO + ?   FIRST ,   GET
RAKE ,   HOE ,   clippers = CUT ,   trim = CUT   WHICH   SMALL   SAW   ITS   TREE   limb = SAW = off
#IF + +   DEAD .   START   INVESTIGATE   TREE + + >   DIFFERENT + ,   SECOND   BUSH +   LET'S-
SEE   WHERE   SAW-OFF   **NEED** .   FINISH$_2$ PICK-UP$_A$ THROW-IN +   DIRTY   large = CAN$_2$.
this = NEXT-TURN = that   RAKE = around   LEAF +   HEAP$_2$,   THROW-IN +   DIRTY   large = CAN$_2$.
NEXT   DIE   FLOWER + ,   W-E-E-D-S   PULL-UP$_A$ ITS +   FLOWER +   "ROW" .   FINISH   HOUSE
OUT   AROUND   **CLEAN** ,   FEEL GOOD   WILL !   READY >   NEW   GROW + .

Glossed Sentences, Translations, and Grammatical Notes

1. GROW = noun +   TIME-PERIOD   OUT +   HEAP₂   WORK

In the springtime, there's always a lot of work

HEAP can refer to any large, voluminous collection of things piled randomly. It can be translated as "heap," "pile," "a lot of." It can be made with one or both hands.

ALWAYS ,   WHY + +   Y-A-R-D   CLEAN +   **NEED** .

to do outside because the yard must be cleaned up.

---

2. EAGER   HELP = you   PICK-UPₐ   *TREE⌣*limb = FALL ,

I'm eager to help you pick up the fallen tree limbs

EAGER can also be translated as "enthusiastic" or "anxious" (to do something). *TREE⌣*limb = FALL is a blend of two signs: after TREE is made, the arm representing the trunk remains in place, while the other hand makes the sign FALL, starting from a place on the upright arm that represents a limb.

SECOND   LEAF +   RAKE = around + +   ALL-OVER

and rake up the leaves all around

HEAP₂   FINISH₂   THROW-IN +   DIRTY⌣large = CAN₂ +   .

into a big pile to throw away in trash cans.

DIRTY can translate as "garbage," "dirt," or "trash."

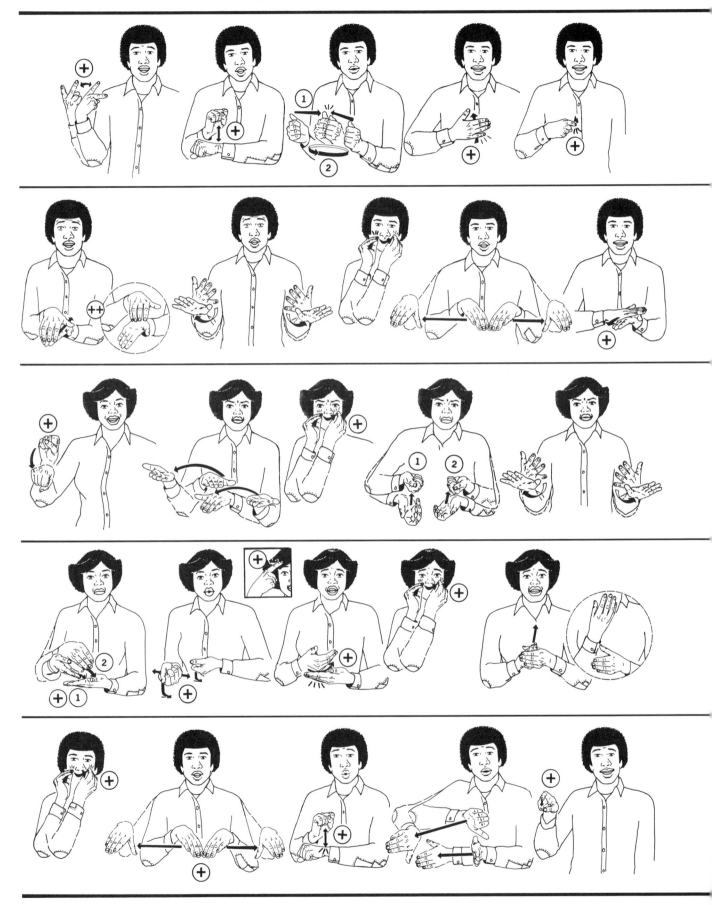

3. we = TWO   WORK+   TOGETHER = around ,   HAPPY   ME !

I'm glad that the two of us can work together!

TOGETHER here moves around in a circle to signify "togetherness in many different situations."

RAKE = around+ +   FINISH₂ ,   FLOWER+   "ROW"   CLEAN+ .

When we finish raking up, we'll clean out the flower beds.

"ROW" here indicates a strip about six inches wide.

4. YES ,   DIE   FLOWER+   PULLₐ   FINISH₂ ,

Yes, and when we finish pulling up the dead flowers,

SPADE+ ,   HOE+   WHAT-FOR+ + ,   NEW+   FLOWER+   GROW+ .

we will turn over the soil for new flowers to grow.

5. FLOWER+   "ROW"+   WORK   ASIDE> ,   NEED+

When the flower bed work is out of the way, we need

See Lesson 4, sentence 5, for explanation of ASIDE>.

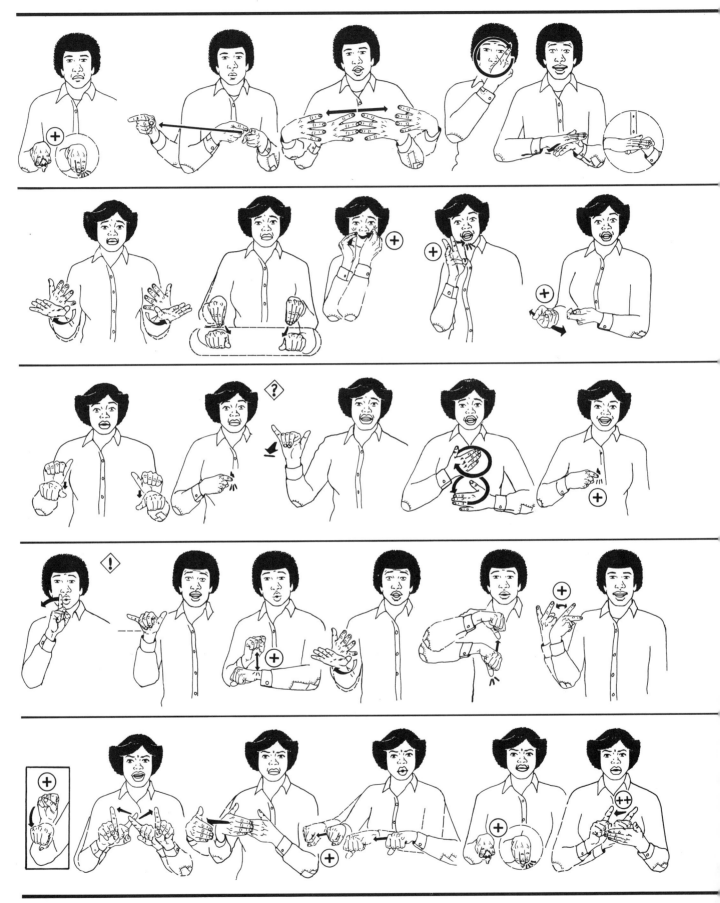

clippers = CUT +   LENGTH   FENCE   FACE   **CLEAN** .

to trim the grass along the fence to make it look neat.

The sign CUT is made as if holding clippers or grass shears.

6. FINISH₂ ,   SOW-SEED   FLOWER + ,   WATER   HOSE +

After that, can I plant the flower seeds and water

CAN   ME ?   THAT   PLEASE = noun₂   ME !

them with the hose? I really enjoy that!

7. **TRUE** !   Y-A-R-D   WORK +   FINISH₁ ,   PRIDE   we = TWO .

Sure thing! We'll have pride when the yard work is all finished.

8. YES ,   BUT   AFTER   MOW + ,   clippers = CUT +   WEEK + + ∨ .

Yes, but afterwards, there will be weekly lawn mowing and trimming.

AFTER can also be translated as "from now on," "hereafter," "from this time forward," etc. WEEK made with short and rapid repetitions, and often moving downward, means "weekly" or "every week."

Vocabulary Review

Test your ability to produce the following signs or sign phrases.

AFTER	FLOWER+	RAKE = around + +
ALIKE	FLOWER+ "ROW"	SAW-OFF
ALL-OVER	GRASS	limb = SAW-OFF
ALWAYS	GROW+	SPADE+
AROUND = area	HOE	START
AUTUMN	water = HOSE	STRONG
BEFORE	ITS	THROW-IN+
wind = BLOW = around	LEAF+	TOGETHER = around
CAN ME ?	LEAVE+	TREE
large = CAN$_2$+	LOUSY	*TREE* limb = FALL
CLEAN = around +	NEXT	TREE + +
trim = CUT	this = NEXT-TURN = that	WATER
DIRTY large = CAN$_2$	PICK-UP$_A$	WEEK + +
EAGER+	PRIDE	WHERE
FEEL GOOD	PULL-UP$_A$	WIND
FIRST	RAKE	WORK+

Notes

Translation Exercises—ASL to English

Translate the following glossed sentences into appropriate English equivalents.

1. PAST+ SATURDAY HOUSE OUT AROUND CLEAN=around+ FINISH$_2$ ME .

2. **MUCH** WORK WHEW+ , **TIRED** , S-T-I-F-F LITTLE-BIT ME ; NOW FEEL BETTER .

3. UP-TO-NOW RAIN++ KNOW+ YOU ; GRASS GROW "TOO-MUCH" , THICK MOW+ **HARD** !

4. MOW+ FINISH$_1$, this=NEXT-TURN=that clippers=CUT+ , FINISH$_2$, LAST RAKE=around ALL-OVER **HEAP$_2$** GRASS .

5. GRASS RAKE=around CLEAN=around+ FINISH$_2$, INVESTIGATE FLOWER+ "ROW" , W-E-E-D-S PULL-UP$_A$.

6. W-E-E-D-S PULL-UP$_A$ "body=BEND" BACK MY+ WHEW !

7. LAST trim=CUT HEAP$_2$++> FINISH$_2$, RAKE++> , THROW-IN+ DIRTY large=CAN$_2$.

8. WORK=continuous **TRUE** SWEAT$_2$, **TIRED** ME+ #BUT FINISH$_2$, FEEL BETTER .

9. #IF RAIN+ NOT MUCH , WORK OUT MOW , RAKE=around EASY , PLEASE=noun$_2$ ME+ .

10. WILL AUTUMN HOUSE OUT AROUND CLEAN=around+ NOT BAD .

11. LEAF+ FALL$_A$, RAKE=around HEAP$_2$++> **PLEASE=noun$_2$** ME .

12. HOUSE OUT AROUND WORK+ CLEAN=around **LIKE** YOU ?

Translation Exercises—English to ASL

Translate the following sentences from English into ASL equivalents.

1. I always enjoy cleaning my yard in the springtime.

2. It feels great to be outside after being inside most of the winter.

3. First, I try to clean out all my flower beds, removing weeds and dead flowers.

4. After that job is finished, I rake up the whole yard.

5. I put all the leaves, dead flowers, fallen tree limbs, and dead grass in trash bags or boxes.

6. When the raking is done, I fertilize my lawn so the grass will grow better.

7. When the raking and picking up is done, it's time to prepare the flower beds.

8. Sometimes we buy new rose bushes or other shrubs to put in the garden.

9. We like to plant new flowers or bedding plants and a few vegetables.

10. I may have to do some spading, hoeing, and raking before planting new flowers.

11. Sometimes there is pruning to do or grass to trim along fences.

12. A clean yard, like a clean house, makes you feel good.

Mixed-Slot Substitution Drills

Practice signing the following target sentences, substituting the suggested vocabulary in each slot. If you have problems with any of the vocabulary, consult your instructor for help.

1. YEAR = ahead + +   OUT +   CLEAN = around   AUTUMN ,   GROW = noun +   TIME-PERIOD
    WORK   #DO ,   <u>Y-A-R-D   PICK-UP$_A$</u> .

    FLOWER   "ROW"   PULL-UP$_A$

    Y-A-R-D   RAKE = around + +

    GRASS   MOW +

    Y-A-R-D   PICK-UP$_A$

2. GRASS   MOW +   FINISH   ME ,   this = NEXT-TURN = that
    <u>RAKE = around   HEAP</u>   **NEED**   ME .
    clippers = CUT +   LENGTH   FENCE
    HOUSE   OUT   clippers = CUT = around
    FLOWER   "ROW"   W-E-E-D   PULL-UP$_A$
    HEAP$_2$ +   trim = CUT +
    RAKE = around   HEAP

3. <u>Y-A-R-D   RAKE = around +</u>   HEAP   FINISH$_2$ ME ,   THROW-IN +   DIRTY   large = CAN$_2$.
    W-E-E-D   PULL-UP$_A$
    TREE   limb = FALL   PICK-UP$_A$
    PAPER ,   T-R-A-S-H   PICK-UP$_A$
    Y-A-R-D   RAKE = around +

4. AUTUMN   FLOWER   "ROW"   DEAD$_A$ PULL-UP$_A$ FINISH,
    <u>SPADE = flower-row +</u>   .
    HOE = flower-row +
    RAKE = back-and-forth
    PUT-IN = ground$_1$ B-U-L-B-S
    WATER   water = HOSE
    SPADE = flower-row +

5. <u>GROW = noun +</u>   TIME-PERIOD   GRASS   MOW   <u>BEGIN</u>   ME .
    SUMMER   WEEK + +
    AUTUMN   SOMETIMES
    WINTER   NEVER
    GROW = noun +   BEGIN

6. PAST SATURDAY HOUSE OUT AROUND <u>MOW = around</u> , FINISH ME .

        RAKE = around

        trim = CUT = around

        W-E-E-D-S PULL-UP$_A$

        WORK = around

        MOW = around

7. HAPPEN RAIN + + , HOUSE OUT <u>MOW = around</u> , CAN'T YOU .

        LEAF + + RAKE = around

        WORK = continuously

        clippers = CUT = around

        MOW = around

8. FLOWER "ROW" + WORK ASIDE> , <u>FENCE ⊥ clippers = CUT</u> NEED + ME .

        HEAP$_2$ + trim = CUT

        FLOWER WATER water = HOSE

        GRASS MOW +

        LEAF + RAKE = around

        FENCE ⊥ clippers = CUT

9. HOUSE OUT AROUND WORK + <u>CLEAN = around</u> , LIKE YOU ?

        MOW = around

        RAKE = around

        W-E-E-D-S PULL-UP$_A$

        HEAP$_2$ + trim = CUT

        CLEAN = around

10. HOUSE OUT AROUND WORK = continuous ALL-DAY , **<u>SWEAT</u>** ME **TRUE** .

        TIRED

        PLEASE = noun$_2$

        FEEL **GOOD**

        HUNGRY

        SWEAT

Suggested Activities

1. Pair off class members to role play the characters in the dialogue used in this lesson. Each pair should proceed with the dialogue while the instructor makes notes of suggestions for improving Sign production, facial expression, etc.

2. Bring to class a picture related to yard cleanup. Be prepared to describe this activity to the class *before* allowing class members to see the picture you have.

3. Practice signing the ASL to English translation exercises *before* translating each sentence.

4. For fingerspelling practice, you may use some of the sentences or selected phrases from the sentences in the English to ASL translations exercises in this lesson. Pair off in class. Partners may then take turns randomly selecting two or three sentences or phrases to fingerspell to each other while the instructor observes.

5. Write an English version of the glossed introductory paragraph.

Death of a Leader

LEADER   DIE

SOMEONE , FRIEND , FAMILY HAPPEN DIE SAD ALWAYS . HAPPEN DEAF LEADER DIE ,
DEAF ALL-OVER heart=TOUCH ! near=RECENT DEAF LEADER NAME+ HIS+ W-A-L-T
W-I-C-K-E-R-S-O-N DIE ! HOW HAPPEN HEART HIT , NOT EXPECT ! DEAF ALL-OVER
MIND FREEZE ! BELIEVE **CAN'T** THEY WHY++ , PAST+ W-W SICK C-A-N-C-E-R
SOMETHING LIE-DOWN=continuously ADD-UP FOUR MONTH++ . **WRONG** WELL , BEAT
C-A-N-C-E-R SEEM+ . DEAF ALL-OVER SURPRISE , HAPPY ! W-W POPULAR ALWAYS .
WORK=continuously HELP=around DEAF PROBLEM+ THEIR REDUCE+ . W-W BEST HIS+
"WHAT" , LISTEN DEAF THEIR STORY-TALK ALWAYS ! HAPPEN HIMSELF=walt **STRONG**
CATHOLIC . WIFE , CHILDREN HIS+ HAPPY FAMILY . CHURCH GO++ HELP=around
DEAF THEY . DEAF RESPECT WHEW ! WILL FUNERAL , PRIEST SIGN EVERY THING ;
LEADER DEAF OTHER+ STORY-TALK PAST+ DO HIS+ . JANE SONG SIGN WILL ,
FINISH₂ BRING BODY BURY AROUND+ LOWER=in-ground.

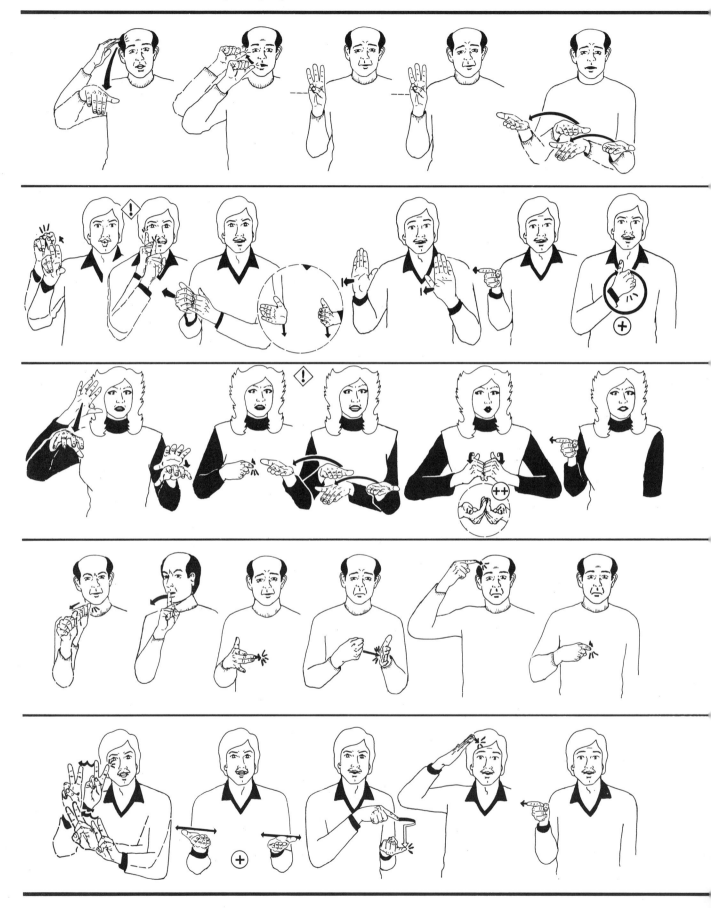

Glossed Sentences, Translations, and Grammatical Notes

1. KNOW‿THAT YESTERDAY W-A-L-T W-I-C-K-E-R-S-O-N DIE ?

   Did you know that Walt Wickerson died yesterday?

   KNOW‿THAT is a blend mentioned in Lesson 1, sentence 7.

2. **NO** ! DEAF LEADER WONDERFUL HE , **SORRY** !

   No! He was a wonderful deaf leader, and I'm very sorry!

3. MIND⌒FREEZE ME ! DIE HOW++ HE ?

   I'm shocked! How did he die?

   MIND⌒FREEZE is an idiomatic compound that can mean "shocked," "speechless," "at a loss for words," "thoughts immobilized," etc. Note that the first part, MIND, is made with more than just the index finger extended.

4. NOT TRUE , HEART⌒HIT THINK ME .

   I'm not sure, but I think from a heart attack.

   HEART⌒HIT is a compound that always means "heart attack" or "cardiac arrest."

5. FUNERAL SERVICE WHEN , KNOW‿YOU ?

   Do you know when the funeral service is?

6. WIFE   HIS   TELL=me   WILL‿THURSDAY   BURY .

His wife told me he will be buried Thursday.

This formal sign for BURY can also mean "grave."

WEDNESDAY   BODY   *LIE-DOWN*   LOOK-AT   CAN .

We can view his body on Wednesday.

The sign LIE-DOWN, which represents the body, is made with one hand and stays in position, while the other hand signs LOOK-AT in the direction of the first hand.

7. W-A-L-T   PAST+   LIE-DOWN=continuously   FOUR   MONTH+ ,

Walt was bedridden for four months before,

The verb LIE-DOWN, moving repeatedly in small even circles, means "to lie down continuously" or "to be bedridden."

REMEMBER   ME ;   C-A-N-C-E-R   SOMETHING ,   RIGHT ?

I recall; he had some kind of cancer, right?

SOMETHING here means "some kind of thing" or "some kind of cancer." In other contexts, it could be translated as "someone" or "some specific person."

8. YES ,   HAPPEN   EVERY‿THING   BETTER+   #BACK   WORK+ .

Yes, but everything got better, and he went back to work again.

The fingerspelled loan sign #BACK moves forward as the hand changes letter shapes. It can also be a directional sign that moves to a specific location.

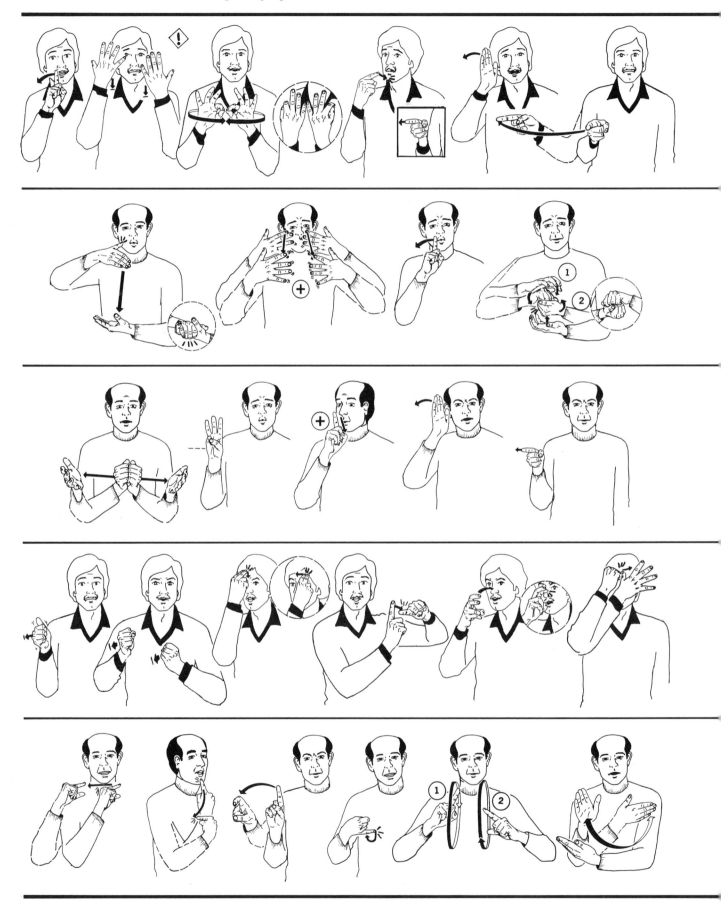

9. TRUE **SAD** ! FAMILY **FEEL-LOSS** HIM , WILL THEY !

It's really sad! The family will really miss him!

FEEL-LOSS means to be disappointed by a loss or absence. It can translate as "disappointed" or as "miss" in the sense of "missing someone or something."

10. WIFE TEARS-FLOW₂ TRUE GRIEF .

His wife cried and cried from grief.

WITHOUT W-A-L-T LONELY WILL SHE .

She will be lonely without Walt.

11. HIMSELF **STRONG** CATHOLIC PLUS STRICT FATHER .

He was a devout Catholic and a strict father.

As in English, **STRONG** can be used in mental, emotional, or spiritual senses, as well as a physical sense.

12. PRIEST TELL=me ASK=her JANE SIGN SONG .

The priest told me to ask Jane to sign a song.

Vocabulary Review

Test your ability to produce the following signs or sign phrases.

ADD-UP   FOUR   MONTH+ +⊥

BEST

BURY

BURY‿AROUND

CAN

CATHOLIC   CHURCH

CHILDREN

DIE/DEAD

DO

EXPECT

FAMILY

FATHER

FEEL-LOSS

FRIEND

FUNERAL

GRIEF

HAPPY

HEART⌒HIT

HELP=around

HIMSELF

KNOW   YOU

LEADER

LIE-DOWN=continuously

LIE-DOWN   LOOK-AT

LISTEN

LONELY

LOWER=body=in-ground

MIND⌒FREEZE

MONTH+ +

NAME

NOT‿EXPECT

OTHER+

POPULAR

PRIEST

REDUCE+

REMEMBER

RESPECT

SAD

SERVICE

SONG   SIGN

SORRY

STRICT

STRONG

heart=TOUCH

WHEN ?

WIFE

WITHOUT

WORK=continuously

WRONG

Notes

Translation Exercises—ASL to English

Translate the following glossed sentences into appropriate English equivalents.

1. near=RECENT **FRIEND** MY+ DIE ; HIMSELF LEADER WONDERFUL TRUE !
2. PEOPLE KNOW HIM MIND FREEZE ; FEEL-LOSS HIM , WILL THEY .
   MYSELF GO FUNERAL HIS+ , CAN'T ME WHY++ **FAR** ⊥ .
4. FRIEND MY+ MAIL=me INFORM=me FUNERAL NICE ; PEOPLE GO=funeral **MANY₂** .
5. FRIEND MY+ TELL=me PEOPLE GIFT_A FLOWERS HEAP₂ WHEW !
6. MONEY GIFT_A ALIKE WHAT-FOR , WILL ESTABLISH SPECIAL REMEMBER
   LOOK-AT=past , HONOR MAN THAT .
7. LIFE ITSELF="object" SAME=continuous₂ ALWAYS ; PEOPLE BORN , PEOPLE LIVE ,
   PEOPLE DIE .
8. HAPPEN PEOPLE DIE , SAD TIME-PERIOD ALWAYS ; FAMILY , FRIEND GRIEF THEY .
9. HAPPEN SOMEONE DIE , FAMILY PLAN+ FUNERAL , BURY **NEED** THEY .
10. PAST+ BROTHER MY+ TWO they=NEXT-TURN=she MOTHER MY+ DIE FINISH₂ .
11. TRUE WISE #WHAT , TRY PLAN+ BEFORE TIME DIE .
12. WANT++ BODY BURN MELT-AWAY , LOWER=in-ground BURY WHICH , DECIDE **NEED**
    YOU .

Translation Exercises—English to ASL

Translate the following sentences from English into ASL equivalents.

1. The unexpected death of a leader is always a very sad time.
2. The death of anyone close to us usually brings some shock.
3. People will plan either a funeral service or a memorial service.
4. Friends and relatives may go to pay last respects at a funeral home.
5. Some people may desire cremation after which their ashes are buried or preserved.
6. Others prefer to have their bodies embalmed for burial in a cemetery or a masoleum.
7. When a leader dies, a memorial fund may be established in that person's name.
8. Sometimes a family may request that expressions of sympathy be a donation to some charity.
9. Some leaders have a building or charity named in their honor.
10. At the funeral of a deaf leader, the priest, minister, or rabbi may sign the service.
11. The service may be interpreted for deaf friends or relatives.
12. Songs may be sung and signed or interpreted.

Single-Slot Substitution Drills

Practice signing the following target sentences, substituting the suggested vocabulary in each slot. If you have problems with any of the vocabulary, consult your instructor for help.

1. near = RECENT   FRIEND   MY +   DIE ,   NOT   EXPECT .

    PAST +   two = MONTH

    WEEK = past

    YEAR = past +

    two = WEEK = past

    near = RECENT

2. FRIEND   MY +   DIE   HOW + + ,   HAPPEN   HEART͡ HIT .

    CAR   COLLISION

    DROWN

    S-T-R-O-K-E

    FALL-OFF = *ladder*

    PLANE = *crash*

    HEART͡ HIT

3. INFORM = me   RECEIVE   FRIEND   DIE ,   **MIND͡ FREEZE**   ME .

    heart = TOUCH

    FEEL-LOSS

    TRUE   **SORRY**

    TRUE   **SAD**

    MIND͡ FREEZE

4. WILL   FUNERAL   CHURCH   **FULL**   WHY + + ,   HIMSELF   POPULAR .

    LEADER

    FAMOUS

    MANY₂   FRIEND

    YOUNG

    POPULAR

5. WIFE ,   CHILDREN   HIS   TEARS-FLOW₂   #ALL = around ,   TRUE   **GRIEF** ,   WHEW .

    MOTHER ,   FATHER

    FAMILY

    BROTHER ,   SISTER

    FRIEND

    WIFE ,   CHILDREN

6. FRIEND   MY +   HIMSELF   **STRONG** <u>CHURCH</u> ,   WHEW .

         STRICT   FATHER

         LOVE   WIFE

         FRIEND   DEAF   GROUP

         LOVE   CHILDREN

         STRONG   CHURCH

7. PAST +   FRIEND   **LOVE**   #WHAT ,   <u>STORY</u> = talk   FUNNY$_2$.

         HELP = around   **ANY**

         TEASE = me = continuous

         WORK = around ,   BUSY   ALWAYS

         CHILDREN   PLAY = around

         STORY = talk   FUNNY$_2$

8. FRIEND   **GONE** ,   FEEL-LOSS   ME   WHY + + ,   <u>FUNNY$_2$</u>   ALWAYS   HE .

         HEART‿LARGE

         HELP = around

         CHEERFUL ,   HAPPY

         TEASE = me +

         FUNNY$_2$

9. HAPPEN   SOMEONE   DIE ,   FAMILY   PLAN +   <u>FUNERAL   SERVICE</u>   **NEED**   THEY .

         BURY   WHERE

         REMEMBER   LOOK-AT = past

         #DO   MONEY   GIFT = them$_2$

         THANK-YOU +   FRIEND

         FUNERAL   SERVICE

10. TRUE   WISE   PLAN +   AHEAD   BEFORE   APPEAR   SOMEONE   DIE   WHY + + ,

    <u>MONEY   **SAVE**</u> .

    READY   EASY

    TROUBLE   REDUCE

    GRIEF   REDUCE

    MONEY   **SAVE**

Suggested Activities

1. Act out the dialogue used in this lesson. Three persons may volunteer or be selected from the group to role play each of the characters. Give special attention to emotions, mental reactions, and facial expression.

2. Practice signing the ASL to English translation exercises *before* translating each of the sentences.

3. Clip an obituary story from a newspaper and bring it to class, prepared to translate the story into ASL.

4. Relate to the class an experience you have had in regard to the death of someone you knew well. Use your own discretion as to what details you might wish to share.

5. For fingerspelling practice, you may use some of the sentences or selected phrases from the sentences in the English to ASL translation exercises in this lesson. Pair off in class. Partners may then take turns randomly selecting two or three sentences or phrases to fingerspell to each other while the instructor observes.

6. Write an English version of the glossed introductory paragraph.

Babysitting Grandson

BABY   TAKE-CARE

HAPPEN BUSY NOTHING , BENNY , GLORIA those = TWO GO-OUT FETCH G-R-A-N-D SON
J-I-M-M-Y SIGN HIS+ JIMMY . those = THREE group = GO WHERE , THAT RIDE +
DIFFERENT + + ITS small = CHILDREN₂ JIMMY RIDE + LOVE "WHAT" , THAT BOAT SMALL ,
FLY = noun + **SMALL** those = TWO ! RIDE + FINISH₁ ONE , HE = jimmy BEG + MONEY RIDE
ONE MORE , PLEASE = noun₂ . BENNY COMPLAIN NOT , HAPPY MONEY GIVE = him-jimmy .
one = HOUR AROUND RIDE + FINISH₂ **SATISFY** , those = THREE GO-OUT EAT_A HOT-DOG ,
MAYBE ICE-CREAM . OTHER TIME-PERIOD those = THREE MAYBE group = GO WHERE ,
Z-O-O WHY + + JIMMY HIMSELF LOVE SEE ANIMAL + DIFFERENT + + ALIKE LION ,
MONKEY , BEAR , REINDEER . SEE ANIMAL + EXCITE HE = jimmy ! EVERYDAY WEEK END
BENNY , GLORIA DAUGHTER THEIR BRING ⊤ JIMMY . those = TWO = benny-gloria BABY
TAKE-CARE WHILE DAUGHTER HERSELF GO-OUT BUY + +   #DO = around₂ DIFFERENT + +
HOUSE HER .

Glossed Sentences, Translations, and Grammatical Notes

1. EVERYDAY WEEK͡ END G-R-A-N-D SON COME = here .

   Every weekend our grandson comes over.

2. BABY TAKE-CARE J-I-M-M-Y , JIMMY , **PLEASE = noun₂** we = TWO !

   We have much pleasure babysitting Jimmy!

3. SATURDAY near = PAST 24 + BIRTH͡ DAY HIS = jimmy .

   Just this past Saturday, the 24th, Jimmy had his birthday.

   Complex numbers like "24" are sometimes repeated for clarity. The compound BIRTH͡ DAY that we show here is just one of many signs that mean "birthday"; there are many regional variations.

4. JIMMY NOW OLD͜ FIVE , "BIG" BOY !

   Jimmy is five years old now and a big boy!

   "BIG" indicates the appropriate height of a person.

5. BIRTH͡ DAY HIS , JIMMY WANT +

   For his birthday, Jimmy wanted

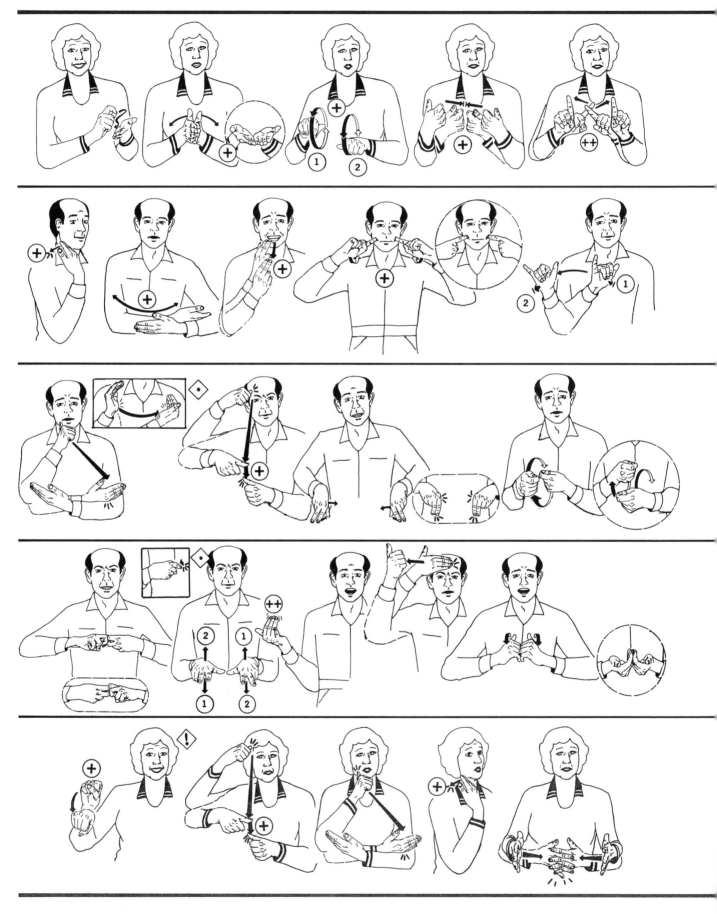

color=WRITE BOOK+ , BICYCLE , GAME+ DIFFERENT+ !

coloring books, a bicycle, and many different games!

color=WRITE is only slightly different from the sign WRITE; it means "to draw or color with crayons." Of course, it can be executed in many different ways, for example, to show "childlike scribbling," etc.

6. PAST+ BABY **CUTE** DIMPLE₂ **he=SAME=she**

Before as a baby, he was very cute and had dimples just like

In **he=SAME=she**, the sign moves in a raised arc between the "locations" of the two people. Emphasis is also shown by depressing the hand once toward each location. Emphatic **SAME** translates as "just the same" or "exactly alike."

DAUGHTER OUR . REMEMBER DIAPER EXCHANGE

our daughter. I remember changing diapers was

EXCHANGE represents one object replacing another; the sign CHANGE refers only to internal changes or modifications that alter the nature of a person or object, such as "changing one's mind," "a change in the weather," etc.

PROBLEM ME . AWKWARD WHY+ + , FORGET HOW !

a problem for me. It was awkward because I had forgotten how!

7. YES ! REMEMBER DAUGHTER PAST+ PREGNANT

Yes! I remember when our daughter was pregnant

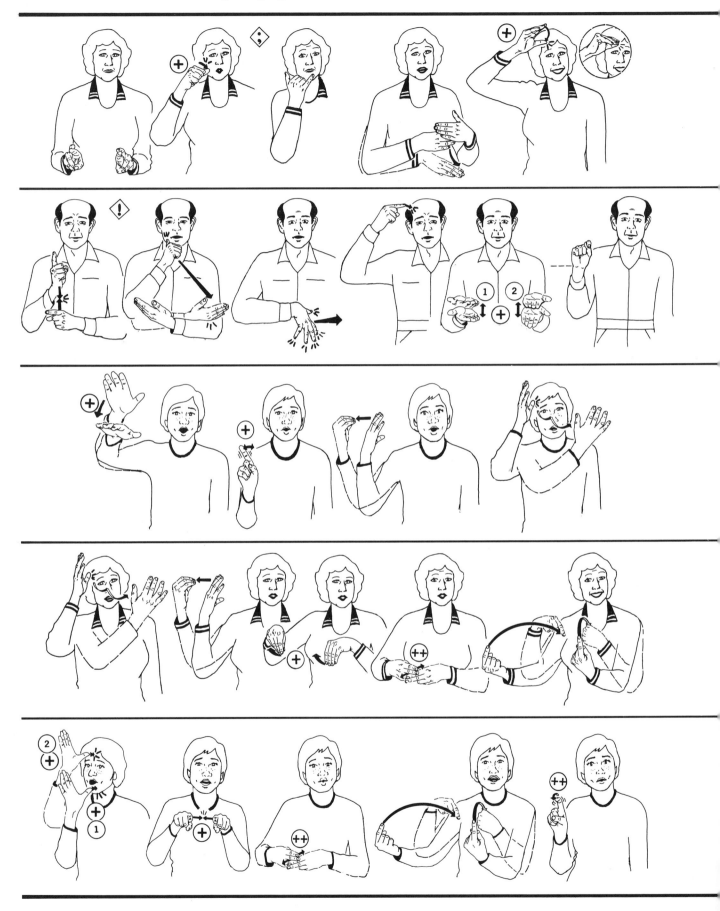

FINGER-CROSS₂ GIRL ; **WRONG** BORN BOY !

she kept hoping for a girl, but when it was born, it was a boy!

FINGER-CROSS, here done with two hands for emphasis, is an informal sign that can mean "hope" or "expectation." The sign **WRONG** can be used figuratively, as in this example, to show that an event did not match expectations. It can be used in either a positive or a negative sense. In many cases, the most appropriate translation is "but."

8. **RIGHT** ! DAUGHTER **STOMACH=big** , THINK MAYBE T-W-I-N !

That's right! Our daughter was big and she thought she might have twins!

STOMACH is made with an exaggerated outward movement to represent an enlarged abdomen, which refers in this context to pregnancy. It could also refer to "obesity" or to a "pot belly."

9. "HEY" , WHERE GO-OUT GRANDPA ?

Grandma, where did grandpa go?

10. GRANDPA GO-OUT SELL=noun+ , SHORT+ COME=here .

Grandpa went to the store; he will come back very soon.

The sign SHORT usually refers to time, and can be translated as "soon," "shortly," or "in a short while." It can also refer to distance, but it can never refer to the height of objects or persons.

11. MAMA , DADDY ALIKE+ SHORT+ COME=here QUESTION++ ?

Will Mama and Daddy come back soon, too?

MAMA and DADDY are simplified, colloquial versions of MOTHER and FATHER, respectively; the hand is held open continuously during the sign, rather than opening from a closed fist.

Vocabulary Review

Test your ability to produce the following signs or sign phrases.

ANIMAL +	FINGER-CROSS$_2$	PREGNANT
AWKWARD	FLY = noun + **SMALL**	QUESTION + +
BEAR	GAME +	**he = SAME = she**
BICYCLE	GIVE = him	SATISFY
"BIG" BOY	GO-OUT WHERE ?	SATURDAY
BIRTH DAY	GRANDPA	SHORT + +
BOAT SMALL	ICE-CREAM	SIGN
small = CHILDREN	LION	G-R-A-N-D SON
DADDY	LOVE	**STOMACH** = big
DIAPER EXCHANGE	MAMA	TAKE-CARE
DIMPLE$_2$	MONEY	those = THREE
#DO = around$_2$	MONKEY	WEEK END
EAT HOT-DOG	NOTHING	WHILE
EVERYDAY	NOW OLD FIVE	color = WRITE BOOK +
EVERYDAY WEEK END	ONE MORE	**WRONG**

Notes

Translation Exercises—ASL to English

Translate the following glossed sentences into appropriate English equivalents.

1. MOST PEOPLE BABY TAKE-CARE EXPERIENCE FINISH THEY .
2. HAPPEN NEXT-DOOR = right PLAN + GO-OUT , MAYBE they = ASK = you BABY TAKE-CARE WILL YOU ?
3. #IF ACCEPT YOU , MAYBE GO = next-door = right WHICH MAYBE BABY BRING т .
4. ANYWAY BABY TAKE-CARE , PLEASE = noun₂ NEED = "soft" you .
5. HAPPEN BABY TAKE-CARE IMPORTANT "WHAT" , DIAPER EXCHANGE KNOW HOW YOU !
6. DIAPER EXCHANGE HOW + + KNOW + , **KNACK** YOU ?
7. PAST + FINISH₂ WIFE we = TWO BABY TAKE-CARE CHILDREN TWO NEXT-DOOR = left .
8. next-door = CHILDREN COME HOUSE MY + , PLAY = around + MY SON ; those = THREE PLEASE = noun₂ .
9. WIFE we = TWO ASK = them = children + + #DO WANT + + YOU ?
10. SON MY + DECIDE WANT + + GO Z-O-O , SEE ANIMAL DIFFERENT + + > .
11. O-K , WIFE we = TWO FETCH CHILDREN those = THREE GO-OUT Z-O-O .
12. we = FIVE GOOD TIME , PLEASE = noun₂ ; TRUE BABY TAKE-CARE **FUN** .

Translation Exercises—English to ASL

Translate the following sentences from English into ASL equivalents.

1. Most of us have had experience babysitting someone's children, maybe our own.
2. Perhaps the most rewarding babysitting involves taking care of your grandchildren.
3. When someone's children are grown, married, or away from home, life gets lonely.
4. Grandchildren can make life exciting and make you feel young again!
5. It's fun to help a grandson or granddaughter celebrate a birthday.
6. Grandpa and Grandma want to join in all the fun.
7. They may give the child something very special that he or she wants.
8. It is also fun to take the child to places like the zoo.
9. At the zoo, you can enjoy yourself like a child.
10. When my grandson was small, we had to take him to kiddie rides.
11. That cost money, but it was fun watching him and his wonderful imagination.
12. He could be almost anything he wanted to be from a train engineer to a pilot!

Mixed-Slot Substitution Drills

Practice signing the following target sentences, substituting the suggested vocabulary in each slot. If you have problems with any of the vocabulary, consult your instructor for help.

1. PAST+   FRIEND   MY+   PREGNANT ,   <u>FINGER-CROSS$_2$</u>   WILL   GIRL ,   **WRONG**   BORN   BOY !

                                    LOOK-AT=her ,   FEEL

                                    DECIDE   FINISH$_2$

                                    DOUBT   NONE$_2$

                                    FEEL   IN+

                                    FINGER-CROSS$_2$

2. BABY   HER+   **<u>DIMPLE</u>**   he=SAME=she   <u>MOTHER</u> ,   WHEW !

                   FACE   STRONG   FATHER

                   HAIR   CURLY   FATHER

                   EAR$_2$ BIG   GRANDFATHER

                   SMILE   **CUTE**   MOTHER

                   DIMPLE   MOTHER

3. BOY+   NAME+   B-A-R-R-Y ;   WILL   OLD   TWO   **<u>"DEVIL"$_2$</u>**   HE !

                                              SWEET

                                              CUTE

                                              ANGEL

                                              STRONG

                                              "DEVIL"$_2$

4. B-A-R-R-Y , WILL   OLD   FOUR ,   HIMSELF   **LOVE**   "WHAT" ,   <u>TRAIN+</u>   .

                                                     AIRPLANE+

                                                     CAR+

                                                     BOAT

                                                     HORSE+

                                                     TRAIN+

5. HIMSELf=barry   COME=here   MY+   HOUSE   WHY++ ,

      <u>G-R-A-N-D   SON   MY+   PLAY+</u>   WANT+   HE .

      ME+   BABY   TAKE-CARE

      T-O-Y-S   MY+   PLAY+

      GAME+   MY+   PLAY+

      EAT+   MY   HOUSE

      G-R-A-N-D   SON   MY+   PLAY+

6. G-R-A-N-D SON MY+ WILL BIRTH DAY HIS+ , WANT+ #WHAT

    <u>BICYCLE</u> **NEW** .

    SMALL CAR ITS PEDAL_A

    color=WRITE BOOK+ SEVERAL₂

    P-O-N-Y TRUE LIFE

    NEW+ GAME+ DIFFERENT+ +>

    BICYCLE **NEW**

7. HIMSELF=grandson GO-OUT+ Z-O-O , **LOVE** HE WHY+ + ,

    FEED=them <u>LION</u> WANT+ HE .

            MONKEY

            ELEPHANT+

            BIRD+

            Z-E-B-R-A

            LION

8. SOMETIMES FETCH=him B-A-R-R-Y , we=FOUR GO=OUT

    <u>Z-O-O</u> ALL-DAY PLEASE-noun₂+ .

    RIDE+

    P-A-R-K

    BOAT+

    FISHING

    Z-O-O

9. SOMETIMES GO-OUT Z-O-O , EAT+ <u>ICE-CREAM</u> PLEASE=noun+₂ we=FOUR .

                          HOT-DOG

                          HAMBURGER

                          PEANUT+

                          "C-O-T-T-O-N" CANDY

                          ICE-CREAM

10. OTHER TIME-PERIOD , we=FOUR GO-OUT RIDE+ DIFFERENT+ +> ALIKE

    <u>ROLLER-COASTER=ride</u>

    FERRIS-WHEEL=ride_A

    small=PLANE

    small=BOAT

    small=CAR

    ROLLER-COASTER=ride

Suggested Activities

1. Share with the class a babysitting incident or experience you have had which you will never forget.

2. Act out the dialogue used in this lesson. Three persons may volunteer or be selected to role play the characters in the dialogue. Others may offer reactions or points of criticisms on sign production, body language used, and facial expression.

3. Practice signing the ASL to English translation exercises *before* translating each sentence.

4. For fingerspelling practice, you may use some of the sentences or selected phrases from the sentences in the English to ASL translation exercises in this lesson. Pair off in class. Partners may then take turns randomly selecting two or three sentences or phrases to fingerspell to each other while the instructor observes.

5. Write an English version of the glossed introductory paragraph.

Getting a Driver's License

FIRST TIME DRIVE+ LICENSE

WEEK = past KEE-KONG , ALEXANDER those = TWO WITH ⊥ D-M-V WHAT-FOR , SHE = kee-kong FIRST TIME TEST ITS DRIVE+ LICENSE . HERSELF = kee-kong **NERVOUS** WHEW ; HE = alexander ENCOURAGE HER = kee-kong RELAX , ANXIOUS **DON'T** + . ARGUE HIM = alexander SHE = kee-kong FINISH₂ BOOK ITS+ RULE+ DRIVE+ STUDY PLUS DRIVE = around+ PRACTICE three = WEEK . BACK-UP PARK+ **GOOD** SHE , PROBLEM NONE₂ . SHE = kee-kong AGREE = him-alexander ; ONE THING AFRAID "WHAT" , MAYBE POLICE HEARING UNDERSTAND+ HARD . ARRIVE D-M-V those = TWO CHAT++ , HAPPEN MAN POLICE APPROACH *TWO* , ASK = them SIGN "*you* = TWO DEAF ?" KEE-KONG **AGAPE** , ASK = him-police officer KNOW+ SIGN HOW++ YOU ? MAN POLICE TELL = her PAST+ LEARN SIGN LITTLE-BIT HOW++ , BROTHER DEAF HAVE ! SHE = kee-kong FEEL BETTER , POLICE SIGN CAN "FINE" , HELP = me WILL HE ! HAPPEN SHE = kee-kong TEST WRITE = page PASS ; TEST DRIVE+ PASS . RECEIVE LICENSE FINISH₂ .

Glossed Sentences, Translations, and Grammatical Notes

1. TEST ITS CAR+ LICENSE

    Do you think it will be easy to pass

    WRITE=page PASS EASY , THINK YOU ?

    the driver's license test?

    In WRITE=page, the nondominant hand is tilted to better represent the concept of a sheet of paper and the writing motion of the dominant hand is usually downwards. In combination with the sign TEST, it means "written test."

2. BOOK ITS DRIVE+⊥ STUDY FINISH₁ YOU ;

    You've studied the driving handbook;

    There is no sign for "handbook," but the context requires this interpretation. DRIVE+⊥ in this sentence moves straight forward repeatedly; it refers to "the action of driving."

    SECOND+ , DRIVE=around+ PRACTICE+ FINISH₂ ;

    second, you've practiced driving around;

    With =around, DRIVE means "to drive" (with no definite distance or location mentioned), or it can mean "to drive in circles."

    THIRD+ , car=PARK+ PRACTICE **GOOD** YOU ;

    third, you did well in parking practice;

    The "3" handshape of car=PARK can represent "vehicles on land or sea." It is most often used to describe cars, however. It is always a part of any sign that describes the spatial arrangement, location, or motion of a car. We will always represent this "3" hand with the lower case gloss "car" unless the context requires another interpretation.

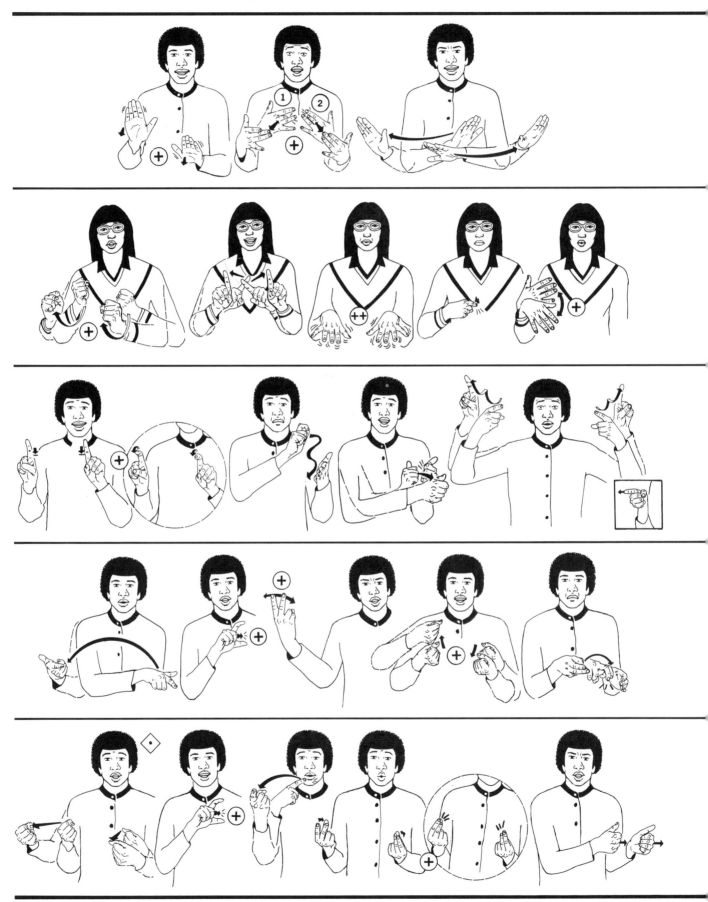

RELAX , ANXIOUS **DON'T** !

so relax and don't worry!

3. ATTEMPT+ BUT **NERVOUS** ME WHEW !

I'm trying, but I'm really nervous!

ATTEMPT is the basis for the sign TRY, which uses a "T" handshape. "Attempt," "try," "strive," etc., are possible translations for both signs.

4. TEST WRITE=page PASS SUCCEED YOU ,

If you succeed in passing the written test,

here=NEXT-TURN=there POLICE you=TWO CAR GET-IN-VEHICLE

next, a police officer will call you to get in the car.

The sign NEXT-TURN indicates a sequence of events, objects, people, or places. In this case, it first points to the left, which is the location for the event of "the written test" and moves to the right, to the location of "the driving test." GET-IN-VEHICLE is used for entering or boarding cars, trains, buses, boats, and planes. (See Lesson 5, sentence 12.)

DRIVE⊥ . POLICE TELL=you #DO+ FOLLOW .

and drive off. Just follow what the police officer tells you to do.

5. DEAF YOU - YOU ? ME HELP ? SIGN KNOW LITTLE-BIT .
    Are you two deaf? Can I help you? I know some signs.

6. KNOW+ SIGN YOU ? SURPRISE ME ! LEARN+ HOW++ ?
    You know signs? I'm surprised! How did you learn?

7. BROTHER = formal DEAF . LEARN PAST BUT FORGET SOME .
    My brother was deaf. I learned in the past, but I've forgotten some.

    NOW TEST . GOOD L-U-C-K !
    It's time for the test now. Good luck!

8. TEST PASS ! WRONG+ ONE , **RELIEVED** ME !
    I passed the test! I only made one mistake, and I'm so relieved!

Vocabulary Review

Test your ability to produce the following signs or sign phrases.

AGAPE	FORGET	RECEIVE
AGREE = him	GOOD L-U-C-K	RELAX
APPROACH	HAVE	RULE +
ARGUE	HEARING = person	STUDY FINISH₁
car = BACK-UP	HELP	SUCCEED
BOOK	KNOW +	THINK YOU ?
BROTHER = formal	LICENSE	THIRD
DRIVE = around	**NERVOUS**	UNDERSTAND
EASY	here = NEXT-TURN = there	three = WEEK
ENCOURAGE	car = PARK +	WILL HE
FIRST TIME	PASS	WITH
FOLLOW	POLICE	test = WRITE = page
	PRACTICE	

Notes

Translation Exercises—ASL to English

Translate the following glossed sentences into appropriate English equivalents.

1. RECEIVE FIRST DRIVE+ LICENSE long=PAST , OLD SEVENTEEN ME .

2. long=PAST THAT TIME-PERIOD , TEST+ ITS DRIVE+ NOT REQUIRED .

3. **WILL** MARRY FINISH₂ , MOVE OTHER S-T-A-T-E TEST WRITE=page , TEST DRIVE⊥ **NEED** ME .

4. PAST+ S-T-A-T-E LAW CONNECT DRIVE+ ITS++ DIFFERENT++ > ; NOW++ S-T-A-T-E-S MORE SAME=around₂ .

5. near=RECENT SON MY+ RECEIVE FIRST DRIVE+ LICENSE ; **EXCITED** HE !

6. FIRST HIMSELF RECEIVE LEARN+ "CARD" FINISH₂ GO SCHOOL TAKE-UP DRIVE+ LEARN++ .

7. WEEK+ FEW HIMSELF STUDY=continuously #WHAT , BOOK ITS+ RULE+ DRIVE+ .

8. DRIVE+ LEARN++ LESSON FINISH₂ , AFTER PRACTICE+ DRIVE=around+ UNDERSTAND++ HE ME SIT=side-by-side₂ .

9. TIME GO TEST WRITE=page , TEST DRIVE ⊥ we=TWO he=WITH=me⊥ "WHERE" , KNOW YOU D-M-V .

10. SON MY+ TEST WRITE=page **PASS** this=NEXT-TURN=that TEST DRIVE ⊥ **PASS** ; RECEIVE LICENSE SHORT++ .

11. WILL SIX MONTH DRIVE=around O-K , GOOD R-E-C-O-R-D , HIMSELF #BACK D-M-V EXCHANGE LICENSE **CONTINUE** FINISH₂ .

Translation Exercises—English to ASL

Translate the following sentences from English into ASL equivalents.

1. Getting your first driver's license is a very exciting, but nervous, experience.

2. Can you remember when you got your first driver's license?

3. When I got my first driver's license, I didn't have to pass any test.

4. That was way back in the late 1940s when I was seventeen.

5. My basic driver education was on a ranch with my father as my instructor.

6. I first learned to drive a pickup and a big cattle feed truck.

7. Most young people now have driver education training in school.

8. Some people have to hire a driving instructor for private lessons.

9. Everyone must now take a written test and a road test for that first license.

10. You must pass the written test by studying a driver's handbook.

11. The road test is the nervous part; you have to do exactly what the police officer says.

12. Once you have your driver's license, you have more independence.

Mixed-Slot Substitution Drills

Practice signing the following target sentences, substituting the suggested vocabulary in each slot. If you have problems with any of the vocabulary, consult your instructor for help.

1. RECEIVE DRIVE+ LICENSE WANT+ YOU , <u>BOOK ITS RULE STUDY</u> **NEED** YOU .

         DRIVE=around+ PRACTICE

         car=BACK-UP+ PRACTICE

         car=PARK PRACTICE

         DRIVE+ TRAFFIC PRACTICE

         BOOK ITS RULE STUDY

2. READY> GO D-M-V RECEIVE DRIVE+ LICENSE ,

    <u>TEST WRITE=page PASS</u> **NEED** YOU .

    TEST DRIVE+ PASS

    TEST car=PARK PASS

    PAY=them MONEY

    TEST WRITE=page PASS

3. FIRST TIME LEARN+ DRIVE+ , TEACH=me WHO , <u>FATHER</u> .

                      UNCLE

                      FRIEND

                      SISTER

                      FATHER

4. PAST+ FIRST TIME GO D-M-V DRIVE+ TEST WRITE=page , <u>NERVOUS</u> YOU ?

                                SUCCEED

                                CONFUSED

                                FAIL

                                PASS

                                NERVOUS

5. <u>TEST WRITE=page PASS FINISH YOU</u> , this=NEXT-TURN=that <u>DRIVE+ TEST</u> .

    DRIVE+ TEST   SUCCEED   car=PARK+ TEST

    car=PARK+ TEST PASS   LICENSE F-E-E

                                        PAY=them

    LICENSE F-E-E   PAY=them   PICTURE shoot=

                                        CAMERA

    PICTURE   LICENSE RECEIVE

    TEST WRITE=page PASS   DRIVE+ TEST

6. <u>FIRST</u>   DRIVE+   LICENSE   RECEIVE   ME ,   WHERE ?   <u>K-A-N-S-A-S</u> .

    SECOND   L-O-U-I-S-I-A-N-A

    THIRD   WASHINGTON,   D.C.

    FOURTH   M-A-R-Y-L-A-N-D

    near = RECENT   M-A-R-Y-L-A-N-D

    FIRST   K-A-N-S-A-S

7. long = PAST   DRIVE+   LEARN+   ME ,   <u>FATHER</u>   SIT = side-by-side   <u>he = TEACH = me</u> .

                                         BROTHER   he = TEACH = me.

                                         UNCLE   he = TEACH = me.

                                         SISTER   she = TEACH = me.

                                         FRIEND   she = TEACH = me.

                                         FATHER   he = TEACH = me.

8. BOOK   DRIVE   RULE+   ITS ,   <u>READ</u>   FINISH   YOU ?

                                  STUDY

                                  LOOK-UP

                                  MEMORIZE

                                  KNOW

                                  READ

9. CAR   <u>DRIVE = around+</u>   PRACTICE   FINISH   YOU .

        car = BACK-UP +

        TRAFFIC   DRIVE +

        car = PASS = *car* +

        car = PARK + ⊤

        DRIVE = around +

10. PAST+   CAR   FIRST‿TIME   TRAFFIC   DRIVE+   **NERVOUS**   YOU ?

                                         SCARED

                                         FEEL‿GOOD

                                         CONFIDENT

                                         LITTLE   NERVOUS

                                         NERVOUS

Suggested Activities

1. Share with the class an incident or experience related to your *first* driving experience or to getting your *first* driver's license. If you don't drive, maybe you know of an incident experienced by someone close to you.

2. Bring a copy of your state's driver's handbook to class. Select a brief portion of the rules or other driving information for translation into ASL. Develop a translation of the material selected and share it with the rest of the class.

3. Act out the dialogue used in this lesson. Three persons may volunteer or be selected from the group to role play each character in the dialogue. Give special attention to body language and to facial expression.

4. Practice signing the ASL to English translation exercises *before* you translate the sentences.

5. For fingerspelling practice, you may use some of the sentences or selected phrases from the sentences in the English to ASL translation exercises in this lesson. Pair off in class. Partners may then take turns randomly selecting two or three sentences or phrases to fingerspell to each other while the instructor observes.

6. Write an English version of the glossed introductory paragraph.

Driving Problems

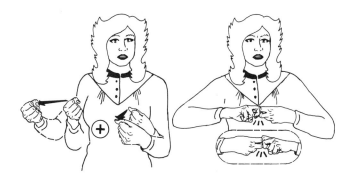

DRIVE+   PROBLEM

early=MORNING TIME GO-OUT WORK . JANE HERSELF GET-IN-VEHICLE CAR KEY PUT-IN=ignition TURN ; MOTOR object=turn=ROUND+ START REFUSE . SHE=jane LET'S SEE TRY AGAIN . SAME₂ START REFUSE ! DECIDE MAN NEXT-DOOR ALEXANDER THAT TAP=him COME-ON LET'S-SEE HELP=me . HE=alexander SMILE , WITH=her LET'S-SEE WRONG+ "WHAT" . KEY she=GIVE=him . ALEXANDER GET-IN-VEHICLE CAR , KEY PUT-IN=ignition TURN-ON=ignition ; MOTOR object=turn=ROUND+ , START REFUSE **SAME₂** ! ALEXANDER GET-OFF-VEHICLE "WALK"=around HOOD=open INVESTIGATE FIND "WHAT" ? WIRE L-O-O-S-E . REPAIR FINISH₁ , "WALK"=around=back GET-IN-VEHICLE TURN-ON=ignition , MOTOR object=turn=ROUND+ AT-LAST running=ROUND MINUTE SMOOTH . HE=alexander GEAR-SHIFT object=PULL-DOWN "R" , BACK-OUT=garage . HAPPEN FEEL+ WHEEL-BUMP+ ; KNOW FINISH₁ FLAT-TIRE ! JANE HERSELF EXCHANGE TIRE "STUPID" . ALEXANDER TIRE EXCHANGE FINISH , SHE=jane GIFT₁ ONE-DOLLAR , GO-OUT WORK !

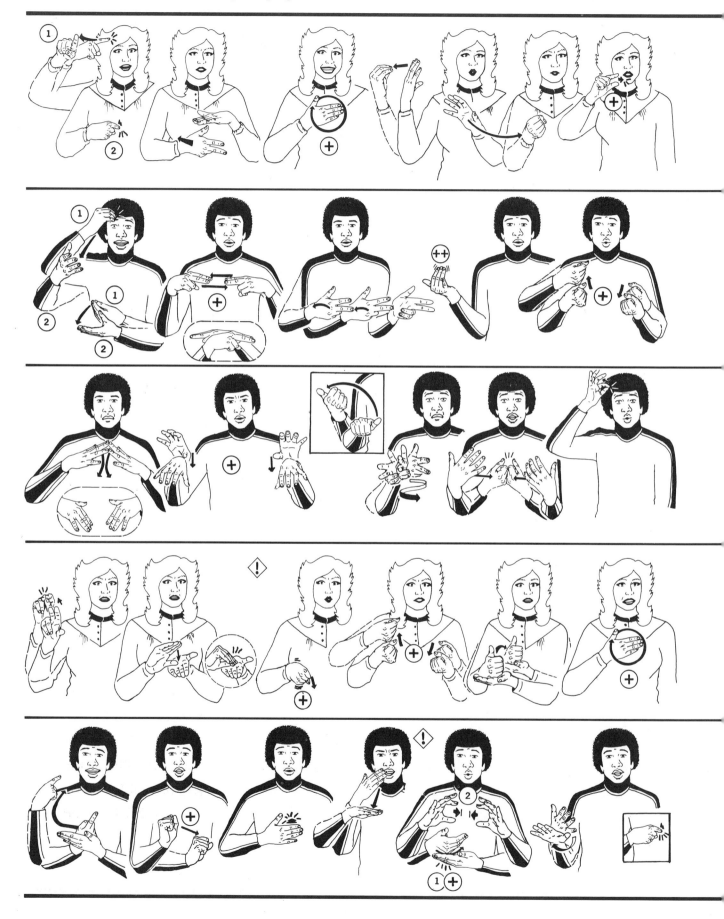

Glossed Sentences, Translations, and Grammatical Notes

1. FOR   ME   car=BACK-OUT=garage   PLEASE ;   GO-OUT   FETCH   GLORIA .

Please back the car out of the garage for me; I'm going to get Gloria.

In car=BACK-OUT=garage, the nondominant hand, palm down, represents an "overhead covering," and the "3" handshape represents the vehicle, "backed out." This sign could also mean "back out of a carport," and the verb is represented by the movement.

2. INFORM=you   FREEWAY   car=LINE-UP$_2$ WHY++ ,   CAR

You should know traffic is backed up on the freeway because a car

FREEWAY could also be translated as "a four-lane highway," "a dual highway," or "an expressway." It could also be modified, with different finger extensions, to show a specific number of lanes in each direction. In car=LINE-UP$_2$, both hands assume the "3" handshape, one in front of the other; the dominant hand then moves back in small, short jumps to represent a line of vehicles forming.

BREAK-DOWN ,   RAIN+ ,   OTHER   car=SKID   COLLISION   "BY-A-HAIR" !

broke down and rain caused another car to skid, just missing a collision!

"BY-A-HAIR" may be translated as "just missing," "almost," or literally "by a hair's breadth."

3. NO !   FLAT-TIRE !   JACK-UP   CAR   HELP=me   PLEASE+ .

Oh no, I have a flat tire! Please help me jack up my car.

4. WEEK=past   BRAKE+   MY+   BAD !   NEW+   BRAKE-SHOE=put-on   FINISH$_1$ ME .

Last week, my brakes went bad! I've already put on new brake shoes.

5. MY+ pedal=PUSH car=MOVE=forward SLOW ; WRONG+ ?

My car has poor pickup; what's wrong?

The sign PUSH is made lower, to indicate "pushing a foot pedal."

6. NEW+ P-L-U-G SPARK NEED+ , MAYBE C-A-R-B CLEAN+ .

It needs new spark plugs and maybe a carburetor cleaning.

7. THANK-YOU ! NEW+ HOME HER+ GLORIA EXIT WHERE ?

Thanks! Where do I exit for Gloria's new house?

8. R-Y-E-S-D-A-L-E R-O-A-D THAT EXIT ; ALMOST-NOTHING TWO B-L-O-C-K .

Exit on Ryesdale Road; it's only two blocks from there.

ALMOST-NOTHING can also be translated "very close" "right by here," "no distance at all," etc. It can sometimes mean "very soon" or "in no time at all." (See also Lesson 10, sentence 9.)

HEADLIGHT-OFF₂ BETTER YOU , BATTERY+ WEAK WILL .

You better turn off your car lights or you'll run down the battery.

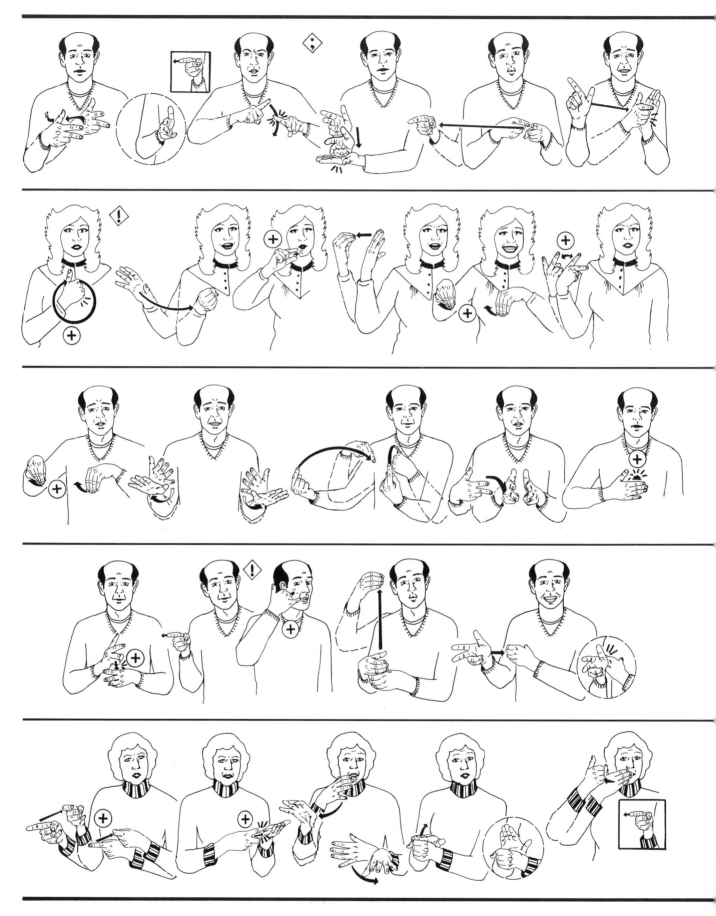

9. car=PARK **CAN'T** YOU ; car=PARK+ + LENGTH **against=LAW** !

You can't park here; this is a no parking zone!

car=PARK moves to indicate the act of "parallel parking." car=PARK+ +, made in a single location, refers to the act of "parking" in general. against=LAW is a singular, emphatic movement. In this sentence, combined with car=PARK, it translates as "no parking," meaning it is illegal to park in this particular place. This sign may also mean "ban," "forbid," "not allowed," "taboo," etc.

10. SORRY ! FETCH GLORIA GO-OUT SELL=noun+ we=TWO .

I'm sorry! I'm getting Gloria so we can go to the store.

11. SELL=noun+ FINISH₂ COME=here , car=ALONGSIDE MY+ .

When you come back from the store, pull up alongside my car.

COME=here moves to a location close to the signer's body. In car=ALONGSIDE, the relative spatial position is shown by two hands.

CAREFUL YOU ! TELEPHONE POLE car=BACK-UP HIT !

Be careful or you'll back into that telephone pole!

12. FAST+ TICKET don't=WANT , pedal=OFF=little BETTER YOU !

If you don't want a ticket for speeding, you'd better let up on the gas a little!

FAST+ can translate as "speed." pedal=OFF=little represents a slight "easing off on the pedal."

Vocabulary Review

Test your ability to produce the following signs or sign phrases.

car = ALONGSIDE MY +	GEAR-SHIFT	MOTOR
car = BACK-OUT = garage	object = PULL-DOWN	object = turn = ROUND +
car = BACK-UP⌣HIT = *barrier*	GET-OFF-VEHICLE	car = MOVE = forward
BATTERY	she = GIVE = him	NEXT-DOOR
BETTER YOU	GO-OUT FETCH	pedal = OFF = little
BRAKE + BAD	HEADLIGHT-OFF$_2$	pedal = PUSH
BRAKE-SHOE = put-on FINISH$_1$	HOME HER +	SAME$_2$
BREAK-DOWN	HOOD-OPEN	car = SKID
"BY-A-HAIR"	JACK-UP	START REFUSE
COLLISION	KEY	"STUPID"
EXCHANGE	KNOW⌣FINISH$_1$	TELEPHONE POLE
EXIT	**against = LAW**	TIRE
FAST +	car = LINE-UP$_2$	TRY
FLAT-TIRE	MINUTE	TURN-ON = ignition
FREEWAY	early = MORNING	"WALK" = around
GEAR-SHIFT	MOTOR	WEAK
	MOTOR	"WHEEL-BUMP"
	object = run = ROUND + +	WIRE

Notes

Translation Exercises—ASL to English

Translate the following glossed sentences into appropriate English equivalents.

1. NOW MORNING TRAFFIC TERRIBLE WHEW !

2. CORRECT ! car=LINE-UP$_2$ car=MOVE=forward$_2$ SLOW ! ARRIVE WORK LATE ME !

3. KNOW YOU HEARING-PEOPLE DRIVE++ "LISTEN" RADIO INFORM=them+ TRAFFIC PROBLEM APPEAR+ , "DEAF" CAN'T !

4. DRIVE++ WORK HAPPEN **RAIN**++ , LIGHTS-ON **NEED** YOU !

5. PAST+ two=MONTH DRIVE+ WORK , ARRIVE FINISH$_2$ HAPPEN FORGET LIGHTS-OFF .

6. READY GO-OUT HOME ME+ GET-IN-VEHICLE=car , KEY PUT-IN=ignition , TURN-ON=ignition , MOTOR object=turn=ROUND+ , START REFUSE !

7. #DO+ ME ? GO ASK=him SOMEONE TELEPHONE HELP=me A-A-A BECKON COME=here BATTERY=charge .

8. FIRST TIME HAPPEN ME QUESTION++ , NO++ ; HAPPEN PAST+ FEW TIME-PERIOD .

9. PAST+ HAPPEN RAIN++ , EYES SEE ME "WHAT" , CAR car=SKID car=OFF-ROAD=right !

10. CAR car=SKID "BY-A-HAIR" COLLISION , **WRONG** car=OFF-ROAD=right car=HIT=object TREE STOP , SAFE !

11. ME+ MIND͡ FREEZE , "HAIR-ON-END"$_2$ NERVOUS , #DO+$_2$, car=MOVE-OVER=right car=STOP .

12. GET-OUT-VEHICLE=car HELP=her=driver CAN'T ME , WHY++ right=leg=COVER , CRUTCHES "WALK=one-leg"$_2$ ME .

Translation Exercises—English to ASL

Translate the following English sentences into ASL equivalents.

1. The other day, a police car pulled up alongside me, and a police officer told me to pull over.

2. I pulled over and the police officer said, "Your lights are off; please turn them on."

3. Can you recall some experiences you've had in driving?

4. One day a few years ago, I ran out of gas on the Parkway!

5. I remember when my sister backed over our cat a long time ago.

6. Someone stole the battery from my new car while I was in class!

7. My car has poor pickup; can you tell me what's wrong?

8. Maybe you should buy a new car.

9. Turn off the freeway when you get to the next exit.

10. There's a gas station where we can buy new windshield wipers.

Mixed-Slot Substitution Drills

Practice signing the following target sentences, substituting the suggested vocabulary in each slot. If you have problems with any of the vocabulary, consult your instructor for help.

1. NOW MORNING TRAFFIC **BAD** WHY++ , <u>SOMEONE COLLISION</u> car=LINE-UP$_2$!

                                                    RAIN+   car=MOVE=forward SLOW$_2$

                                                    SOMEONE STUCK   CAR BREAK-DOWN

                                                    SNOW+   car=MOVE=forward SLOW$_2$

                                                    SOMEONE COLLISION car=LINE-UP$_2$!

2. PAST+ DRIVE+ WORK car=PARK+ FINISH ME , HAPPEN FORGET

      <u>HEADLIGHTS-OFF$_2$</u>

      TURN-OFF=ignition

      WALLET LEAVE HOME

      DRIVE+ LICENSE

      HEADLIGHTS-OFF$_2$

3. HAPPEN FORGET <u>car=HEADLIGHTS-OFF$_2$</u> , **WRONG** <u>BATTERY "DIE"</u> !

                              TURN-OFF=ignition   motor=run=ROUND+ , ALL-GONE GAS

                              KEY PUT-IN=ignition   DOOR LOCK , KEY NONE

                              DRIVE+ LICENSE   POLICE CATCH=me , LICENSE NONE$_2$

                              car=HEADLIGHTS-OFF$_2$ BATTERY "DIE"

4. CAR MY+ pedal=PUSH can=MOVE=forward=slow , SEEM+ NEED+

      <u>NEW P-L-U-G SPARK</u> .

      C-A-R-B CLEAN+

      T-U-N-E U-P

      GAS, BY-A-HAIR ALL-GONE

      NEW P-L-U-G SPARK

5. CAR MY+ TROUBLE #WHAT , <u>BRAKE+ BAD</u> .

                              BATTERY WEAK

                              TURN-ON=ignition HARD

                              MOTOR object=run=ROUND++ SMOOTH NOT

                              C-A-R-B STUCK+

                              BRAKE+ BAD

6. PAST+ NEW CAR MY+ FLAT-TIRE , WHY++ <u>N-A-I-L PUNCTURE</u>=tire .

                                                   BREAK+ GLASS

                                                   S-C-R-E-W PUNCTURE=tire

                                                   DON'T-KNOW

                                                   TIRE CUT

                                                   N-A-I-L PUNCTURE=tire

7. <u>car=SKID</u> EXPERIENCE FINISH YOU ?

    FLAT-TIRE

    BRAKE+ FAIL

    GAS ALL-GONE

    car=SKID

8. PAST+ CAR "BY-A-HAIR" COLLISION SEE FINISH YOU ?

                        car=SKID car=OFF-ROAD=left

                        MOTOR FIRE

                        HIT TREE

                        OVERTURN

                        "BY-A-HAIR" COLLISION

9. DRIVE++⊥ WORK , HAPPEN POP-UP **RAIN++** , <u>LIGHTS-ON</u> **NEED** YOU !

                                               SLOW DRIVE+

                                               WIPERS TURN-ON=wipers

                                               CAREFUL DRIVE+

                                               ATTENTION DRIVE+

                                             LIGHTS-ON

10. YOU DRIVE++⊥ , HAPPEN POP-UP <u>FLAT-TIRE</u> #DO YOU ?

                                        MOTOR "DIE"

                                        WATER *radiator-cap*=**GUSH**

                                        TRAFFIC car=LINE-UP$_2$

                                        CAR car=SKID

                                        FLAT-TIRE

Suggested Activities

1. Act out the dialogue used in this lesson. Four persons may volunteer or be selected from the group to role play each character in the dialogue. Watch facial expression and body language.

2. Relate to the class an incident you have encountered in your driving experience that you will never forget.

3. Describe a traffic incident that you have recently experienced *or* tell about a car problem you have had, how you discovered the problem, and what you did about it or how you solved it.

4. Find out from deaf people *how* they detect problems with their autos. Discuss what you find out in class.

5. Practice signing the ASL to English translation exercises *before* you translate the sentences.

6. For fingerspelling practice, you may use some of the sentences or selected phrases from the sentences in the English to ASL translation exercises in this lesson. Pair off in class. Partners may then take turns randomly selecting two or three sentences or phrases to fingerspell to each other while the instructor observes.

7. Write an English version of the glossed introductory paragraph.

Train Trip to New York City

NEW-YORK TRAIN GO

FIRST TIME TRAIN GO NEW-YORK those=TWO ALEXANDER , JENNIFER ; TOUCH PAST+
NEVER ! PLAN+ three=WEEK EXCITED those=TWO ! HE=alexander GO TRAIN TICKET+
BUY RESERVE FINISH₂ . WILL those=TWO GET-IN-VEHICLE FANCY₁ M-E-T-R-O-L-I-N-E-R ,
KNOW YOU . SHE=jennifer PAST MAIL=it NEW-YORK RECEIVE PAPER‿THIN=object
INFORM=them those=TWO HOTEL DIFFERENT++ EATₐ FANCY₁ WHERE PLUS
SIGHTSEE=around HOW++ . TIME GO-OUT those=TWO GET-IN-VEHICLE TRAIN
early=MORNING TIME‿EIGHT . TRAIN COMFORTABLE WHEW ! those=TWO "STRETCH=leg₂"
CAN , "FINE" ! TRAIN RIDE LOOK-AT=outside=right WINDOW , LOOK-AT=outside=left
WINDOW , ONE-PAST=headₐ PLEASE=noun+₂ those=TWO ! TRAIN STOP++⊥ BALTIMORE ,
W-I-L-M-I-N-G-T-O-N , PHILADELPHIA , AT-LAST ARRIVE NEW-YORK ! GET-OFF-VEHICLE
TRAIN FINISH₂ those=TWO GET-IN-VEHICLE T-A-X-I GO-OUT HOTEL , BAGGAGE₂ PUT-IN+₂
FINISH₂ , DISCUSS #DO=around AFTER .

Glossed Sentences, Translations, and Grammatical Notes

1. WEEK = past FRIDAY we = TWO = alexander TRAIN GO-OUT

   Last Friday, Alexander and I went by train to

   In we = TWO = alexander, the directional pronoun TWO moves alternately towards the signer and (the location of) Alexander.

NEW-YORK ; **WONDERFUL** TIME-PERIOD , NEVER FORGET !

New York City; we had a most wonderful time and I will never forget it!

---

2. TOUCH = around + DIFFERENT + FINISH₂ ? TELL = me WHAT'S-UP + + .

   Did you get around to see different places? Tell me about the highlights.

   The verb TOUCH can also mean "to experience" (especially a place), "to visit" (a place), or "to be" (in a place). In the context of travel, it can be translated as "see." See TOUCH in sentence 4.

---

3. RESERVE , TICKET BUY FINISH₁ PAST + FANCY₁

   We had our reservations and bought our tickets earlier for the plush

   FANCY₁ can mean "plush," "well-appointed," "very comfortable," "above the ordinary," etc.

M-E-T-R-O-L-I-N-E-R , LEAVE WASHINGTON early = MORNING TIME EIGHT .

Metroliner and left Washington in the morning at 8:00.

early = MORNING is made with a single, abrupt horizontal movement forward. It can also be translated in other contexts as "daybreak," "crack of dawn," etc.

4. FIRST TIME NEW-YORK , TOUCH‿FINISH₂ PAST+ NEVER .

It was our first time in New York; we've never been there before.

See note on TOUCH in sentence 2.

we=TWO ARRIVE AROUND NOON , T-A-X-I RIDE

We arrived around noon and rode a taxi to our

HOTEL . TRUE AGAPE SKYSCRAPER+ , TALL-STRUCTURE_A+ !

hotel. We were really astounded at the skyscrapers and tall buildings!

AGAPE can be translated by any verb that means "to express amazement." TALL-STRUCTURE most often refers to buildings but can refer to other man-made structures as well.

5. BAGGAGE₂ PUT-IN₂+ HOTEL FINISH₁ , we=TWO

After we checked in and put our bags in the hotel, we

WALK TWO=forward+ ARRIVE BUILDING E-M-P-I-R-E S-T-A-T-E ,

walked together to the Empire State Building and

The directional verb TWO=forward in this case indicates motion toward a place, and it is marked for two people doing the action.

ELEVATOR STAND∧ GET-OFF LOOK-AT = noun+ FLOOR LOOK-AT = down = around₂+ .
took the elevator to the observation area and viewed the city.

LOOK-AT = noun+ involves short repetitions which give it the sense of "looking" or "observation." LOOK-AT = down = around₂+ , made with two hands, involves a "downward" direction and the movement in arcs that is typical of multiple, indefinite activities.

---

6. AFTERNOON we = TWO SUBWAY RIDE this = NEXT-TURN = that car = FERRY-BOAT
In the afternoon, we took the subway to catch a ferry boat

NEXT-TURN first moves to indicate the activity of "riding" and then to the place where FERRY-BOAT will be signed.

GO L-I-B-E-R-T-Y ISLAND SEE STATUE ITS FREE !
to Liberty Island to see the Statue of Liberty!

ITS can sometimes be used to link a noun and an adjective that describes one of its inherent qualities. FREE can be translated "freedom," "liberty," etc.

---

7. all = EVENING GO-OUT RESTAURANT , THEATRE , DANCE we = TWO .
During the evening, we went out to eat, to the theatre, and to dance.

all = EVENING is made with a continual, slow arc that moves past the normal position for EVENING.

---

8. WONDERFUL TRIP NEW-YORK you = TWO **TRUE** !
You two certainly had a wonderful trip to New York City!

Vocabulary Review

Test your ability to produce the following signs or sign phrases.

AFTERNOON	MAIL = it	SUBWAY
BAGGAGE$_2$	NEVER	TALL-STRUCTURE$_A$ +
BALTIMORE	NEW-YORK	THEATRE
BUY‿FINISH$_1$	NOON	three = HOUR
COMFORTABLE	ONE-PAST = head$_A$	TICKET
DEPART	PAPER THIN = object	TIME‿EIGHT
DISCUSS	PHILADELPHIA	TOUCH = around + >
ELEVATOR	baggage = PUT-IN$_2$	TOUCH‿FINISH$_2$
all = EVENING	RESERVE	TRAIN TICKET
FANCY$_1$	RESTAURANT	TRIP
car = *FERRY-BOAT*	RIDE	TRUE
FREE	SIGHTSEE = around	TWO = forward +
FRIDAY	SKYSCRAPER	WALK
HOTEL	STAND ∧	WASHINGTON
KNOW YOU	STATUE	WONDERFUL
LOOK-AT = down = around	STOP + +⊥	**WONDERFUL**
LOOK-AT = noun$_2$	"STRETCH = leg$_2$"	

Notes

Translation Exercises—ASL to English

Translate the following glossed sentences into appropriate English equivalents.

1. NEW-YORK TOUCH‿FINISH, ONCE , GO++ AGAIN++ WANT++ , WILL YOU !

2. WASHINGTON NEW-YORK you=FLY=there ARRIVE TIME+ ALMOST-NOTHING SHORT .

3. #IF WASHINGTON NEW-YORK GO TRAIN , ARRIVE TIME+ AROUND three=HOUR .

4. WASHINGTON NEW-YORK DRIVE++⊥ PLEASE=noun₂+ ME+ #BUT STRIKE-CHANCE N-J FREEWAY , TRAFFIC WHEW !

5. KNOW THAT TRAIN RIDE ITS+ M-E-T-R-O-L-I-N-E-R "STRETCH-LEG₂" CAN YOU , "FINE" COMFORTABLE TRUE .

6. TRAIN RIDE LOOK-AT=outside=right WINDOW , LOOK-AT=outside=left WINDOW , ONE-PAST=head_A PLEASE=noun₂+ YOU ?

7. FIRST TIME NEW-YORK YOU ? TOUCH NEVER BEFORE , TRUE AGAPE SKYSCRAPER+ , TALL-STRUCTURE_A+ WILL YOU !

8. BUILDING SKYSCRAPER NAME+ E-M-P-I-R-E S-T-A-T-E KNOW YOU ; TRUE WORTH ELEVATOR STAND ∧ GET-OFF LOOK-AT=noun+ FLOOR .

9. STRIKE-CHANCE CLEAR DAY , LUCKY YOU ; LOOK-AT=down=around₂+ SEE FAR CAN YOU !

10. GO L-I-B-E-R-T-Y ISLAND WHAT-FOR , SEE STATUE ITS FREE , **NEED** YOU !

11. GO L-I-B-E-R-T-Y ISLAND HOW++ , GET-IN-VEHICLE SUBWAY RIDE this=NEXT-TURN=that car=FERRY-BOAT ARRIVE ISLAND WILL YOU .

Translation Exercises—English to ASL

Translate the following sentences from English into ASL equivalents.

1. New York City is always an exciting place to visit.

2. Our first time in New York City was a short weekend trip several years ago.

3. The whole family went by train from Washington to Penn Station.

4. The first things you notice about New York are the skyscrapers and tall buildings.

5. They are really impressive, both from a distance and from the streets.

6. No trip to New York is complete without an elevator ride up the Empire State Building.

7. The elevators are fast and smooth and before you know it, you're on the observation floor.

8. The views from there are magnificent, both day and night, if the weather is clear.

9. A ferry boat ride to Liberty Island to see the Statue of Liberty is also a must

10. We took a walking tour around Rockefeller Center and Times Square.

11. Our hotel was across from Madison Square Garden which we had seen on TV many times.

12. A weekend train trip is not enough; you want to go back again!

Mixed-Slot Substitution Drills

Practice signing the following target sentences, substituting the suggested vocabulary in each slot. If you have problems with any of the vocabulary, consult your instructor for help.

1. <u>NEW-YORK</u> TOUCH ‿FINISH$_2$ PAST+   MANY$_2$∧ YOU ?
   CHICAGO
   WASHINGTON
   SEATTLE
   HOUSTON
   NEW-YORK

2. WASHINGTON   <u>NEW-YORK</u> you=FLY=there , ARRIVE TIME+   <u>ALMOST-NOTHING</u> , SHORT !
                 NEW-ORLEANS   AROUND two=HOUR
                 BOSTON   BELOW two=HOUR
                 SEATTLE   AROUND five=HOUR
                 NEW-YORK   ALMOST-NOTHING

3. WASHINGTON   NEW-YORK DRIVE++   PLEASE=noun$_2$+   ME , UNDERSTAND++
   <u>TRAFFIC   car=MOVE=forward$_2$</u> .
   DRIVE+   PROBLEM   NONE$_2$
   ENOUGH   TIME+
   FREEWAY   SMOOTH
   WEATHER   CLEAR
   TRAFFIC   car=MOVE=forward$_2$

4. PAST+   FAMILY MY+   group=GO NEW-YORK HOW++   <u>CAR</u> .
                                                      TRAIN
                                                      PLANE
                                                      B-U-S
                                                      BOAT
                                                      CAR

5. SIGHTSEE$_2$ NEW-YORK WIFE we=TWO PLEASE=noun$_2$ "WHAT" ,
   <u>WALK   TWO=forward+</u> .
   GET-IN-VEHICLE   SUBWAY
   LOOK-AT   TALL-STRUCTURE$_A$+
   VISIT   DIFFERENT++>
   EAT$_A$ DIFFERENT++>
   WALK   TWO=forward+

6. FIRST   TIME   GO   NEW-YORK ,   TRUE   AGAPE   #WHAT ,   <u>SKYSCRAPER</u>++ .
    TALL-STRUCTURE_A+
    T-I-M-E-S   SQUARE
    STATUE   ITS   FREE
    RESTAURANT   DIFFERENT + + >
    SKYSCRAPER + +

7. LONG-AGO+   TRAVEL   GO   <u>CHICAGO</u>   HOW++ ,   TRAIN .
    NEW-ORLEANS
    S-T.   L-O-U-I-S
    WASHINGTON
    HOUSTON
    K.C.
    CHICAGO

8. FIRST   TIME   <u>NEW-YORK</u>   TOUCH   FINISH ,   PAST+   NEVER   YOU ?
    CHICAGO
    WASHINGTON
    NEW-ORLEANS
    L-A
    SEATTLE
    NEW-YORK

9. GO   NEW-YORK ,   VISIT   <u>E-M-P-I-R-E   S-T-A-T-E   BUILDING</u>   **NEED**   you=TWO !
    STATUE   ITS   FREE
    R-O-C-K-E-F-E-L-L-E-R   CENTER
    T-I-M-E-S   SQUARE
    NEW-YORK   UNIVERSITY
    WORLD   T-R-A-D-E   CENTER
    U-N
    E-M-P-I-R-E   S-T-A-T-E   BUILDING

10. you=TWO   GO-OUT   NEW-YORK ,   GET-IN-VEHICLE   TRAIN
    TOMORROW   **MORNING**   TIME   <u>EIGHT</u> .
        FIVE
        SEVEN
        SIX
        NINE
        EIGHT

Suggested Activities

1. Have you ever traveled by train, here in this country, or in Europe or elsewhere? If so, you might have an interesting experience to share with others in your class.

2. If you have ever gone sightseeing in the "Big Apple" or in some other large city in the U.S. or elsewhere, perhaps you will have some short incident or experience to recall and share with members of your class.

3. Act out the dialogue used in this lesson. Three persons may volunteer or be selected from the group to role play the characters in the dialogue. Watch facial expression and body language.

4. Practice signing the ASL to English translation exercises *before* translating the sentences.

5. For fingerspelling practice, you may use some of the sentences or selected phrases from the sentences in the English to ASL translation exercises in this lesson. Pair off in class. Partners may then take turns randomly selecting two or three sentences or phrases to fingerspell to each other while the instructor observes.

6. Write an English version of the glossed introductory paragraph.

Visitors from San Francisco

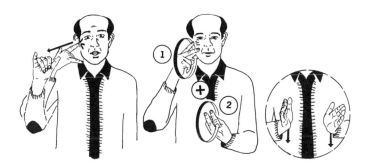

CALIFORNIA VISITOR

ONCE-IN-A-WHILE FRIEND+ THEIR BENNY , GLORIA COME=here VISIT FROM PLACE+ DIFFERENT++ ALIKE CALIFORNIA , SECOND NEW-YORK , F-L-A , VARIOUS . FRIEND DEAF COME=here SEE NEW+ HOME , MAYBE STAY one=WEEK two=WEEK . FETCH FRIEND SIGHTSEE=around WASHINGTON , D.C. , PLEASE=noun$_2$ those=TWO . FIRST , ALWAYS PATRONIZE U-S CAPITOL BUILDING , SECOND , WASHINGTON SKYSCRAPER , ALSO big=HOUSE WHITE ITS PRESIDENT . ATTEMPT+ go=THROUGH , come=THROUGH ITS+ S-M-I-T-H-S-O-N-I-A-N , "KNOW YOU" . IN+ DIFFERENT++ INTEREST , OLD LONG-AGO FLY=noun+ , TRAIN MOTOR+ , CAR+ , VARIOUS . REQUIRE HOUR++ LOOK-AT=around ALL ! #IF++ DAY PRETTY , those=TWO FETCH FRIEND GO-OUT M-T V-E-R-N-O-N , SEE big=HOUSE BEAUTIFUL HIS+ G-E-O-R-G-E WASHINGTON HOME LONG-AGO . ONCE-IN-A-WHILE group=GO HOW++ BOAT ITS P-O-T-O-M-A-C RIVER . ALWAYS SIGHTSEE WASHINGTON WHAT'S-UP !

Glossed Sentences, Translations, and Grammatical Notes

1. "HEY" , GO-OUT FLY = noun + FETCH TOM , BARBARA

Benny, we've got to go to the airport to pick up Tom and

When in its repeated form, FLY can be translated as "airport" or "airplane."

NEED we = TWO . those = TWO MAIL = me INFORM = me

Barbara. They sent a letter informing me that they're

S-F + FLY = here one = WEEK VISIT REMEMBER + ?

flying here from San Francisco to visit for one week, remember?

FLY = here moves toward the signer.

---

2. PLAN SIGHTSEE = around WASHINGTON **NEED** we = TWO .

We must plan some sightseeing around Washington.

TIME + plane = LAND , WHICH D-U-L-L-E-S , B-W-I ?

What time is the plane landing and where, Dulles or Baltimore-Washington International?

When choices are specified, use the interrogative WHICH rather than WHAT.

3. D-U-L-L-E-S TIME FOUR NOW AFTERNOON ; FLY = here

    Dulles Airport at 4:00 this afternoon; they're flying

    AMERICA 354 . "COME-ON" EARLY BETTER we = TWO .

    American Flight 354. Come on, it will be better if we're early.

4. HI ! ARRIVE AT-LAST HAPPY ME .

    Hi, Benny and Gloria! I'm so glad we've finally arrived.

    we = TWO LOOK-AT = ahead + TRIP LONG TIME-PERIOD !

    We've looked forward to this trip for a long time!

5. you = TWO COME = here , HAPPY we = TWO = gloria ; FLY = here GOOD ?

    Gloria and I are happy you've come; did you have a good flight?

6. "OK" , PLEASE=noun₂ we=TWO=barbara ! EAGER

The flight was perfect and Barbara and I really enjoyed it. We're eager

While the sign OK means "OK" or "all right," the familiar gesture "OK" (the one used by hearing people, also) means "great" or "perfect."

SIGHTSEE=around , shoot=CAMERA++> FAMOUS LINCOLN M-E-M-O-R-I-A-L ,

WASHINGTON

to go sightseeing and take pictures of the famous Lincoln Memorial and the Washington

SKYSCRAPER ; TOUCH++ DIFFERENT++ FUN NEED="soft"+ .

Monument; it should be fun going to all those different places.

The "soft" version of NEED, as opposed to the regular or emphatic versions, means "should."

7. READY TRY ASCEND WASHINGTON SKYSCRAPER ME+ .

I'm ready to try walking up the Washington Monument.

8. FIRST we=FOUR GROUP=go RESTAURANT FANCY₁ .

First, we'll all go to a classy restaurant.

Vocabulary Review

Test your ability to produce the following signs or sign phrases.

ALL	FLY = noun +	PRESIDENT
AMERICAN	we = FOUR	RIVER
ASCEND	FROM	THEIR
BETTER	HOUR + +	go = THROUGH
BOAT	big = HOUSE	come = THROUGH
CALIFORNIA	plane = LAND	TIME FOUR
shoot = CAMERA + + >	LINCOLN	TOUCH + +
CAPITOL	MAIL = me	WASHNGTON SKYSCRAPER
FLY	NEED = "soft" + +	WHAT'S-UP
FLY = here	"PERFECT"	WHITE HOUSE
	PLACE +	

Notes

Translation Exercises—ASL to English

Translate the following glossed sentences into appropriate English equivalents.

1. FRIEND GROUP CALIFORNIA FLY=here ARRIVE=here TIME+ , FLY+ NUMBER , KNOW YOU ?

2. ARRIVE=here TIME+ ? NEED="soft"+ TIME+ AROUND 4:50 , T-W-A 113 .

3. NOW⁀NIGHT EAT_A RESTAURANT FANCY₁ GOOD IDEA , THINK YOU ?

4. YES , #BUT WAIT , FRIEND ARRIVE=here++ , GROUP=together FINISH₂ , WHERE EAT_A DECIDE O-K ?

5. HERE LUCKY , RESTAURANT FANCY₁ PLENTY=around+ , LUCKY TRUE .

6. KNOW THAT FRIEND GROUP CALIFORNIA FLY=here LONG , ARRIVE=here TIRED ; GO-OUT EAT_A MAYBE DON'T-WANT THEY .

7. DISBELIEVE++ ME ; KNOW FRIEND GROUP ARRIVE=here , TRUE EXCITED , GO-OUT EAT_A , CHAT++ , WILL THEY !

8. FRIEND GROUP LONG TIME-PERIOD SEE NONE₂ , CORRECT ME ?

9. CORRECT ! TWENTY YEAR AROUND , THINK ME ; WONDER FACE SAME₂ PAST ?

10. SILLY YOU ! FACE SAME₂ OF-COURSE ; REMEMBER near=RECENT PICTURE RECEIVE , FACE SAME₂ , CHANGE NONE₂ !

11. NOW⁀NIGHT FRIEND GROUP SLEEP GOOD , REST , TOMORROW group=GO SIGHTSEE=around DIFFERENT++ .

12. SURPRISE WILL THEY ! HERE CHANGE MANY₂+ UP-TO-NOW TWENTY YEAR !

Translation Exercises—English to ASL

Translate the following sentences from English into ASL equivalents.

1. Living in the Washington area has many advantages.

2. One of them is ready-made sightseeing for out-of-town visitors.

3. There are so many attractions to see in the Washington area.

4. The monuments and memorials are a must on a sightseeing tour.

5. Washington also has some fabulous museums that take hours and hours to go through.

6. The Smithsonian is perhaps the most interesting museum because of its historical preservation.

7. A trip to Mount Vernon and to Arlington Cemetery can take a whole day's time.

8. If you like to take pictures, the best time to come is Cherry Blossom time.

9. But Washington is beautiful any time of the year.

10. Washington also has some great restaurants and eating places.

11. If there are kids among your visitors, take them to the National Zoo.

12. And don't forget to visit Gallaudet University, the Washington Cathedral, and the National Shrine.

Single-Slot Substitution Drills

Practice signing the following target sentences, substituting the suggested vocabulary in each slot. If you have problems with any of the vocabulary, consult your instructor for help.

1. FRIEND   MY+   THERE   <u>CALIFORNIA</u>   INFORM=me   FLY=here   WEEK=ahead .

                                            NEW-YORK

                                            ENGLAND

                                            CANADA

                                            HOUSTON

                                            CALIFORNIA

2. FRIEND   MY+   those=TWO   COME=here   WASHINGTON   WHAT-FOR ,

    <u>SIGHTSEE=around$_2$</u> .

    TOUCH   NEVER   PAST+

    VOLUNTEER   WORK+

    SEARCH=around   HOUSE

    SIGHTSEE=around$_2$

3. FETCH   FRIEND   GO-OUT   <u>SIGHTSEE=around$_2$+</u>   PLEASE=noun$_2$+   ME !

                                   RESTAURANT   EAT$_A$

                                   CAPTION   MOVIE

                                   DEAF   C-L-U-B

                                   BUY=around++

                                   SIGHTSEE=around$_2$+

4. FRIEND   MY+   ARRIVE=here   TIME+ ,   NEED="soft"++   AROUND   <u>2:30</u> .

                                                               NOON

                                                                 9:00

                                                                 4:15

                                                                  2:30

5. TOMORROW   MORNING   GO   FLY=noun+   MEET   FRIEND   YOU ,   REMEMBER   FLY+

    NUMBER   <u>T-W-A   147</u> .

                     U-N-I-T-E-D   35

                     AMERICAN   327

                     WESTERN   275

                     EASTERN   333

                     T-W-A   147

6. FLY+   TICKET   RESERVE ,   BUY ,   <u>FINISH</u>   ME .

   LATE

   WILL

   TOMORROW+

   MAYBE

   FINISH

7. FRIEND   GROUP   ARRIVE = here ,   group = GO   SIGHTSEE + +   WHERE ,

   <u>WHITE   HOUSE</u> .

   WASHINGTON   SKYSCRAPER

   CAPITOL

   LINCOLN   M-E-M-O-R-I-A-L

   M-T   V-E-R-N-O-N

   WHITE   HOUSE

8. TOMORROW   ALL-DAY   <u>SIGHTSEE = around</u> ,   EAGER   YOU ?

   PICTURE   shoot = CAMERA + + >

   FISHING

   SWIMMING

   BICYCLE = around

   SIGHTSEE = around

9. <u>WHITE   HOUSE</u>   TOUCH   FINISH   PAST+   YOU ?

   S-M-I-T-H-S-O-N-I-A-N

   WASHINGTON   SKYSCRAPER

   M-T   V-E-R-N-O-N

   LINCOLN   M-E-M-O-R-I-A-L

   U-S   CAPITOL

   WHITE   HOUSE

10. WEEK = ahead   FRIEND   YOUR+   <u>CALIFORNIA</u>   FLY = here   #DO   you = TWO ?

    ENGLAND

    FRANCE

    CANADA

    ALASKA

    ATLANTA

    CALIFORNIA

Suggested Activities

1. Act out the dialogue used in this lesson. Four persons may volunteer or be selected from the group to portray the characters in the dialogue. Watch facial expression and body language.

2. Tell about your first airplane trip to visit friends or family in another area of the country.

3. If you have never traveled by air, perhaps you know of an incident or experience that someone close to you has had that is related to air travel. Share that story with the class.

4. Pair off in class to practice signing the ASL to English translation exercises in dialogue form *before* translating the sentences.

5. For fingerspelling practice, you may use some of the sentences or selected phrases from the sentences in the English to ASL translation exercises in this lesson. Pair off in class. Partners may then take turns randomly selecting two or three sentences or phrases to fingerspell to each other while the instructor observes.

6. Write an English version of the glossed introductory paragraph.

Alexander and Jennifer Become Engaged

ENGAGE FINISH₁ ALEXANDER , JENNIFER

NEW-YORK FINISH₁ COME = here those = TWO ALEXANDER , JENNIFER SECRET HAVE
"WHAT" ? ENGAGE FINISH₁ PLAN+ MARRY . one = WEEK "HOLD = mouth₂" , ANNOUNCE
FRIEND NONE₂ . WILL one = WEEK PASS JENNIFER "HOLD = mouth₂" MORE+ CAN'T SHE !
HAPPEN APPEAR JANE , LAWRENCE those = TWO COME = here VISIT those = TWO = jennifer-
alexander WHAT-FOR ? ASK = them_A NEW-YORK WHAT'S-UP ? those = TWO = jane-
lawrence SURPRISE FIND ENGAGE FINISH₁ those = TWO = jennifer-alexander . HERSELF = jennifer
PRIDE LOOK-AT = ring , DIAMOND = ring LARGE-JEWEL ! those = TWO = jane-lawrence IMPRESS
WHEW ! RING BEAUTIFUL TRUE ! MARRY WHEN , those = TWO = jennifer-alexander DECIDE
WILL A-P-R-I-L . EXCITED REDUCE , those = FOUR OFF-POINT CHAT++ all = EVENING !
STORY-TALK NEW-YORK WHAT'S-UP ; SECOND , YEAR = ahead OFF-WORK++ GO-OUT
WHERE ; THIRD , those = TWO = jane-lawrence GO-OUT M-I-A-M-I B-E-A-C-H WILL
two = WEEK = ahead !

Glossed Sentences, Translations, and Grammatical Notes

1. WHAT'S-UP   KNOW   YOU ?   SECRET   INFORM = you   we = TWO = alexander   !

   Do you know what? Alexander and I have a secret to tell you!

   SECRET can also mean "private."

   REMEMBER   near = PAST   we = TWO = alexander   GO-OUT   NEW-YORK ?

   You remember Alexander and I recently went to New York City?

2. REMEMBER , YES ;   WHAT'S-UP   SECRET   TELL = me !

   Yes, I remember now; tell me, what's the secret?

3. DECIDE   MARRY   we = TWO ;   ENGAGE   FINISH₁ !

   We've decided to get married; we're engaged!

4. SURPRISE !   HOPE   HAPPY   WILL   you = TWO = alexander .

   What a surprise! I hope you two will be happy.

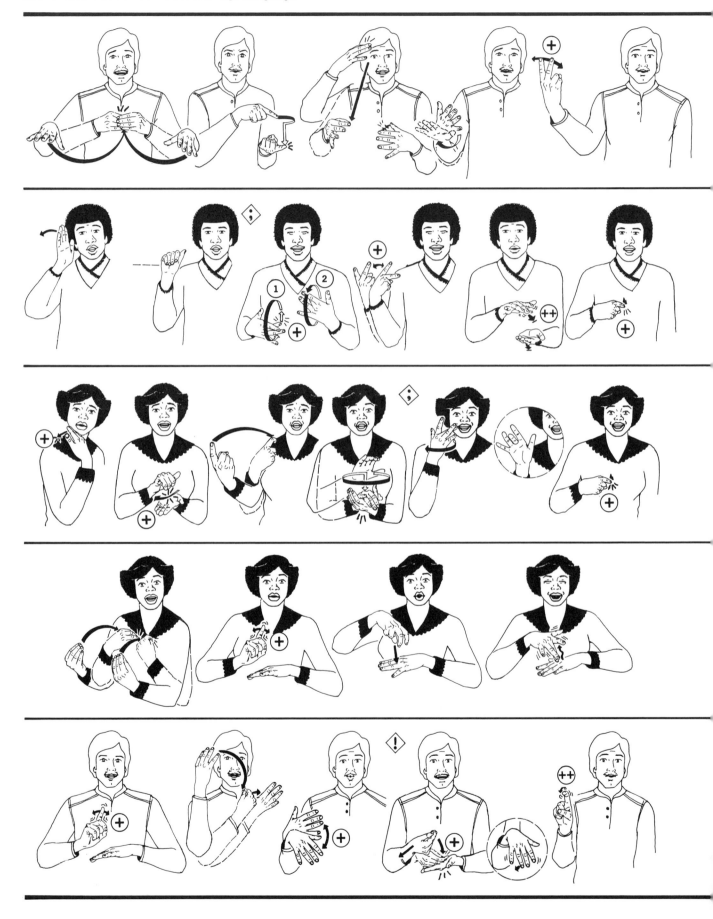

5. WEDDING   WHEN ,   DECIDE   FINISH, you = TWO ?

Have you decided on a wedding date?

6. WILL   A-P-R-I-L ;   EXCITED   we = TWO = jennifer !   WAIT + +   ME + .

It will be in April, and we're excited! I've waited a long time.

7. PAST +   NEW-YORK   alexander = ASK = me   MARRY ;   LUCKY   ME !

Alexander asked me to marry him when we were in New York City; I'm lucky!

ASK originates from the direction that represents Alexander and moves toward the signer.

GIVE = me   DIAMOND = *ring*   LARGE-JEWEL ,   SHINY₂ .

He gave me a large, sparkling diamond ring.

The sign DIAMOND is made over the "ring finger" to represent a "diamond ring."

8. DIAMOND = *ring*   BEAUTIFUL   WHEW !   EXPENSIVE   QUESTION + + ?

It's really a beautiful ring! Was it expensive?

9. YES ! PAY PORTION-OFF + + , ANXIOUS NOT ME .

Yes, but I'll pay on monthly installments so I'm not worried.

The sign PORTION-OFF refers to any "regular decrements" of something. In the context of pay, it means "installments," or "regular payments." When speaking of food, PORTION-OFF means "diet."

MONEY ⌣ STACK PUT-IN = savings + FINISH$_1$, PROBLEM NONE$_1$.

I have money saved up so there's really no problem.

MONEY STACK means "a lot of money." PUT-IN, when repeated, means the "act of saving," "putting away for the future," "stocking up," or "savings." In the context of MONEY, it can refer to a "savings account."

10. LOOK-AT = *ring* + SHINY$_1$ PRIDE ME ! TOMORROW

I'm very proud to show off my sparkling diamond! Tomorrow

LOOK-AT is directed at the ring finger of the nondominant hand.

ANNOUNCE FRIEND + ENGAGE we = TWO !

we'll announce our engagement to friends!

11. LOOK-AT = *past*$_2$ you = TWO MARRY FUTURE PREDICT , RIGHT ME .

Looking back, I predicted you two would get married, and I was right.

In LOOK-AT = past$_2$, both hands move past the face and over the shoulder. It can translate as "reminisce," "look back in time," "reflect upon the past," etc.

Vocabulary Review

Test your ability to produce the following signs or sign phrases.

ANNOUNCE	FUTURE	OFF-POINT
ANXIOUS NOT	"HOLD = mouth$_2$"	OFF-WORK + +
he = ASK = me	HOPE	PORTION-OFF + +
CORRECT	IMPRESS	PREDICT
DECIDE͜ FINISH$_1$	LARGE-JEWEL = *ring*	PUT-IN = savings +
DIAMOND = *ring*	LOOK-AT = past$_2$	RING
ENGAGE FINISH$_1$	LOOK-AT = *ring*	SHINY = *ring*
EXPENSIVE	LUCKY ME	WEDDING WHEN ?
those = FOUR	MONEY͜ STACK	

Notes

Translation Exercises—ASL to English

Translate the following glossed sentences into appropriate English equivalents.

1. LOOK-AT = past₂ + REMEMBER ENGAGE YOUR + O-R FRIEND HIS + , REMEMBER CAN YOU ?

2. LOOK-AT = past₂ ENGAGE MY + REMEMBER ME ; long = PAST , ABOVE 25 YEAR .

3. GO-OUT BUY DIAMOND = *ring* MEDIUM-JEWEL SHINY FINISH₂ ME , UNDERSTAND + + PAY HOW + + , PORTION-OFF + + .

4. PLAN + GIFT = her₂ SWEETHEART HOW + + , SURPRISE = her WANT + + ME !

5. DECIDE BEST "WHAT" , INVITE = her MY A-P-T EAT_A we = TWO .

6. TIME NEAR + , EXCITED , NERVOUS ME ; MIND QUESTION APPEAR , "ACCEPT RING WILL SHE ?"

7. EAT = noun + PLAN + "WHAT" , SPAGHETTI MEAT BALL + PLUS SALAD .

8. GIRL FRIEND APPEAR FINISH we = TWO TABLE SIT = opposite EAT_A START , WRONG NERVOUS , EXCITED , WAIT CAN'T ME !

9. MYSELF EXCUSE ME , GET-UP GO-OUT FETCH small = BOX RING ITS + FINISH₁ , BRING = here TELL = her "SURPRISE GIFT = you ."

10. HERSELF SWEETHEART THINK FREEZE MINUTE , ACCEPT DIAMOND = *ring* FINISH₂ we = TWO HUG , "KISS" !

11. EAT_A #DO DROP , EXCITED we = TWO ; EAT + CAN'T ; GO-OUT INFORM = her CLOSE FRIEND .

Translation Exercises—English to ASL

Translate the following sentences from English into ASL equivalents.

1. People often have interesting stories about how they became engaged to marry.

2. Do you remember when you decided to get married?

3. How did you pop the question to your sweetheart?

4. How did you feel when you first became engaged?

5. What kind of engagement ring did you buy, a large-size diamond, a medium-size diamond, or a small-size diamond?

6. Did you pick out the ring together, or was it a surprise gift?

7. Did you pay cash for the ring, or did you buy it on the installment plan?

8. Who was the first person you told about your engagement?

9. Did you have a long engagement or a short engagement?

10. Will you tell us about your marriage proposal or is that very private?

11. If you had to go through this again, would you do it in the same way?

Single-Slot Substitution Drills

Practice signing the following target sentences, substituting the suggested vocabulary in each slot. If you have problems with any of the vocabulary, consult your instructor for help.

1. long = PAST   WIFE   we = TWO   BECOME   ENGAGE ,   "HOLD = mouth"$_2$ **one = WEEK**

   <u>**SUCCEED**</u>   we = TWO .

   CAN'T

   TRY

   FAIL

   SUCCEED

2. recent = PAST   FRIEND   MY +   BECOME   ENGAGE ,   HERSELF   RECEIVE   DIAMOND = *ring*

   <u>LARGE-JEWEL</u> .

   MEDIUM-JEWEL

   SMALL-JEWEL

   SMALL-JEWEL + +

   three = MEDIUM-JEWEL

   LARGE-JEWEL

3. FIRST   TIME   ENGAGE   GIRL ,   ME   GIFT$_2$ <u>F-R-A-T   PIN</u> .

                                            NECKLACE

                                            CLASS   RING

                                            NOTHING

                                            F-R-A-T   PIN

4. FRIEND   MY +   ENGAGE ,   those = TWO   WEDDING   DECIDE   #WHEN ,

   WILL   <u>SPRING</u> .

          F-E-B   14

          CHRISTMAS

          AUTUMN

          J-U-N-E   15

          SPRING

5. FRIEND   MY +   GIFT$_2$ GIRL   DIAMOND = *ring*   LARGE-JEWEL ,   PAY   HOW + +

   <u>PORTION-OFF + +</u> .

   MONEY   PAY-CASH

   L-O-A-N

   MONEY   BORROW   FATHER

   PORTION-OFF + +

6. those=TWO   LOOK-AT=*ring*++   **SHINY** ,   FEEL   <u>**PRIDE**</u>   those=TWO .
                                          HAPPY
                                          EXCITE
                                          WORTH
                                          GOOD
                                          PRIDE

7. PLAN+   MARRY   you=TWO ,   BETTER   <u>MONEY   PUT-IN=savings++</u>   FIRST !
                                      CAR   BUY
                                      L-O-A-N   PAY-OFF
                                      FURNITURE   BUY
                                      RING+   PAY-OFF
                                      MONEY   PUT-IN=savings++

8. PEOPLE   SEVERAL$_2$ PLAN+   MARRY   DECIDE   FINISH ,   ENGAGE
      <u>one=YEAR</u>   those=TWO .
      NEVER
      LONG
      SHORT
      SECRET
      one=YEAR

9. PEOPLE   SEVERAL$_2$ BECOME   ENGAGE   WHERE ,   <u>HOME   O-R   A-P-T</u> .
                                        RESTAURANT
                                        FRIEND   HOUSE   HIS++
                                        CAR
                                        MOVIE   HOUSE
                                        B-E-A-C-H
                                        HOME   O-R   A-P-T

10. long=PAST   COLLEGE   MAN   ENGAGE   GIRL   WANT++   HIM ,   he=GIFT=her$_2$
      <u>F-R-A-T   PIN</u> .
      FRIEND   RING
      CLASS   RING
      FALSE   DIAMOND=*ring*
      F-R-A-T   PIN

Suggested Activities

1. Act out the dialogue used in this lesson. Four persons may volunteer or be selected to role play the characters in the dialogue. Give special attention to facial expression, to emotion, and to body language.

2. Are you willing to share a short story related either to your own engagement *or* that of someone you know very well? If so, prepare, in advance, how you will present your story. Keep it brief.

3. Clip an engagement or a wedding story from the newspaper and prepare to give an ASL version of the story.

4. Describe your own or someone else's diamond ring or other bejeweled ring.

5. Practice signing the ASL to English translation exercises *before* translating the sentences.

6. For fingerspelling practice, you may use some of the sentences or selected phrases from the sentences in the English to ASL translation exercises in this lesson. Pair off in class. Partners may then take turns randomly selecting two or three sentences or phrases to fingerspell to each other while the instructor observes.

7. Write an English version of the glossed introductory paragraph.

Vacation Flight: Miami and Back

MIAMI   OFF-WORK+

TOUCH‿FINISH₁ M-I-A-M-I B-E-A-C-H YOU = around ? WEEK = past JANE , LAWRENCE
those = TWO FIRST TIME FLY = there F-L-A . WEATHER "PERFECT" , PLEASE = noun₂ +
those = TWO ! PLAY , SWIM , sun = SHINE + + , EAT_A , SLEEP , SIGHTSEE , WORK
NOTHING₂ one = WEEK , PLEASE = noun₂ those = TWO ! HE = lawrence + "SMOOTH-LIP₂"
TEASE = jane + "WHAT" ? TELL = her = jane CAREFUL SEE FINISH₁ , S-H-A-R-K out = THERE
water = WAVE₂ ! SHE = jane GULLIBLE WHEW , BELIEVE STORY-TALK HIS = lawrence + ! TRUE
S-H-A-R-K NONE ! WILL SHE = jane FIND LIE = talk HIM = lawrence , CROSS SHE WHEW !
HIMSELF = lawrence LAUGH + + ; LATER + HERSELF = jane WONDER₂ REVENGE HIM = lawrence
HOW + + . IDEA APPEAR ; WAIT LIE-DOWN B-E-A-C-H SLEEP-HARD HE = lawrence ,
SHE = jane "SMOOTH-LIP₂" TAP = hard = him-lawrence , "HEY" CRAB LARGE HELP = me !
HE = lawrence WAKE-UP FINISH₂ LOOK-AT = around₂ , JUMP = stand WHERE ? HERSELF = jane
LAUGH + + ! HE = lawrence + TEASE = her = jane AGAIN DON'T !

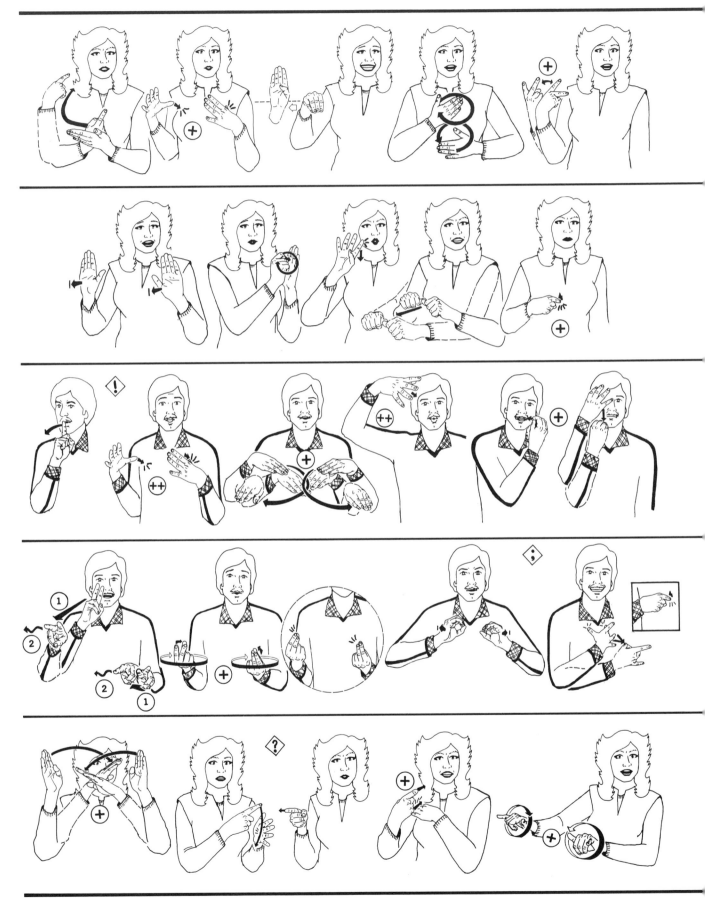

Glossed Sentences, Translations, and Grammatical Notes

1. WEEK = past   OFF-WORK +   M-I-A-M-I   B-E-A-C-H   PLEASE = noun$_2$ we = TWO = lawrence .

Last week, Lawrence and I enjoyed our vacation in Miami Beach.

OFF-WORK can apply to a single day as well as longer periods, in which case it is repeated and is best translated as "vacation" or permanently, in which case it translates as "retired."

WONDERFUL   TIME-PERIOD ,   DROOL   CONTINUE   ME + !

We had a wonderful time, and I wish I could stay there!

CONTINUE can also be translated as "stay" or "remain."

---

2. TRUE !   OFF-WORK + + ,   SWIM ,   sun = SHINE + + ,   EAT + ,   SLEEP ,

You can say that again! Loafing, swimming, sunning, eating, sleeping,

In some colloquial situations, OFF-WORK, repeated more than once, can mean "loafing" or "goofing off." sun = SHINE refers to the sun's rays, but it can translate as "sunning" or "sunbathing."

SIGHTSEE = around ,   #DO = around +   NONE$_2$;   LIKE   ME .

sightseeing, and just doing nothing; that I like.

#DO is a fingerspelled loan sign that derives from D-O. When moved in circles to indicate = around, it can mean "chores," "regular work duties," or "busy work."

---

3. TROUBLE   "WHAT" ?   HE = lawrence   TEASE = me   SAME = continuous$_2$.

Lawrence gave me a lot of trouble teasing me all the time.

"WHAT" is the general, informal interrogative sign. SAME = continuous$_2$ can mean "the same old thing," "unchanging," "constantly," "all the time," etc.

TELL = me CAREFUL S-H-A-R-K , TRUE **NONE₂** !

He kept telling me to be careful of sharks when really there were none!

4. JEALOUS ME ! FUTURE TOUCH M-I-A-M-I B-E-A-C-H HOPE .

I'm jealous! I hope to go to Miami Beach sometime in the future.

5. SHE = jennifer + EARTH TOUCH = around + + **THIRSTY₁** SHE .

Jennifer really craves to go all over the world.

In TOUCH = around + +, the nondominant hand, from the preceding sign EARTH, represents "the globe" and the TOUCH sign contacts it repeatedly, as if moving around it. This sign could be translated "globetrotting," "going around the world," etc.

6. FLY = there , FLY = here SMOOTH QUESTION + + ?

Was your flight there and back smooth all the way?

7. FLY = there FRIDAY FINE ! FLY = here THURSDAY **BAD**

The flight there last Friday was just fine! The return flight on Thursday was very bad

The emphatic form **BAD** has a slow movement upwards from the mouth and then a firm downward movement.

WHY++ LIGHTNING‿STORM TERRIBLE !

because of a severe thunderstorm!

---

8. CORRECT ! FLY=noun+ ARRIVE , PUT-AWAY$_2$ BAGGAGE$_2$,

That's right! We just arrived at the airport, checked in our baggage,

PUT-AWAY$_2$, in this case, does not mean "to store something," but simply to "put something out of the way," and in the context of airport travel and baggage, translates as "check baggage." (See note on "BY-A-HAIR" in Lesson 17, sentence 2.)

"BY-A-HAIR" GET-IN-VEHICLE=plane ! ALMOST-NOTHING plane=TAKE-OFF .

and barely got on the plane before it took off.

---

9. LIGHTNING‿STORM STRIKE-CHANCE , plane=BOUNCE , FASTEN-SEAT-BELT+ **NEED** !

We all had to fasten our seat belts with the plane bouncing up and down as the thunderstorm hit hard!

The sign BOUNCE is made with the handshape representing a "plane."

---

10. LOOK-AT=down$_2$+ AFRAID+ ME ! AT-LAST plane=LAND **RELIEVED** !

I was afraid looking out the plane window, and when we finally landed, I was so relieved!

In LAND, the "plane" handshape contacts the flat surface of the other hand (or another flat surface).

Vocabulary Review

Test your ability to produce the following signs or sign phrases.

AFRAID+	LARGE	TAP = him
plane = BOUNCE	LAUGH+ +	TEASE = him/her/you
CRAB	LIE = talk	TEASE = me
CROSS	LIE-DOWN	out = THERE
EARTH	LIGHTNING	**THIRSTY**$_1$
FASTEN-SEAT-BELT	LIKE ME	THURSDAY
FINE	OFF-WORK+	TOUCH
FLY = there	PLAY	TOUCH⌣FINISH$_1$
FRIDAY	PUT-AWAY$_2$	TROUBLE
GET-UP	REVENGE	WAIT
GULLIBLE	SAME = continuous	WAKE-UP FINISH$_2$
HERSELF	SEE⌣FINISH$_1$	water = WAVE$_2$
IMPROVE	sun = SHINE+ +	WEATHER
JEALOUS ME	SLEEP-HARD	one = WEEK
JUMP = stand	"SMOOTH-LIP"$_2$+	WONDER$_A$
plane = LAND	STORM	WORK NOTHING$_2$
	plane = TAKE-OFF	

Notes

Translation Exercises—ASL to English

Translate the following glossed sentences into appropriate English equivalents.

1. OFF-WORK+ TIME-PERIOD WONDERFUL ALWAYS ; LOOK-AT=ahead₂+ OFF-WORK+ YEAR=ahead++ YOU ?

2. OFF-WORK+ GO-OUT DRIVE⊥ , **TRAIN** , FLY=there NO-MATTER , PLEASE=noun₂+ WILL YOU !

3. "WHEN" OFF-WORK+ GO **FAR** WANT YOU , BETTER FLY=there WHY++ **TIME** SAVE !

4. OFF-WORK+ TIME-PERIOD GO "WHERE" , DIFFERENT++> LIKE ME .

5. SOMETIMES FAMILY MY+ GROUP=go WATER WAVES SAME A-T-L-A-N-T-I-C CITY alternate=TWO O-C , KNOW YOU O-C-E-A-N C-I-T-Y .

6. B-E-A-C-H LIE-DOWN sun=SHINE+ mind=BLANK #DO NOTHING , LIKE ME !

7. SUMMER TIME-PERIOD OFF-WORK MAYBE GO MOUNTAINS WHY++ , CAMPING , FISHING , COOL .

8. WINTER TIME-PERIOD OFF-WORK+ FLY=there M-I-A-M-I WHY++ **WARM** , "FINE" !

9. WINTER TIME-PERIOD SOME PEOPLE OFF-WORK+ GO-OUT MOUNTAINS WHY++ , SKI+ LIKE THEY .

10. EUROPE TOUCH FINISH YOU ? EUROPE FLY=there OFF-WORK+ **WONDERFUL** WHY++ HISTORY , SIGHTSEE=around DIFFERENT++> , INTEREST TRUE !

11. SOMETIMES OFF-WORK+ TIME-PERIOD **BEST** #DO #WHAT , STAY HOME !

Translation Exercises—English to ASL

Translate the following sentences from English into ASL equivalents.

1. Everyone looks forward to a vacation, right?

2. A real vacation means having nothing to do except resting and enjoying yourself.

3. If your vacation includes a flight to some far-off place, make your reservations early.

4. Where did you go on your last vacation?

5. I remember a vacation we once took to the Rocky Mountain National Park in Colorado.

6. We were surprised by a July snowstorm on the mountain tops, and we had no snowtires on our car!

7. A vacation at the ocean is great, too. You can sunbathe, swim, ride the waves, and so on.

8. In the winter time, some people like to vacation in the mountains where they can go skiing.

9. Other people like to fly south for a winter vacation because it's a warmer place at that time of the year.

10. Have you ever vacationed in Europe? It's a great experience because there's so much history there.

11. There's plenty to see in America, too. We have lots of history here in our country.

12. No matter where you go for a vacation, planning ahead will help you save money and enjoy it more.

Single-Slot Substitution Drills

Practice signing the following target sentences, substituting the suggested vocabulary in each slot. If you have problems with any of the vocabulary, consult your instructor for help.

1. two = WEEK = past OFF-WORK + YOUR + , GO-OUT <u>M-I-A-M-I</u> , PLEASE = noun$_2$ + YOU ?

                                                                  NEW-YORK

                                                                   CANADA

                                                                   ENGLAND

                                                                   NEW ORLEANS

                                                                   M-I-A-M-I

2. OFF-WORK + GO-OUT B-E-A-C-H **LIKE** ME WHY + + , <u>SWIM +</u> CAN ME .

                                                                   LIE-DOWN   sun = SHINE + +

                                                                   SEARCH = around S-H-E-L-L-S

                                                                   water = WAVE FLOAT >

                                                                   PLAY +   S-A-N-D

                                                                   BICYCLE +   B-O-A-R-D-W-A-L-K

                                                                   SWIM +

3. PAST +   GET-IN-VEHICLE = *plane* ALMOST-NOTHING *plane = TAKE-OFF* , EXPERIENCE

    <u>FINISH$_1$</u> ME .

    TWICE

    NEVER

    ONCE

    LATE +

    FINISH$_1$

4. FIRST TIME FLY = there LONG-AGO PLEASE = noun$_2$ + ME , **WRONG**

    STRIKE-CHANCE <u>LIGHTNING⌣STORM</u> .

                                         plane = BOUNCE + +

                                         plane = TAKE-OFF POSTPONE + +

                                         plane = CIRCLE = continuous

                                         LIGHTNING⌣STORM

5. PAST + FRIEND MY + "SMOOTH-LIP" + TEASE = me , STORY = talk , ME <u>GULLIBLE</u> !

                                                                          IGNORE = him

                                                                          GET-EVEN

                                                                           LAUGH

                                                                          GULLIBLE

6. SOMETIMES OFF-WORK+ SUMMER GO MOUNTAIN WHY++ , <u>CAMPING</u> LIKE ME !
    FISHING
    WALK+ +
    COOL
    LOOK-AT+ ANIMAL
    CAMPING

7. PAST+ OFF-WORK+ ME STAY HOME #DO , <u>PAINT = object HOUSE</u> .
    NOTHING
    READ+ +
    WORK = around LITTLE-BIT
    POEM WRITE = page
    PAINT = object HOUSE

8. NOW YEAR TRUE OFF-WORK+ NONE₂ ME WHY+ + , <u>BOOK WRITE = page</u> .
    MEETING FLY = there ,
     FLY = here
    YEAR = ahead PLAN+
    WORK NEW DIFFERENT
    MONEY PUT-IN+ + WANT+
    BOOK WRITE = page

9. YEAR = ahead OFF-WORK+ WIFE we = TWO PLAN+ FLY = there alternate = TWO = *two*
  <u>ENGLAND , DENMARK</u> .
  ITALY , GERMANY
  SPAIN , GREECE
  FRANCE , HOLLAND
  SWEDEN , FINLAND
  ENGLAND , DENMARK

10. YEAR = ahead OFF-WORK+ PLAN+ #WHAT YOU , <u>FLY = there SOMETHING</u> ?
    TRAIN
    DRIVE+
    STAY HOME
    SHIP = cruise
    BICYCLE
    FLY = there SOMETHING

Suggested Activities

1. Prepare a short story describing an unforgettable vacation trip you have experienced at some time in the past.

2. If you have traveled by air, perhaps you have experienced a flight that was unusual in some way—bad weather delays, a rough flight, a missed plane, missing baggage, a lost ticket, etc. Describe this experience to the class.

3. Act out the dialogue used in this lesson. Four persons may volunteer or be selected from the group to role play the characters in the dialogue. Give particular attention to facial expression, to emotions, and to body language.

4. Tell about how you have "SMOOTH-LIPPED"+ someone you like.

5. Practice signing the ASL to English translation exercises *before* translating the sentences.

6. For fingerspelling practice, you may use some of the sentences or selected phrases from the sentences in the English to ASL translation exercises in this lesson. Pair off in class. Partners may then take turns randomly selecting two or three sentences or phrases to fingerspell to each other while the instructor observes.

7. Write an English version of the glossed introductory paragraph.

VOTE+   TIME-PERIOD

YEAR = ahead + +   AUTUMN   DEAF   C-L-U-B   many = CONVERGE   WHAT'S-UP ?   VOTE +   NIGHT
ITS + .   VOTE   OFFICER₂   NEW + ,   PRESIDENT ,   V-P ,   SECRETARY ,   TREASURER .
BEFORE   DIE   W-A-L-T   W-I-C-K-E-R-S-O-N   PRESIDENT   CONTINUE   FOUR   YEAR .   NOW   DEAF
"STUCK" ;   NEW   PRESIDENT   VOTE   **NEED** !   JENNIFER ,   ALEXANDER ,   JANE
those = THREE   ATTEMPT +   LET'S-SEE   PERSUADE   LAWRENCE   RACE   PRESIDENT ,   V-P ,
alternate = TWO = *two* .   HE = lawrence   STRADDLE = back-and-forth   DECIDE⏜LATE .   JENNIFER
THINK   #IF + +   MAYBE   JANE   APPLY   SECRETARY   she = TWO = lawrence   TEAM   "FINE" !
those = TWO   POPULAR ,   WIN   EASY   CAN .   PROBLEM: those = TWO   OFFICER +
PAST   NEVER ;   EXPERIENCE   NONE !   NO-MATTER   those = TWO   YOUNG ,   SECOND
INTELLIGENT ,   EAGER ,   WORK + +   WILL   those = TWO .   those = TWO   LOOK-AT = each-other
WONDER₂ ,   DECIDE   ACCEPT   SEEM + .   HE = lawrence   ENCOURAGE   ALEXANDER   APPLY
BOARD .   #IF + +   WIN   those = THREE ,   STRONG   GROUP   UNITY .   DEAF   C-L-U-B   IMPROVE
WILL !

Glossed Sentences, Translations, and Grammatical Notes

1. TOMORROW   NIGHT   DEAF   C-L-U-B   MEETING   VOTE = noun +

   Are you two going to the Deaf Club meeting tomorrow night

   NEW +   OFFICER₂   FOR   YEAR = ahead   GO-OUT   you = TWO = alexander = jennifer

   for the election of new officers for next year?

   OFFICER₂ means "officers" or "officials." Made with one hand, the sign often translates as "boss" or "chairperson." In YEAR = ahead, the circular movement of YEAR is omitted.

2. CORRECT !   PRESIDENT ,   V-P ,   SECRETARY ,   TREASURER

   That's right! We have to vote for the president, vice president,

   VOTE   **NEED** ;   FORGET   ALMOST   we = TWO .

   secretary, and treasurer; we almost forgot all about it.

3. "HEY" ,   RACE   PRESIDENT ,   V-P   ACCEPT   YOU = lawrence ?

   Lawrence, would you agree to run for president or for vice president?

   Here, RACE has the general meaning of "compete" or "run for."

4. TRUE don't=KNOW , LET'S-SEE , DECIDE MAYBE ME .

I really don't know; we'll see; maybe I'll decide.

5. NEED="soft"+ YOU ; PRESIDENT GOOD CAN YOU .

You should; you could be a very good president.

6. SECOND=you ! SUPPOSE+ YOU=jane APPLY SECRETARY ;

I agree with you! Jane, suppose you run for secretary;

APPLY can mean "volunteer" or "become a candidate." Compare this sentence with how the concept was expressed in sentence 3.

BEAT=around+ + EASY CAN WHY+ + POPULAR YOU !

you can easily beat all the others because you are popular!

See Lesson 3, sentence 4 for another use of BEAT. The sign POPULAR only translates in the sense of "well-liked" or "to have a following." Rarely, it can take on negative senses, also, in which case it would mean "being mobbed" or "being ganged upon."

7. OTHER+ BETTER ; ARGUE WILL THEY=deaf .

Others are much better; the deaf members will surely argue about it.

THEY points in the direction that was already established for "the deaf members."

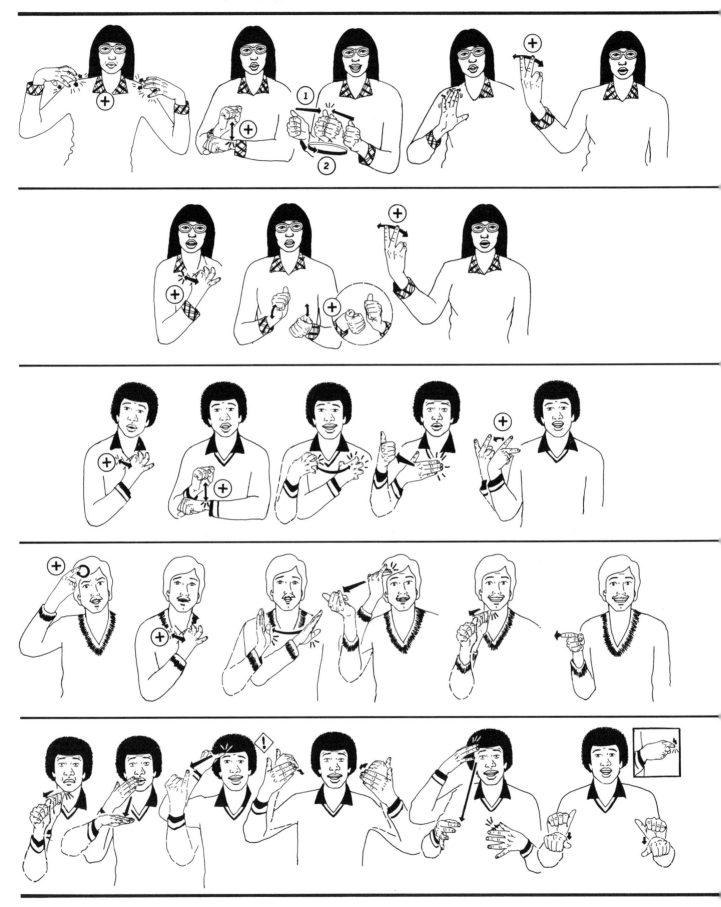

8. OFFICER₂ WORK TOGETHER = around FINE you = TWO = jane = lawrence .

You and Lawrence would work very well together as officers.

APPLY RACE you = TWO = jennifer = alexander ?

Jennifer and Alexander, are you two going to run?

9. APPLY WORK COMMITTEE PREFER we = TWO = jennifer .

Jennifer and I prefer to volunteer for committee work.

10. WONDER APPLY BOARD WHY‿NOT YOU = alexander ?

Why don't you consider running for the board, Alexander?

11. NOT BAD IDEA ! "AUTHORITY" DECIDE+ CAN ME !

That's not a bad idea at all! I could do more decision making!

"AUTHORITY," meaning "having the full freedom to do something," differs from AUTHORITY in the sense of "power." It is made with a fleeting backward movement of the hands past the head. See also Lesson 24, sentence 3.

Vocabulary Review

Test your ability to produce the following signs or sign phrases.

ACCEPT͜ YOU ?	IMPROVE	TOMORROW͜ NIGHT
ALMOST	INTELLIGENT	TREASURER
"AUTHORITY" DECIDE	LOOK-AT = each-other	alternate = TWO = *two*
BEAT = around + +	NOT BAD IDEA	UNITY
BOARD	OFFICER$_2$	VOTE
COMMITTEE	PERSUADE	VOTE = noun +
many = CONVERGE	POPULAR YOU	WHY͜ NOT
DEAF C-L-U-B	PREFER	WIN EASY
DECIDE͜ LATE	SECRETARY	WONDER
DECIDE = noun +	STRONG GROUP	WONDER$_A$
EXPERIENCE	"STUCK"	WORK = around
FOUR YEAR	TEAM	YOUNG

Notes

Translation Exercises—ASL to English

Translate the following glossed sentences into appropriate English equivalents.

1. NEW+ PRESIDENT VOTE **NEED** WHY++ , PRESIDENT NOW+ , HIMSELF=*one* RESIGN .

2. DEAF C-L-U-B PRESIDENT APPLY RACE WHO , KNOW YOU ?

3. APPLY NAME DON'T-KNOW$_2$ ME ; KNOW+ APPLY ALTOGETHER FOUR .

4. DEAF C-L-U-B PRESIDENT RACE JOIN WHY NOT YOU ? POPULAR YOU , WHEW , WIN **EASY** !

5. REASON MY+ WANT+$_1$ YOU ? FIRST , FEEL EXPERIENCE NOT ENOUGH ME ; SECOND , PREFER RACE SECRETARY POSITION .

6. #IF SECRETARY POSITION WIN NOT , APPLY TREASURER ACCEPT ME ; alternate=TWO=*two* FINE .

7. #BUT PRESIDENT RACE , VOTE WIN YOU , "AUTHORITY" YOU , WHEW !

8. SECRETARY , TREASURER VOTE+ NOW NOT ; one=YEAR=*ahead* .

9. KNOW THAT ME ; NO-MATTER NOW+ WORK=*around* COMMITTEE HELP=*them* CAN ME . EXPERIENCE EARN++ .

10. SUPPOSE++ DEAF C-L-U-B OFFER=*you* RACE BOARD , ACCEPT YOU ?

11. DECIDE LATE ME . TELL=*you* FINISH PREFER ME+ #WHAT : SECRETARY , TREASURER alternate=TWO=*two* , ENOUGH .

12. WEEK=*ahead* DEAF C-L-U-B VOTE=*noun* PRESIDENT , many=CONVERGE , FEEL YOU ?

Translation Exercises—English to ASL

Translate the following sentences from English into ASL equivalents.

1. Most deaf clubs, like any other clubs, have an annual election of officers.

2. Some members may volunteer to run for office; others wait until nominated.

3. Sometimes a popular member will be persuaded to run for a certain office.

4. Club members usually vote for a president, a vice president, a secretary, and a treasurer.

5. There may be other officers such as a sergeant at arms or a house manager.

6. Whoever is elected to office knows that the job requires a lot of responsibility.

7. The president has to run regular meetings and help plan activities for the members.

8. The treasurer must see that members pay their dues regularly.

9. He will also have to pay bills and prepare monthly financial reports.

10. Most deaf clubs are open only on weekends.

11. If there is no program or special activity, members may just visit, play games, chat, etc.

12. Deaf clubs often sponsor a basketball team and a softball team.

Double-Slot Substitution Drills

Practice signing the following target sentences, substituting the suggested vocabulary in each slot. If you have problems with any of the vocabulary, consult your instructor for help.

1. <u>SUPPOSE++</u> DEAF C-L-U-B OFFER=you RACE <u>PRESIDENT</u> , ACCEPT YOU ?

      #IF   V-P

      HAPPEN   SECRETARY

      HAPPEN   PARLIAMENTARIAN

      #IF   BOARD

      SUPPOSE++   PRESIDENT

2. DEAF C-L-U-B <u>PRESIDENT</u> RACE , JOIN WHY NOT YOU ? <u>POPULAR YOU</u> !

                     V-P   RACE NONE₂

                     SECRETARY   WIN EASY YOU

                     TREASURER   RACE you=TWO

                     BOARD   WIN EASY YOU

                     PRESIDENT   POPULAR YOU

3. TOMORROW NIGHT DEAF many=CONVERGE MEETING , WHAT'S-UP ,

      <u>VOTE=noun+ OFFICER₂ NEW</u> .

      PROPOSE_A IDEA NEW+

      DISCUSS=around , MAYBE BUY HOUSE

      MEETING FINISH CAPTION MOVIE

      VOTE=noun+ OFFICER₂ NEW

4. DEAF C-L-U-B APPLY <u>PRESIDENT</u> FINISH₁ , ME ; #IF WIN FAIL <u>V-P</u> ACCEPT ME .

                      V-P   SECRETARY

                     SECRETARY   TREASURER

                     TREASURER   BOARD

                     BOARD   COMMITTEE ANY

                     PRESIDENT   V-P

5. ME+ STRADDLE=back-and-forth , APPLY <u>SECRETARY , TREASURER</u> alternate=TWO=*two* .

                                     TREASURER , BOARD

                                     OFFICER₂ , NOTHING

                                     PRESIDENT , V-P

                                     PRESIDENT , SECRETARY

                                     SECRETARY , TREASURER

6. <u>WEEK=ahead</u> DEAF C-L-U-B <u>CAPTION FILM</u> , many=CONVERGE FEEL YOU ?

two=WEEK=ahead   VOTE CONSTITUTION NEW

WILL SATURDAY   B-A-N-K NIGHT

TOMORROW NIGHT   DRAMA , DANCE

WILL SATURDAY   VOTE=noun+ PRESIDENT NEW

WEEK=ahead   CAPTION FILM

7. DEAF C-L-U-B MEETING DISCUSS=around

<u>NEW HOUSE BUY</u> , many=CONVERGE <u>FEW</u> !

NEW CONSTITUTION   NOT ENOUGH

MEMBER PAY=club INCREASE   BY-A-HAIR

PROGRAM YEAR=ahead   NOT ENOUGH

CHANGE NAME   GOOD

NEW HOUSE BUY   FEW

8. DEAF C-L-U-B <u>NEW HOUSE BUY HARD+</u> WHY++ , <u>MONEY NOT ENOUGH</u> !

NEW CONSTITUTION VOTE PASS   many=converge FEW

MEMBER PAY=club VOTE+ PASS   NEW HOUSE WANT+ THEY

PROGRAM YEAR=ahead BETTER   NEW+ , DIFFERENT

CHANGE NAME VOTE+ PASS   many=CONVERGE GOOD

NEW HOUSE BUY HARD+   MONEY NOT ENOUGH

9. DEAF C-L-U-B <u>PRESIDENT</u> DUTY HIS #WHAT , <u>MANAGE MEETING MONTH++</u> .

V-P   PROGRAM MONTH++ PLAN+

SECRETARY   WRITE=page MEETING MONTH++

TREASURER   MONEY PAY=him EARN MONTH++

BOARD   MEETING GO++

PRESIDENT   MANAGE MEETING MONTH++

10. <u>YEAR=ahead</u> DEAF C-L-U-B <u>BASKETBALL</u> JOIN YOU ?

WILL AUTUMN   DRAMA GROUP

WILL GROW=noun+   BASEBALL

WEEK=ahead   NEW HOUSE COMMITTEE

WILL FRIDAY   "FUN NIGHT"

TOMORROW NIGHT   B-A-N-K NIGHT

YEAR=ahead   BASKETBALL

Suggested Activities

1. Act out the dialogue used in this lesson. Five persons may volunteer or be selected from the group to role play the characters in the dialogue.

2. Conduct a mock election of officers in class for a hypothetical organization such as a drama club, a PTA organization, a garden club, etc. Go through the processes of making nominations for each office; of having candidates present themselves and their goals for the "organization," if elected; and of the actual voting by raised hand or ballot.

3. Have your instructor arrange a visit to the local deaf club, if there is one in your community, or invite local deaf persons to participate in your class to observe your mock election and make comments or give feedback on your sign performances.

4. Practice signing the ASL to English translation exercises *before* translating the sentences.

5. For fingerspelling practice, you may use some of the sentences or selected phrases from the sentences in the English to ASL translation exercises in this lesson. Pair off in class. Partners may then take turns randomly selecting two or three sentences or phrases to fingerspell to each other while the instructor observes.

6. Write an English version of the glossed introductory paragraph.

Getting Ready for Christmas

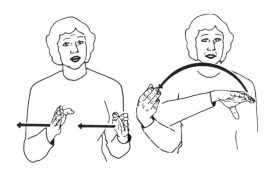

CHRISTMAS TIME-PERIOD

TIME-PERIOD APPROACH ⊥ CHRISTMAS , BENNY , GLORIA those = TWO DISCUSS NEW+
HOUSE DECORATE+ HOW++ . NOW FIRST TIME CHRISTMAS **NEW** HOUSE . **NEW**
HOUSE DECORATE+ PRETTY , IMPRESS = you WANT+ those = TWO . HIMSELF = benny
WONDER_A CHRISTMAS TREE BUY TRUE , FALSE+ WHICH . CHRISTMAS TREE FALSE+
don't = WANT HER = gloria WHY++ TREE **TRUE** "WHIFF" "FINE" , LIKE SHE . HE = benny
GO-OUT TREE++> SEARCH = around STRIKE-CHANCE **PERFECT** TREE , CHOP = *tree*
FINISH₁ BRING HOME . WIFE HAPPY , EXCITED START DECORATE++ WANT++
SHE ! those = TWO TALK = each-other , AGREE COLOR LIGHT₂> ITS CHRISTMAS PLUS
"BALL"+ DECORATE+ DIFFERENT++> #WHAT . WILL TOMORROW MORNING GET-UP
those = TWO , START DECORATE = around+ HOUSE , IN+ , OUT BOTH . WORK = around
FINISH₂ , LAST TREE DECORATE+∨ , **WRONG** LIGHT-ON-OFF+ DOOR WHO ?
APPEAR WHO THINK YOU , DAUGHTER PLUS JIMMY . those = TWO = jimmy = mother
HELP = them TREE DECORATE++∨ FINISH₂ , **BEAUTIFUL** WHEW !

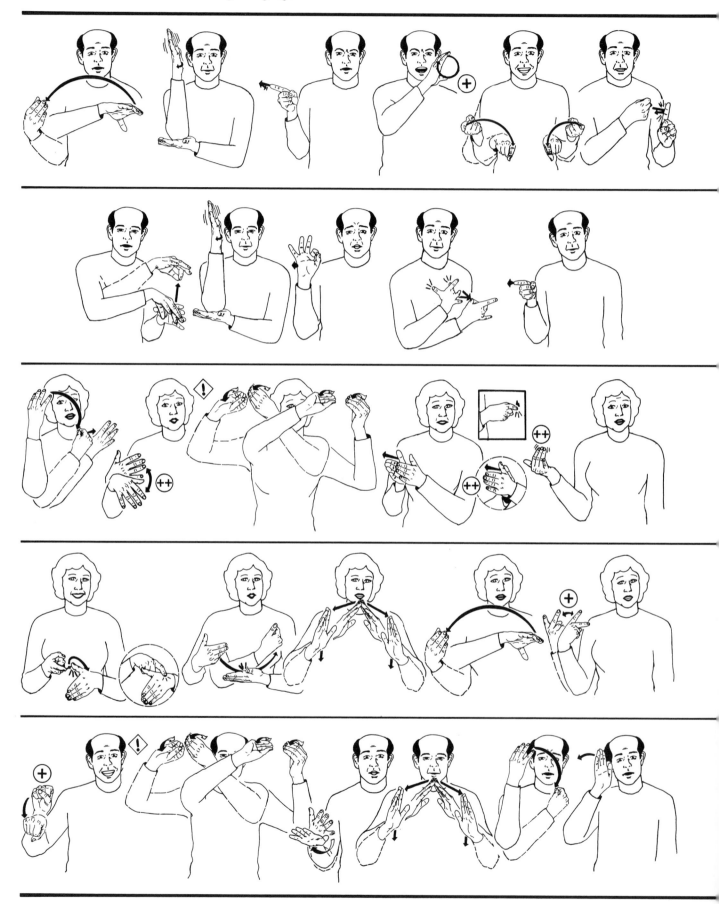

Glossed Sentences, Translations, and Grammatical Notes

1. CHRISTMAS TREE+ +> **THERE**=far SEARCH=around HAPPEN

   I went far into the woods to look around for a perfect Christmas

   THERE=far is made by holding the pointing finger at a steep angle and moving it back abruptly.

   STRIKE-CHANCE FIND "PERFECT" , LIKE YOU=gloria ?

   tree and I made a lucky find; do you like it, Gloria?

   Compare STRIKE-CHANCE here with its use in Lesson 1, sentence 14.

---

2. **BEAUTIFUL** WHEW ! DECORATE **EAGER** ME WHY+ + ,

   It's gorgeous! I'm so eager to decorate because

   FIRST‿TIME NEW HOUSE CHRISTMAS we=TWO !

   it's our first Christmas in our new house!

---

3. YES ! DECORATE FINISH₂ HOUSE PRETTY WILL !

   Yes! When we finish decorating the house, it will be very pretty!

4. NOW   YEAR   TREE   DECORATE   RED ,

This year I want to decorate the tree in red,

WHITE ,   GOLD ,   MAYBE   FLOWER   KNOW   YOU   P-O-I-N-S-E-T-T-I-A

white, and gold and maybe put poinsettias

PUT = around$_2$ ME   WANT ;   THINK   PRETTY   YOU ?

around it; do you think that will be pretty?

PUT = around$_2$ here represents the placing of objects (poinsettias) around a Christmas tree. Compare this with the use of PUT = around$_2$ in Lesson 3, sentence 7, and in Lesson 4, sentence 10.

5. AGREE   ME !   ME   WANT   FIX   FIRE   MANTEL ,

I agree with you! I want to fix up the fireplace mantelpiece

For review of FIRE   MANTEL, see Lesson 8, sentence 3.

PUT$_2$ GREEN   DIFFERENT+   PLUS   SET = noun + + >

and put different greens plus set up

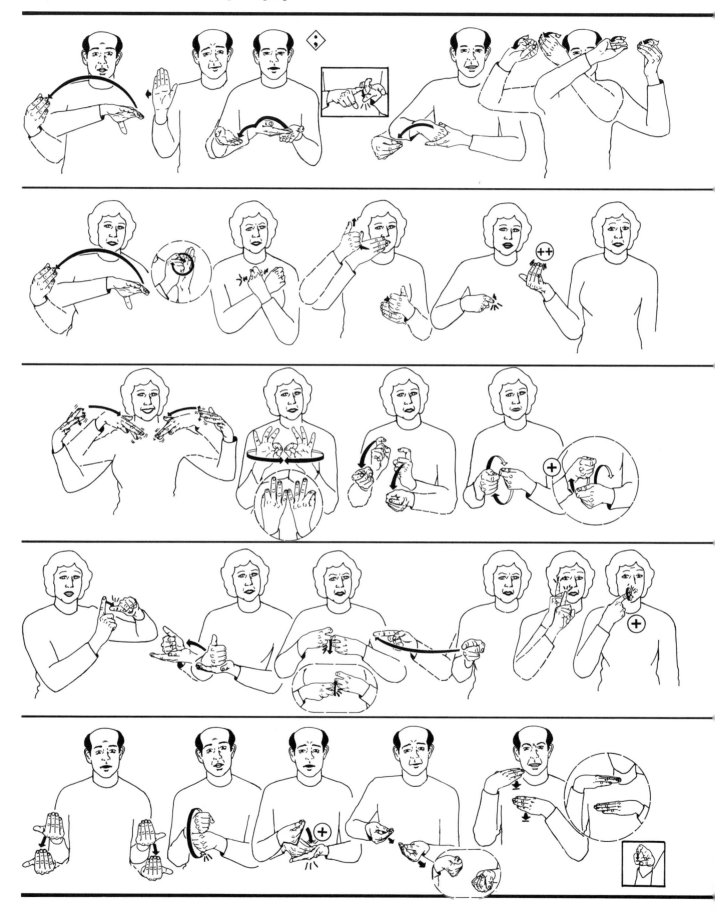

CHRISTMAS ITS THING+ ; SECOND , OUT+ DECORATE .

Christmas things; then, I want to decorate outside.

6. CHRISTMAS TIME-PERIOD LOVE BEST ME , WHY+ +

I love Christmas time the best because

FAMILY many = CONVERGE GIFT$_2$+ EXCHANGE+ + ,

the family comes together to exchange gifts,

many = CONVERGE can be used in a number of situations where individual things come to a central location. In this context, it could be translated as "reunion" or "get-together." It could also be used to represent people entering a lecture hall or traffic entering a stadium parking lot. For EXCHANGE, see Lesson 15, sentence 6.

PLUS HELP = them NEEDY THEY DEAF = colloquial , HEARING .

and we help those who are needy, whether they are deaf or hearing.

7. NOW YEAR MONEY SPEND$_2$ **LIMIT NEED** .

This year we have to limit the amount of money we spend.

Vocabulary Review

Test your ability to produce the following signs or sign phrases.

AGREE   ME

BEAUTIFUL   WHEW !

CHOP = *tree*

CHRISTMAS

CHRISTMAS   TIME-PERIOD

CHRISTMAS   TREE

DEAF = colloquial ,   HEARING

DECORATE +

DECORATE = around +

DECORATE   FINISH$_2$

DECORATE = noun + +   ITS
   CHRISTMAS

EAGER   ME

FAMILY   many = CONVERGE

GIFT$_2$ EXCHANGE

GOLD

GREEN

HELP = them   NEEDY

HOUSE   PRETTY

IMPRESS = you

LIGHT$_2$>   ITS   CHRISTMAS

LIMIT   NEED

LOVE   BEST

MONEY   SPEND$_2$

PUT = around$_2$

RED

SEARCH = around

SET = noun + + >

STRIKE-CHANCE   FIND

TALK = each-other

THERE = far

WHITE

Notes

Translation Exercises—ASL to English

Translate the following glossed sentences into appropriate English equivalents.

1. CHRISTMAS TIME-PERIOD BUSY ALWAYS WHY++ MANY THINGS #DO=around SAME CLEAN=around++ , DECORATE=around , BUY++ , GIFT₂ WRAP+ .

2. YEAR=ahead+ OUT+ ELECTRIC LIGHT-ON+ ITS CHRISTMAS PUT=up₂ LIKE ME .

3. HOUSE DECORATE=around FINISH₂ , READY CHRISTMAS , SHINY₂ ATTRACT-TO₂ TRUE !

4. PAST+ WIFE we=TWO GO-OUT SEARCH=around , PICK , BUY CHRISTMAS TREE NEW+ CUT=down FINISH , BRING HOME , SET-UP ; LATER DECORATE+∨ PRETTY .

5. **WILL** CHANGE , DECIDE BUY CHRISTMAS TREE FALSE FINISH₂ ; **AFTER** BUY YEAR=ahead+ NOT **NEED** .

6. PAST+ CHRISTMAS TREE DECORATE++∨ DIFFERENT++ COLOR SAME+ RED *GREEN* BLUE *WHITE* GOLD , FINISH₂ ME .

7. ONCE-IN-A-WHILE CHRISTMAS TREE DECORATE++∨ LIMIT TWO COLOR SAME+ RED , WHITE alternate=*TWO* BLUE , GOLD LIKE ME .

8. FIRE MANTEL DECORATE+> #WHAT , NEW++ GREEN "ROPE" IT+ P-I-N-E LIKE ME , WHY++ SMELL "FINE" .

9. ONE THING don't=LIKE ME #WHAT , GO SELL=noun+ BUY=around++ LAST MINUTE , PEOPLE **many=CONVERGE** , CROWDED WHEW !

10. CHRISTMAS TIME-PERIOD NEAR+⊥ , FAMILY MY+ LIKE #WHAT , GET-IN-VEHICLE+ DRIVE⊥ LOOK-AT=around₂++ HOUSE+ DECORATE+ DIFFERENT++ THEIR .

11. SOMETIMES FAMILY+ , FRIEND many=CONVERGE GROUP=together CHRISTMAS EVE , WHAT-FOR GIFT₂+ EXCHANGE++ , EAT_A , DRINK_A , GOOD TIME .

Translation Exercises—English to ASL

Translate the following sentences from English into ASL equivalents.

1. Decorating for Christmas is a real family affair in many homes.
2. Some families go to the woods to look for a Christmas tree.
3. Other families may own an artificial tree or go out and buy a real tree.
4. When the tree is set up, you first string lights around it.
5. After that, you may hang different ornaments and decorations around the tree.
6. Tinsel and icicles are put on last, and the tree is ready to light up.
7. Some people also like to put lights on trees outside the house and on the house.
8. If you have a fireplace, you will want to decorate the mantelpiece, too.
9. Shopping for gifts, wrapping them, and placing them under the tree helps your Christmas spirit.
10. Christmas is a time also to give and to share with needy people.

Single-Slot Substitution Drills

Practice signing the following target sentences, substituting the suggested vocabulary in each slot. If you have problems with any of the vocabulary, consult your instructor for help.

1. YEAR = ahead + + APPROACH + CHRISTMAS TIME-PERIOD FAMILY MY **BUSY** WHY + + ,
   <u>HOUSE CLEAN = around</u> **NEED** .
   CHRISTMAS GIFT$_2$ + BUY + +
   FAMILY CHRISTMAS LETTER WRITE = page
   CHRISTMAS CARD + MAIL = them +
   CHRISTMAS GIFT$_2$ + WRAP = object
   HOUSE CLEAN = around

2. HOUSE , WINDOW + , EVERY THING **CLEAN** FINISH$_2$, PROCEED
   <u>DECORATE + + > HOUSE IN + , OUT</u> .
   DECORATE + + > FIRE MANTEL
   COOK + CHRISTMAS THING + DIFFERENT + + >
   CHRISTMAS LIGHT + PUT-UP$_2$ +
   DECORATE + + > HOUSE IN + , OUT

3. NOW YEAR CHRISTMAS TREE DECORATE COLOR #WHAT , <u>RED , WHITE , *GOLD*</u> .
                                                                       BLUE , SHINY = silver
                                                                       GOLD #ALL
                                                                       DIFFERENT + +
                                                                       RED , WHITE , *GOLD*

4. HOUSE DECORATE = around FINISH$_2$, READY CHRISTMAS ,
   <u>SHINY$_2$, ATTRACT-TO$_2$ TRUE</u> .
   FAMILY PLEASE = noun$_2$ + CAN
   FEEL RELIEVED ME +
   INVITE$_A$ FRIEND CAN
   SHINY$_2$, ATTRACT-TO$_2$

5. NOW YEAR MONEY SPEND$_2$ CHRISTMAS LIMIT **NEED** WHY + + , <u>MONEY SMALL +</u> .
                                                                       MONTH + + SPEND$_1$
                                                                       HIGH
                                                                       MONEY PUT-IN +
                                                                       WILL NEW HOUSE
                                                                       COST INCREASE + +
                                                                        MONEY SMALL +

6. CHRISTMAS TIME-PERIOD LOVE ME WHY++ , FAMILY many=CONVERGE
   <u>GIFT₂ EXCHANGE</u> .
   EAT_A
   SING+ CHRISTMAS ITS+
   GROUP=go CHURCH
   GIFT₂ EXCHANGE

7. CHRISTMAS TIME-PERIOD BUY++ HEAD=pain ONE #WHAT ,
   <u>SELL=noun+ CROWDED</u> .
   TRAFFIC WHEW
   MONEY SPEND₂ LIMIT
   GIFT=this , GIFT=that , DECIDE WHICH
   LAST MINUTE FORGET SOMEONE
   SELL=noun+ CROWDED

8. YEAR=recent-past FAMILY GO-OUT OFF-WORK+ ;
   <u>OUT ELECTRIC LIGHT+ PUT-UP₂+ NONE₂</u> .
   HOUSE DECORATE++ **LITTLE**
   GIFT₂ BUY++ FEW
   PARTY NONE₂
   OUT ELECTRIC LIGHT+ PUT-UP₂+ NONE₂

9. CHRISTMAS EVE FAMILY , FRIEND many=CONVERGE GROUP=together
   WHAT-FOR , <u>GIFT₂ EXCHANGE+</u> .
          SING+
          DECORATE++∨ TREE
          EAT_A
          PARTY
          GIFT₂ EXCHANGE+

10. CHRISTMAS TIME-PERIOD FINISH₂ , WORK+ "WHAT" ,
    <u>DECORATE++ TAKE-DOWN=object_A</u> .
    DECORATE++ PUT-IN_A BOX+
    TREE THROW-AWAY=object
    HOUSE CLEAN=around++
    PLAN+ CHRISTMAS YEAR=
      ahead
    DECORATE++ TAKE-DOWN=object_A

Suggested Activities

1. Act out the dialogue used in this lesson. Two persons may volunteer or be selected from the group to role play the characters in the dialogue, or the class may be paired off so that everyone participates in the dialogue.

2. Describe Christmas or Chanukah preparations in your family tradition or in your own home. Tell how you decorate for the holiday season, the kinds of foods you prepare especially for it, and any other family customs you may wish to share with the class.

3. Find pictures showing various aspects of the Christmas season and bring them to class, prepared to pair off and to describe your picture to your partner before allowing other members of the class to see your picture.

4. Try your hand at signing some carols or other songs or poems that may relate to the season. (Translation of songs and poems will be covered in Lesson 25, but you can experiment at this time, and later try again to see how you might change what you do now.)

5. Practice signing the ASL to English translation exercises *before* translating the sentences.

6. For fingerspelling practice, you may use some of the sentences or selected phrases from the sentences in the English to ASL translation exercises in this lesson. Pair off in class. Partners may then take turns randomly selecting two or three sentences or phrases to fingerspell to each other while the instructor observes.

7. Write an English version of the glossed introductory paragraph.

Reunion at PRSD

many = CONVERGE   INSTITUTION   P-R-S-D

three = YEAR = ahead + +   DEAF WORLD   many = CONVERGE   INSTITUTION   P-R-S-D .   DEAF
INSTITUTION   SAME = around₂   TRADITION   ITS + .   HAPPEN   INSTITUTION   P-R-S-D   WHAT'S   UP
many = CONVERGE   COLLABORATE   P-R-A-D ,   ITS   P-I-N-E   R-I-D-G-E   ASSOCIATION   DEAF .
ALWAYS   three = YEAR = ahead + +   PRESIDENT   DEAF   INSTITUTION   LECTURE ,   INFORM = them
DEAF   IN +   INSTITUTION   NEW ,   CHANGE ,   IMPROVE   BETTER   "WHAT" .   ALSO
INFORM = them   PROBLEM   APPEAR + ,   NEED +   MONEY ,   FUTURE   PLAN +   #WHAT ,
VARIOUS .   PRESIDENT   LECTURE + ,   DEAF   LOOK-AT = him₂   PLEASE = noun₂ +   ALWAYS
WHY + + ,   HIMSELF = president   SIGN   CLEAR ,   DEAF   THEY   UNDERSTAND ,   FEEL
COOPERATE = him .   SECOND ,   PRESIDENT   "COME-ON"₂ +   DEAF   THEIR   IDEA   IMPROVE
INSTITUTION   HOW + + .   MEETING   FINISH₂ ,   DEAF   GROUP = together +   CHAT + + ,   LOOK-
AT = past₂   OLD   TIME-PERIOD ,   REMEMBER   APPEAR + +   HAPPEN   YOUR + + .   OTHER
#DO = around ,   MEETING   VOTE + ,   BUSINESS ,   EAT_A ,   MEET = around   OLD   FRIEND ,
MAYBE   CAPTION   MOVIE ,   PICNIC .

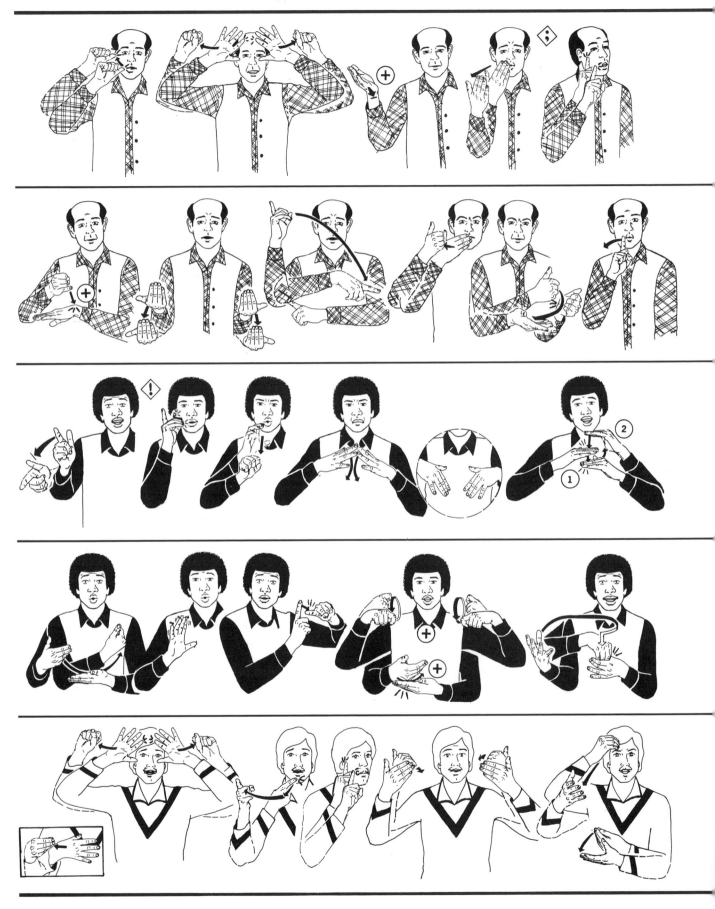

Glossed Sentences, Translations, and Grammatical Notes

1. YESTERDAY   PRESIDENT   LECTURE   GOOD ;   DEAF

The superintendent gave a good talk yesterday; the State

PRESIDENT is translatable as "president," "superintendent," and is sometimes used in formally addressing a "chairperson" or other titular head.

INSTITUTION   NOW   DAY   BETTER+ EVERYTHING   TRUE .

School for the Deaf is really better in every way.

INSTITUTION is frequently used to refer to a "state school for the deaf" or a "residential school." BETTER+ EVERYTHING is a blend which means "better in every way" or "better all around."

---

2. SECOND = you !   DORMITORY   OLD   BREAK-DOWN ,   BUILDING

I agree with you! The old dormitory has been torn down and a

DORMITORY is a modification of HOME, made with a "D" handshape. Fingerspelled D-O-R-M is also common. BREAK-DOWN can mean "breakdown," "tear down," "collapse," or "demolish."

NEW   "FINE" ,   PLUS   GYM   NEW+   **all = INCLUDE** .

swell brand new one built plus a new gym with everything.

In the colloquial form of FINE, the thumb remains in contact with the chest and the fingers alternately and repeatedly wiggle. The emphatic all = INCLUDE means that "everything possible is included" or "nothing is left out."

---

3. AND   PRESIDENT   TELL = them   DEAF   "AUTHORITY"   INFORM = him +

And the superintendent told us we have the freedom to let him know

For explanation of "AUTHORITY", see Lesson 22, sentence 11.

LIKE , don't = LIKE , HELP LEARN = noun + BETTER .

what we like and what we don't like to help improve education here.

In don't = LIKE, as in don't = WANT, the negation is shown by the outward twisting of the hand. (See Lesson 4, sentences 5 and 6.) LEARN = noun + BETTER is a blend that means "improve education."

4. NOW AFTERNOON MEETING LET'S-SEE VOTE WHO

This afternoon there's a meeting, and we will see whom they elect

PRESIDENT P-R-A-D NEXT TWO YEAR + .

to run the Pine Ridge Association of the Deaf over the next two years.

PRESIDENT here is translated as one who will "run" or "control" a group.

5. PAST NIGHT GROUP = together CHAT + + all = NIGHT .

Last night a group of us got together and chatted all night.

In GROUP = together, the hands move directly toward each other rather than in the usual arched orientation for GROUP.

6. YES ! PLEASE = noun$_2$ LOOK-AT = past$_2$ TIME-PERIOD **LONG-AGO** .

Yes! It's a pleasure to look back on old times.

7. long = PAST +   HE = lawrence   AVOID   ME ;   NOW   LOOK-AT = us₂   we = TWO .

In the past, Lawrence avoided me; now look at the two of us.

In LOOK-AT = us₂, the fingers are oriented directly toward the signer's face, contrasted with LOOK-AT = past₂ in which the movement is back past the face and over the shoulder.

8. BLAME = yourself ;   DIFFERENT + + >   BOY +   ATTRACT-TO + >   YOU !

That's your fault; you were always attracted to different boys!

BLAME = yourself is a directional complex sign which may be translated as "that's your fault," "you have no one to blame but yourself," or simply "blame yourself." DIFFERENT here moves slightly toward the right with each repetition as does the sign ATTRACT-TO, which refers, in this case, to the idea of "attraction to different boys."

9. he = SAME = alexander ,   PAST +   BOTHER = me + ;   ME   IGNORE = alexander .

It was the same with Alexander; he used to bother me, but I ignored him.

10. NOW   ENGAGE   FINISH₁,   we = TWO ;   HAPPY   YOU ?

Now we're engaged; aren't you happy?

11. PAST + +   LOOK-AT = ahead₂ +   COLLEGE   GO-OUT   ME ,   WRONG   MARRY !

I used to look forward to going to college, but I got married!

LOOK-AT = ahead always moves directly out from the signer and may mean "look forward to" or "anticipate."

Vocabulary Review

Test your ability to produce the following signs or sign phrases.

ASSOCIATION	COLLABORATE	LECTURE
ATTRACT-TO	COLLEGE	don't = LIKE
"AUTHORITY"	DEAF = colloquial "AUTHORITY"	LOOK-AT = past$_2$
AVOID	DEAF = colloquial INSTITUTION	LOOK-AT = us$_2$
BETTER +⌣ EVERYTHING	DEAF⌣ WORLD	MEET = around
BLAME = yourself	DORMITORY	MEETING
BOTHER = me	GROUP = together	all = NIGHT
BOY +	GYM NEW +	SAME = around
BREAK-DOWN	IGNORE = him/her/you	TRADITION
BUILDING	INFORM = him/her/you	three = YEAR = ahead + +
BUSINESS	LEARN = noun +⌣ BETTER	

Notes

Translation Exercises—ASL to English

Translate the following glossed sentences into appropriate English equivalents.

1. DEAF   INSTITUTION   many=CONVERGE   OFTEN   COLLABORATE   S-T-A-T-E   ASSOCIATION   ITS   DEAF .

2. FIRST‿TIME   ME+   GO   DEAF   INSTITUTION   many=CONVERGE   THAT   PAST+   M-A-Y   1977 .   ITS   K-A-D ,   K-A-N-S-A-S   ASSOCIATION   ITS   DEAF   MEETING .

3. HAPPEN   **THIRTY**   YEAR   MY   CLASS   INSTITUTION   ITS   K-A-N-S-A-S   SEE   NONE₂   EXCEPT   1-2 ,   1-2   SEE   FEW   TIME-PERIOD .

4. #ALL   CLASS   MY+   many=CONVERGE   NOT ;   SAY   AROUND   SIX .   CLASS   MY+   ALTOGETHER   TEN ,   GRADUATE   FINISH₁   LONG-AGO   1947.

5. CLASS   MY+   group=TOGETHER   CHAT ,   STORY-TALK ,   LOOK-AT=past₂   OLD   TIME-PERIOD   HAPPEN+ +>   PLEASE=noun₂+   TRUE !

6. MEET=around   OLD   FRIEND   KNOW+   **MANY**   SEE   **NONE₂**   LONG   TIME-PERIOD ,   PLEASE=noun₂   ME .

7. SEE   FINISH₁   PAST+   DEAF   INSTITUTION   NOW-AND-THEN ,   BUT   **NEW**   BUILDING   SEE   LATE   ME .

8. **GONE**   OLD   SCHOOL   BUILDING ,   EXCHANGE   **NEW**   BUILDING ,   "FINE" ,   **NICE** !

9. **NEW**   BUILDING   IN+   HAVE   CLASS   ROOM ,   FANCY₁+   T-V   S-T-U-D-I-O ,   PLUS   DEAF   HISTORY   M-U-S-E-U-M ;   TRUE   **IMPRESS=me** !

10. NEW+   BUILDING   OTHER   #WHAT ,   GYM   ADD-ON ,   WHAT-FOR   SWIMMING   P-O-O-L ;   MY   TIME-PERIOD   **NONE₂** !

11. WILL   1997 ,   **FIFTY**   YEAR ,   CLASS   MY+   many=CONVERGE   DEAF   INSTITUTION ,   HOPE   ME !

Translation Exercises—English to ASL

Translate the following sentences from English into ASL equivalents.

1. Deaf persons who graduate from state residential schools like to attend reunions.

2. It may not be possible to attend every reunion every two or three years.

3. Some reunions are often in conjunction with the state association of the deaf convention.

4. You may find old buildings gone or new buildings being erected.

5. The school superintendent likes to encourage old grads to give him ideas for improving the school.

6. Suppose you haven't gone to a school reunion for many years.

7. You will probably find yourself staying up all night chatting with old friends and classmates.

8. Everyone always enjoys looking back on old times and things they did when young.

9. A reunion may offer a chance to go back to school or classes.

10. There will be business meetings, elections, and planning for future reunions.

Single-Slot Substitution Drills

Practice signing the following target sentences, substituting the suggested vocabulary in each slot. If you have problems with any of the vocabulary, consult your instructor for help.

1. TOMORROW AFTERNOON GROUP=together MEETING WHAT-FOR ,
   <u>PRESIDENT LECTURE</u>
   DISCUSS PLAN+ FUTURE
   NEW BUSINESS
   R-E-S-O-L-U-T-I-O-N-S
   PRESIDENT LECTURE

2. NOW AFTERNOON MEETING , VOTE+ <u>PRESIDENT</u> ; WIN WHO , FEEL YOU ?
   V-P
   TREASURER
   PARLIAMENTARIAN
   PRESIDENT

3. <u>DORMITORY</u> **OLD** BREAK-DOWN FINISH$_2$; EXCHANGE BUILD NEW , FANCY$_A$.
   SCHOOL BUILDING
   GYM
   INFIRMARY
   LIBRARY
   DORMITORY

4. NOW NIGHT GROUP=together WHAT-FOR , <u>CHAT++</u> .
   GROUP=go EAT$_A$
   LOOK-AT=past$_2$ TIME-PERIOD LONG-AGO+
   DANCE+
   GROUP=go DRAMA
   CAPTION MOVIE
   CHAT++

5. INSTITUTION MY+ CHANGE , NEW+ #WHAT ,
   <u>SWIMMING P-O-O-L</u> ; MY TIME-PERIOD NONE !
   CAFETERIA A-C
   DEAF HISTORY M-U-S-E-U-M
   T-V S-T-U-D-I-O
   PLAY-POOL ROOM
   SWIMMING P-O-O-L

6. three=YEAR=ahead++   DEAF INSTITUTION many=CONVERGE SEEM <u>BETTER+</u> .

                                                                                                     EXPAND++

                                                                                                     EXCITED

                                                                                                     SAME=continuous$_2$

                                                                                   BETTER+

7. PAST+   DEAF INSTITUTION many=CONVERGE ALTOGETHER AROUND <u>200</u> DEAF .

                                                                                                                 150

                                                                                                                 300

                                                                                                                 225

                                                                                                                 200

8. LONG-AGO+   DEAF INSTITUTION ME+ "AUTHORITY" WHY++ ,

      <u>SENIOR CLASS PRESIDENT</u> .

      SCOUT LEADER

      DORM LEADER

      CANDY SELL+

      FOOTBALL OFFICER$_1$

      CHEERLEAD OFFICER$_1$

      SENIOR CLASS PRESIDENT

9. LONG-AGO+   THINK MAYBE COLLEGE ME , PLAN+ , WRONG <u>MARRY</u> .

                                                                                                         FATHER DIE

                                                                                                         FAIL

                                                                                                   MONEY NOT ENOUGH+

                                                                                       FALL-IN-LOVE BOY

                                                                                  MOTHER

                                                                                         SICK=continuous$_2$

                                                                                  MARRY

10. WILL 1990 , <u>THIRTY</u> YEAR , CLASS MY+ many=CONVERGE DEAF INSTITUTION .

                FORTY

                TWENTY

                TWENTY-FIVE

                FIFTEEN

                FIFTY

                THIRTY

Suggested Activities

1. Have you ever attended a reunion of your high school class or of your college class? If so, you may have some experiences you'd like to share with your class here. Prepare to relate a brief reminiscence from bygone days that a reunion brought back to mind.

2. Act out the dialogue used in this lesson. Seven persons may volunteer or be selected from the group to portray each character in the dialogue. Give special attention to facial expression, emotions, and body language.

3. Invite deaf speakers to come to your class to share some of their anecdotes and/or memories from their days at the state school or at college.

4. Practice signing the ASL to English translation exercises *before* translating the sentences.

5. For fingerspelling practice, you may use some of the sentences or selected phrases from the sentences in the English to ASL translation exercises in this lesson. Pair off in class. Partners may then take turns randomly selecting two or three sentences or phrases to fingerspell to each other while the instructor observes.

6. Write an English version of the glossed introductory paragraph.

Lesson 25

Signing Poetry and Song

The intermediate student of Sign Language may wish to learn how to sign poetry and/or songs. Very little poetry has been written that may easily be classified as "ASL poetry." ASL poetry cannot be written simply because ASL itself is not a written language. A glossing system must be used in order to show how ASL poetry would be signed. Dorothy Miles, Ella Lentz, Clayton Valli, and Pat Graybill are all known for their ASL poetry, which is not written or glossed. Such poetry has been developed in recent years as a natural art form that sometimes uses visual rhyme schemes and sometimes is free verse, but is never a translation of a written poem.

Most poetry and all songs, we know, were written for auditory presentation rather than for visual presentation and, therefore, follow English syntax and structure. Students, who have learned basic signs, often enjoy trying their hand at "interpreting" songs from live music or records. What ordinarily happens, however, is a rendition which is little more than a transliteration of the song(s), and many signs used are based on single-word concepts which do not always fit the meaning the song should convey. Since these songs are English-language based songs, such transliterations can hardly be avoided. But what about the student of ASL who wants to present an "ASL version" of a particular song or poem?

First of all, the student quickly learns that it is not possible to give a *complete* translation into the target language but rather, at best, only a *partial* translation. What are some of the problems involved in this process? In attempting to work out a suitable translation, one must take the song or poem, line by line, and try to determine the meaning or concept behind each phrase or sentence. This analysis does not always produce immediate satisfaction because there are also problems of rhythm and often of rhyme which need to be retained as closely as possible. This is especially true of a translation of a song one may wish to present in accompaniment to music. In a rendition of a poem, this is less of a problem. However, once one has worked out some kind of translation, it is then necessary to "test" the translation, first, to see if the signs selected adequately convey the meaning from a visual point of view and, second, to see if it retains the basic flow or rhythm. One must also be concerned with aesthetic values since music is a form of emotional entertainment. For this reason, the Sign translation must include signs which are rhythmic and graceful in motion.

In another sense, translation of songs and poems from English into ASL allows one to utilize creative or discovery processes to come up with the best possible result. This can only be done in collaboration with another person who acts as visual critic and who can help you determine when you have a suitable translation. The song, "Let There Be Peace on Earth," illustrated in this lesson, with the permission of its authors, makes full use of these processes. The translation finally accepted here may not be the only possible translation, but it has been tested and does seem to meet the criteria discussed in this introduction. As you analyze the final product, discussion will help bring out the reasons for the translation of each line in the song.

Glossed Sentences, Translations, and Grammatical Notes

1. ALLOW   PEACE   SPREAD = globe   EARTH

Let there be peace on earth

ALLOW may be translated as "allow," "let," "permit," or "chance." The sign SPREAD here moves in a circumferential direction rather than the usual horizontal plane to give the impression of covering the globe.

AND   ALLOW   PEACE   START   OUT = me   "ME = poetic" ,

And let it begin with me,

START can be translated as "start," "begin," "initiate," or "originate." OUT = me is made close to the body to give the impression of something coming from within oneself. "ME = poetic" is a sign which is used chiefly in translation of poetry or song.

2. ALLOW   PEACE   SPREAD = globe   EARTH

Let there be peace on earth

PEACE   INTEND   FOR   CONTINUE .

The peace that was meant to be.

INTEND is a complex sign incorporating the ideas of "thought" and "meaning." It is also translatable as "purpose" in some contexts. Since ASL does not have the equivalent forms of the English verb, "to be," we select signs in translation to show approximate meaning. "To be," here, implies "to last"; hence the signs FOR CONTINUE.

3. BECAUSE   GOD   "THERE = poetic"   OUR   FATHER

As God is our Father

BROTHER͜UNITY   all = GROUP .

Brothers all are we.

BROTHER͜UNITY is a blend meaning "brothers altogether" or "brothers in cooperation." GROUP here is made with the same handshapes we would use for LINE-UP but the hands move out and forward arc-like.

4. ALLOW   *"ME = poetic"*₁   MY   BROTHER͜UNITY   *ONE = forward*   FIVE = forward

Let me walk with my brothers

ME here is made with the nondominant hand to allow it to establish a referent for *ONE* in the same line. *ONE = forward* FIVE = forward is a special blend in which both hands move forward simultaneously, *ONE* representing "me" and FIVE referring to "brothers."

WITH   PERFECT   HARMONIZE .

In perfect harmony.

5. ALLOW PEACE START OUT=me "ME=poetic"

Let peace begin with me

ALLOW THIS MOMENT HAPPEN+ NOW ,

Let this moment be now,

The English verb "be" here implies "occurrence" or "taking place," hence the sign HAPPEN+ which is translatable as "happen," "occur," "take place," etc.

6. WITH EVERY STEP MYSELF WALK

With every step I take

"To take" is another English verb form which must be considered for its real meaning before attempting translation into Sign.

ALLOW MY HUMBLE PROMISE CONTINUE :

Let this be my solemn vow:

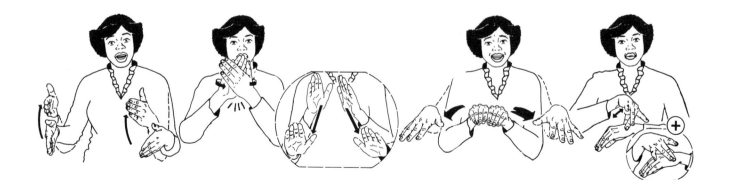

7. ACCEPT_A EACH MOMENT

To take each moment

"To take" here has a different meaning from that in sentence 6; hence it is translated as ACCEPT_A.

AND LIVE EACH MOMENT WITH PEACE ALWAYS‿STILL₁ .

And live each moment in peace eternally.

ALWAYS‿STILL₁ is translatable as "forever," "everlasting," "eternal," etc.

8. ALLOW PEACE SPREAD = globe EARTH

Let there be peace on earth

ALLOW PEACE START OUT=me "ME=poetic" .

Let it begin with me.

9. ALLOW PEACE START OUT=me "ME=poetic" .

Let it begin with me.

SONG: "Let There Be Peace on Earth"
Sy Miller & Jill Jackson

Copyright © 1955 by Jan-Lee Music, Beverly Hills, California
By Permission.

Vocabulary Review

Test your ability to produce the following signs or sign phrases.

ACCEPT$_A$	all = GROUP	*ONE = forward* FIVE = forward +
ALLOW	HAPPEN +	OUT = me
ALWAYS $\frown$ STILL$_1$	HARMONIZE	PEACE
BECAUSE	HUMBLE	PERFECT
BROTHER $\smile$ UNITY	INTEND	PROMISE
CONTINUE	LIVE	SPREAD = globe
EACH	"ME = poetic"	START
EARTH	*"ME = poetic"$_1$*	STEP
EVERY	MOMENT	THIS
FATHER	MY	WALK
FOR CONTINUE	MYSELF	WITH
GOD "THERE = poetic"	NOW	

Notes

Translation Exercises—English to ASL

Try your hand at translating the following old-time songs. The songs may not be used much today, but they are still included in classical collections of American songs.

"Grandfather's Clock"

My grandfather's clock was too large for the shelf,
So it stood ninety years on the floor;
It was taller by half than the old man himself,
Though it weighed not a pennyweight more.
It was bought on the morn of the day that he was born,
And was always his treasure and pride.
But it stopp'd short never to go again
When the old man died.

CHORUS:

Ninety years, without slumbering Tick, tock, tick, tock,
His life seconds numbering Tick, tock, tick, tock,
It stopp'd short never to go again
When the old man died.

In watching its pendulum swing to and fro,
Many hours had he spent while a boy;
And in childhood and manhood the clock seem'd to know
And to share both his grief and his joy.
For it struck twenty-four when he enter'd at the door,
With a blooming and beautiful bride.
But it stopp'd short never to go again
When the old man died.

Repeat CHORUS

"Red River Valley"

From this valley they say you are going,
We will miss your bright eyes and sweet smile,
For they say you are taking the sunshine,
That brightens our pathway a while.

CHORUS:

Come and sit by my side if you love me,
Do not hasten to bid me adieu,
But remember the Red River Valley,
And the girl that has loved you so true—.

Won't you think of the valley you're leaving?
Oh, how lonely, how sad it will be,
Oh—think of the fond heart you're breaking,
And the grief you are causing me.

Repeat CHORUS

From this valley they say you are going,
When you go, may your darling go, too?
Would you leave her behind unprotected
When she loves no other but you?

Repeat CHORUS

I have promised you, darling, that never
Will a word from my lips cause you pain;
And my life, it will be yours forever
If you only will love me again.

Repeat CHORUS

The poem quoted here was written by the author in 1978. It was first used in the production of the Gallaudet University Theatre Touring Company's production of "How?", an original play written by Richard Peterson. The poem is offered here as a translation exercise for the student of ASL.

"My Rainbow, My World"

You know I'm deaf; my ears they do not hear;
And yet I neither cry nor do I fear.
I see, I feel, I smell, I even touch,
And let my hands create the world as such
As mind perceives; it does not matter much.

You see a rainbow now before your eyes;
Some birds in flight, some brilliant butterflies,
And shining lakes or mountains far away,
And puffy clouds of white and deer at play;
And this is what my hands do everyday.

You see the world is one large orchestra
A constant melody that sets us free;
And if I choose, I can by some design
Create a marvelous world that's all mine,
And do it with this language we call SIGN!

Do you see the rainbow in the sky?
Do you ever wonder, "Can I fly?"
And if you could, would you like to go
And sit atop the arch of a rainbow,
And view the whole wide world down below?

Or sit, perhaps, upon a grassy hill
And marvel at its colors, if you will
The brilliant yellow, orange, and red or blue
And purple fantasy or bright green hue,
With birds and butterflies as free as you!

Willard J. Madsen, 1978

Suggested Activities

1. After going through the illustrated lesson which gives a translation of "Let There Be Peace on Earth," try signing the translation in time to actual music or to a record containing the music and song.

2. Bring to class at least one of your favorite songs and attempt to work out a translation that follows the guidelines given in this lesson. You may wish to work with a deaf person who knows how to sign songs. If such a person(s) is known in your community, you might invite that person to assist you with this work.

3. Consider putting on a performance of poetry and song at the end of this course for the deaf people in your community and for other Sign Language classes and other interested people. You could advertise this performance in your community, if you wish, and call it "An Experiment in Sign." Involve every person in your class in the production. It should be an enjoyable experience.

4. If you can, obtain a copy of *Gestures* by Dorothy Miles, and try your hand at signing some of this poetry, or invite a deaf poet in your community, if there is one, to give a "reading" of some of his/her poetry.

Vocabularies

Students will find the vocabularies a useful reference in locating the meaning of a gloss or in finding the gloss to use for an English word or phrase. Glosses representing ASL signs are listed first (for example, ACCEPT), and the English or English equivalents are indented under the glosses (for example, Accept).

ACCEPT
  Accept

ACCEPT$_A$
  Accept this, accept that

ACCEPT‿YOU ?
  Do you accept; do you agree to (this)?

ADD
  Add

ADD-ON = object
  Addition or attachment to existing object

ADDRESS
  Address

ADD-UP
  Add up; altogether; the sum/total

ADVERTISE = noun +
  Advertisement

AFRAID(+)
  Afraid; scared; frightened

AFTER
  After (in time); afterwards; from now on; from then on

AFTERNOON

Afternoon; during the afternoon

AGAIN

Again; repeat

AGAPE

Agape; mouth fell open; jaws dropped

AGREE

Agree; think the same

AGREE‿FINISH₁

Agreed; agreed to; already made an agreement

AGREE ME

I agree very strongly

me = AGREE = him

I agree with him

he = AGREE = me

He agrees with me

taste = AGREE

Becoming; appropriate in taste; agrees with (you/him/her)

ALEXANDER (arbitrary name sign)

Alexander

ALIKE

The same; too

ALL

All; entire; whole

#ALL

All of; the whole thing

ALL-OVER

All over; all around; the whole area; area

ALLOW

Allow; let; permit

ALL-RIGHT

All right; OK

ALMOST

Almost; very nearly

ALMOST-NOTHING

Very litte; very few; hardly any; almost nothing at all. Very close; right by here; no distance at all. Very soon; in no time at all.

car = ALONGSIDE

Pull up (vehicle/car) beside; pull up (vehicle/car) alongside

ALSO

Also; in addition to; too

ALTOGETHER

Altogether; total

ALTOGETHER MANY₂ ∧ ?

Altogether how many; how many in all?

ALWAYS

Always

ALWAYS‿STILL₁

Forever; everlasting

AMERICA

America; U.S.A.; the U.S.; American

ANALYSIS

Analysis; analyze

AND

And; in addition

ANIMAL +

Animals

ANNOUNCE

Announce; tell; declare; announcement

ANXIOUS

Emotionally anxious or worried

ANXIOUS NOT

Not anxious or emotionally worried

ANY

Any

APPEAR

Appear; pop up; show up; surface

APPLE PIE

Apple pie

APPLY

Volunteer; apply for; application (for something)

APPOINTMENT

Appointment

APPROACH ⊥

Approach; come closer to

ARGUE

Argue; argument; debate

AROUND = area

Around; approximately; area; a plot

AROUND 11:00

Around eleven o'clock

AROUND TWO = approximate

Approximately at two o'clock; around two o'clock

ARRIVE

Arrive; reach destination

ARRIVE +

Arrival of more than one

ASCEND

Ascend; climb; walk up

ASIDE <

Out of the way; finished; to one side (left)

ASIDE >

Out of the way; finished; to one side (right)

ASK = her (you, him)

Ask or question her/you/him

ASK = them + +

Ask or question them, one by one

he = ASK = me

He asked or questioned me

ASSISTANT

Assistant; helper; assistance

ASSOCIATION

An association

AT-LAST

Finally; at last

ATTEMPT +

Attempted; try and try

ATTRACT-TO

Attracted to; attractive; pulled toward

ATTRACT-TO

Fascinated; held (my) attention; spellbound

"AUTHORITY"

Have the power, freedom, or authority to act or do something

"AUTHORITY" DECIDE

Having the freedom, power, or authority to make decisions

AUTUMN

Autumn; fall; fall season

AVERAGE

Average; median

AVOID

Avoid; stay away from; get out of; keep (your) distance

AWKWARD

Awkward; clumsy; not smooth

B-B-Q

Barbecue; cookout

BABY

Baby; infant

#BACK

Go back; come back; return

car = BACK-OUT = garage

Back (the car/vehicle) out of the garage or carport

car = BACK-UP

Back up (the car/vehicle); put (car/vehicle) in reverse

car = BACK-UP ⌣ HIT = barrier

Back (the car/vehicle) up into a barrier

BACON

Bacon

BAD

Bad

BAD

Very bad

BAD NOT

Not bad at all

BAGGAGE₂

Baggage; bags; suitcases

"BALL" + (Christmas)

Various sizes of Christmas ball-shaped ornaments

BALTIMORE

Baltimore, Maryland

BAR

Drinking bar

BARBARA (arbitrary name sign)

Barbara

BASEMENT

Basement; sublevel

BATH ROOM

Bathroom

BATTERY +

Battery (generally vehicular type)

BEANS ITS GREEN

Green beans

BEAR

A bear; bears

BEAT

Beat; defeat. Better than

BEAT = around + +

Beat or defeat everyone in a given contest or competition

BEAUTIFUL

Beautiful

BEAUTIFUL WHEW

Absolutely beautiful; gorgeous

BECAUSE

Because; since; as

BED ROOM

Bedroom

BEER

Beer; drinking

BEFORE(+)

Before (in time); prior to

BEG

Beg

BELIEVE

Believe

BENNY   (arbitrary name sign)

Benny

BEST

Best

BEST

The very best (thing or whatever)

BETTER

Better

BETTER+

Becoming better and better; improving

BETTER+⌣EVERYTHING

Everything is much better than before

BETTER⌣YOU

You had better

BETWEEN

Between; in between

BETWEEN   FOUR>EIGHT

Between the hours of 4:00 and 8:00

BICYCLE

A bicycle; a bike

"BIG"

Big in the sense of not being a baby anymore

BIRTH⌢DAY

Birthday; day of birth

BLACK

Black

BLAME=yourself

Blame yourself; you have no one to blame but yourself; it's all your fault

BLOOD

Blood

wind=BLOW=around₂

Wind-blown; wind-strewn

BLOW-NOSE

A head cold; an upper respiratory infection

BLUE

Blue

BOARD

Board; a governing group

BOAT

Boat

BOAT⌣SMALL

A small boat

BODY

Body; physical; health

BOOK

Book

BORN

Born

BOTH

Both; two together

BOTHER=me

Bother me; a bother to me; an interruption

BOTTLE

A bottle (of wine, for example)

plane = BOUNCE +

    An aircraft hitting air pockets or a turbulence

BOX +

    Boxes

BOY

    Boy; a boy

BOY +

    Boys

BRAKE +

    Brakes

BRAKE-SHOE = put-on₂

    Install or put on brake shoes

BREAK

    Break; broken

BREAK-DOWN

    Break down; collapse; tear down

BREAST

    Breast part of body

BRICK + + >

    Bricks; made of brick

BRIGHT

    Bright; light-colored

BRING T

    Bring here

BRING ⊥

    Bring or take elsewhere

BROIL

    Broil; cook in a broiler

BROKE

    Broke; having no money

BROTHER (formal)

    Brother

BROTHER (informal)

    Brother

BROTHER‿UNITY

    Brothers all; all are brothers; brothers together

tooth = BRUSH

    A toothbrush; act of brushing teeth

BUILD

    To build; to construct; to erect

BUILDING

    A building; a structure

BURY

    Bury; burial; a grave

BURY AROUND

    Burial area; a cemetery; a graveyard

BUSINESS

    Business

BUSY

    Busy

BUT

    But; on the other hand; however

#BUT

    But

BUY

    Buy

BUY +

    Buy and buy

BUY + +

    Shopping

BUY‿FINISH₁

    Bought; having bought

"BY-A-HAIR"

    Almost; just missing; by a hair's breadth

CABINET+

    Cabinets; cupboards

CAKE DELICIOUS

    Delicious cake; very tasty cake

CALCULATOR

    Calculator

"PALM-SIZE" CALCULATOR

    A hand calculator; a pocket calculator

CALIFORNIA

    California; gold

shoot = CAMERA+ + >

    Take pictures; act of shooting a camera or taking pictures

CAN

    Can; may

CAN ME !

    I can do that! I have that ability!

CAN‿ME ?

    May I; can I?

large = CAN₂

    Large (trash) can, receptacle, or container

tin = CAN+ +

    Canned foods or goods

CAN'T

    Can't; unable to

CAN'T ME

    I just can't do that; I wouldn't dare try that

CAN'T‿SHE

    She can't do that

CAPITOL

    Capitol building; the capital city; government

CAPTION MOVIE

    Captioned film; captioned movie or TV show

CAR

    Car; automobile

CAREFUL

    Be careful; take care

CAREFUL

    Be very careful; use extreme caution

CATHOLIC

    Catholic

CENT

    A penny; one cent; cents

CHANGE

    Change; not remain the same as before

CHARGE = around+ +

    Buy on charge account at different stores; go on a charge-account shopping spree

CHARGE-PLATE

    To charge by credit card

CHARGE-PLATE CARD

    A charge-plate card; a credit card

CHAT+ +

    Chat; talk casually with someone else

CHEESE

    Cheese

CHEST

    Chest

CHEST = around

    Chest area

CHICKEN BREAST

    Chicken breasts

CHILDREN

    Children

small = CHILDREN

    Very young children; tiny tots

CHILLY +

    Chilly; chills; very cool; almost cold

CHOOSE

    Choose; pick out; select

CHOP +

    Chop up; cut up; dice (vegetables, etc.)

CHOP = *tree*

    Cut down a tree

CHRISTMAS

    Christmas; Yule

CHRISTMAS TIME-PERIOD

    Christmas time; yuletide

CHRISTMAS TREE

    Christmas tree; yule tree

CHURCH

    Church

CLEAN

    Clean; neat

CLEAN

    Very clean; immaculate; "spic and span"

CLEAN +

    Clean up; cleaning

CLEAN = around + +

    Clean up all around or all over

CLEAR

    Clear

"CLOSE-UP"

    Closely situated; in close proximity; also a close-up view

CLOTHES

    Clothes

CLOTHES_A +

    Clothing fashions; stylish

CLOTHES⌣CLOSET-RACK

    A clothes closet

COAT

    A coat; a jacket

COAT⌢PANTS

    A suit

COFFEE

    Coffee

COLD

    Cold

COLD

    Very cold; extremely cold; bitter cold

COLD EAT = noun +

    Cold food

COLLABORATE

    Collaborate; join together; come together; work together

COLLEGE

    College

COLLISION

    Collision; wreck; crash

COLOR

Color

COLOR$_A$

Different colors; colorful

COME = here

Come over; come here

COME = here$_1$

Come here; come over here

"COME-ON"

Come on (as a gesture)

COMFORTABLE

Comfortable; comfort; comforting

COMMITTEE

A committee; a council

COMPLAIN +

Complaining; a gripe; griping about

CONTINUE

To continue; to keep and not give up; to be; to remain

many = CONVERGE

A reunion; a coming together; a gathering of a group of people or things

COOK

To cook; to prepare food with or without heat

COOK +

Cooking; the act of cooking or preparing food

CORRECT

Correct; right

CORRECT ?

Is that right; is that correct?

CORRECT>WRONG

Right or wrong

COST

Cost; price; fee

COST MANY$_1$

How much does (it) cost; what's the price?

COST +

Taxes

COST

A fine; a charge

COUGH

Cough; a cough; a chest cold

COUNT +

Count; counting

left = forearm = COVER

A cast on the left forearm

CRAB

A crab; crabs

CRACKER

Crackers

CREAM

Cream

CROCHET

Crochet

CROSS

Cross; angry-faced

CURTAIN +

Curtains

clippers = CUT

Trim or cut with clippers or shears

CUT = finger

Cut one of your fingers

scissors = CUT

Cut out with scissors

trim = CUT

Trim as with grass shears

CUT = coupon

Coupons to clip or cut out

CUTE

Cute; darling

DADDY

Dad; daddy; colloquial form of father

DANCE +

Dance; dancing

DAUGHTER

Daughter

DAUGHTER OUR

Our daughter

DAY

Day; daytime

all = DAY

All day long; throughout the day

DAY-BEFORE-YESTERDAY

The day before yesterday; the other day; two days ago

DEAF = colloquial

Deaf (archaic: deaf-mute)

DEAF = formal

Deaf

DEAF = coll. "AUTHORITY"

The deaf have the authority, freedom, or power to act

DEAF = coll. C-L-U-B

A club for the deaf

DEAF , HEARING

Both deaf and hearing

DEAF INSTITUTION

A state school for the deaf

DEAF WORLD

The deaf world; the deaf community

DECIDE

Decide; make up one's mind; come to a decision; determine

DECIDE +

Decisions; making decisions

DECIDE FINISH₁

Decided; made up one's mind; already decided

DECIDE LATE

Haven't decided yet; haven't made up one's mind yet

DECIDE = noun

A decision; a determination

DECORATE

Decorate; fix up

DECORATE = around +

To decorate all around or everywhere

DECORATE FINISH₂

Decorated; already decorated or fixed up

DECORATE = noun + + ITS CHRISTMAS

Christmas decorations

DELICIOUS

Delicious; tasty to the palate

DELICIOUS₂

Very delicious

DENTIST

Dental; dentist

DEPART

    Depart; leave; departure

DEPEND

    Depend on; dependence; pending

DEPEND͜ CAN'T

    Can't depend upon; undependable

DIAMOND

    A diamond

DIAMOND = *ring*

    A diamond ring; a diamond set in a ring

DIAPER

    Diapers

DIAPER EXCHANGE

    To change diapers; a change of diapers

DIE

    To die; to be dead; death; dead; deceased

DIFFERENT

    Different; not the same

DIFFERENT +

    Differences

DIFFERENT + + >

    Many different (things)

DIMPLE

    Having dimples; to be dimpled

DIRTY

    Dirt; dirty; soiled; not clean

DIRTY͜ large = CAN$_2$

    Garbage can; trash can

DISCUSS

    Discuss; talk about

DIVE

    To dive from a diving board

DO

    Do (something); act or action

#DO +

    What to do? What shall I do?

#DO +

    What *can* (I) do; what *would* (you) do?

#DO = around$_2$ +

    To do many things all around the place

DOCTOR

    A doctor; a physician

DOLLAR

    A dollar; a dollar bill

DON'T

    Don't; don't do that

DON'T

    Don't do that!

DOOR

    A door; a doorway

DORMITORY

    A dormitory

DRAIN = arm +

    Extract or take blood sample from the arm

DRAPE +

    Drapes; draperies

DRESS

    A dress

DRESS ITS AUTUMN

    A fall dress

DRESS+ "TRY-ON"

    Try on dresses

tooth = DRILL

    Drilling a tooth

DRINK_A

    Having drinks; drinking

DRIVE

    To drive (a vehicle)

DRIVE+ +⊥

    To drive and drive

DRIVE = around +

    To drive around and around

DROOL

    Mouthwatering; crave; strongly desire or wish for; a craving

DROP

    Drop the idea of; drop something

DRY CLEAN+

    Dry clean; dry cleaning

DRY ROLL₁+

    A dryer, specifically a clothes dryer

DUTY HIS

    His duty; his job

EACH

    Each; each one

EAGER

    Eager; enthusiastic; earnest; anxious to do

EAGER ME

    I'm very eager; I'm very anxious to (do something)

EARLY

    Early

EARN+

    Earnings; income

EARTH

    The earth; the world; the globe

EASY

    Easy; simple; uncomplicated

EAT+

    To eat

EAT_A

    Dinner; banquet; eating and eating

EAT_A FULL = eat

    Very full; had more than enough to eat

EAT HOT-DOG

    Eat hot dogs

EAT = noun +

    Food; groceries

EGG

    Egg; eggs

EGG "ROLL"

    Egg rolls

EITHER

    Either

ELECTRIC

    Electric; electrical; electricity

ELECTRIC EVERYTHING

    All-electric; everything run by electricity

ELECTRIC all = INCLUDE

    All-electric

ELECTRIC OFF

    Electricity off; electricity cut off

ELEVATOR

Elevator; lift

ELIMINATE = right-side

Remove or take out from the right side

EMERGENCY

An emergency

ENCOURAGE

To encourage; to boost; encouragement

ENGAGE

Engagement prior to marriage

ENGAGE   FINISH₁

Engaged; having become engaged to marry

ENOUGH +

Enough

ENOUGH

Plenty

ENTER

Enter; go into

EQUAL

Being equal; being fair

ESTABLISH

Establish; established; founded; set up; put into place

EVENING

Evening; dusk

EVENING   CHILLY

A chilly or very cool evening

all = EVENING

All evening; the entire evening

EVERY ͡ THING

Everything

EVERY

Every

EVERYDAY

Everyday; daily; the usual (thing); ordinary; ordinarily

EVERYDAY   WEEK ͡ END

Every weekend

EXAGGERATE

Stretch out of proportion; exaggeration

EXAMINE₂

Examine; look over; search over

EXCHANGE

Exchange; change one for another

EXCITED

Excited; turned on

EXIT

Exit; directional turn-off

EXPECT

To expect; with expectation

EXPENSIVE

Expensive; costly; very high in price

EXPERIENCE

Having experience; act of experiencing

FACE

Face

FACE   FINE

Look just fine; look well

FALL

A fall; fall down

FALSE +

False; not real; artificial; a lie

FAMILY

A family; the family

FAMILY   many = CONVERGE

A family gathering; a family reunion

FAMOUS

Famous; well-known; famed

FANCY₁

Formal; the best in quality

FANCYₐ

Exquisite; "high class"; elaborate; stylish

FAST

Fast; speedy; fast work

FAST +

Speed; speeding

FASTEN-SEAT-BELT

Fasten seat belt; secure yourself in seat

FATHER

Father

FEEL

Feel

FEEL +

Guess; an estimate or guess based on intuition

FEEL   BETTER

Feel much better about

FEEL   GOOD

Feel good about

FEEL-LOSS

Miss very much; pine for (someone or something)

FEEL   **WHEW**

Feel hurt; sensitive

FEEL   YOU ?

How do you feel about that; what are your feelings about that?

FENCE

A fence; a barrier

car = FERRY-BOAT

A car ferry

FETCH

To fetch; get; obtain

FETCH   FINISH₁

Having fetched; gotten; obtained; picked up (someone or something)

FEW

A few; not many

FEW

Very few

FIFTEEN

Fifteen (15)

FIFTY>FIFTY

A 50-50 proposition; equal; equally shared; half and half

FIND

Find; discover; find out

FINE

Fine

FINE₂

Just fine; very well

FINE

That's just fine

"FINE"

Swell; dandy; exceptionally fine quality

FINE = "soft"

    That's fine; no problem

FINGER-CROSS$_2$

    With fingers crossed; hope; hoping for

FINGERSPELL

    Fingerspell; fingerspelling; spell out on your fingers

FINISH$_1$

    Finished; completed; having done; already

FINISH$_2$

    Finished; completed; having done; already

FINISH$_1$ +

    Stop; that's enough (of that)

FINISH = you

    You stop that right now

FINISH‿YOU ?

    Have you finished; are you through? Have you ever?

FIRE

    A fire

FIRE‿MANTEL

    A fireplace; a mantelpiece

FIRE WARM

    A cozy fire

FIRST

    First as in "the first thing"

FIRST‿TIME

    The very first time

FIX

    Fix; make; prepare

FLAT$_2$

    Lay flat or smooth; a flat surface

FLAT = finger

    A smashed finger

FLAT-TIRE

    A flat tire; a deflated tire

FLATTER ME

    You flatter me; I'm flattered

FLIP = over

    Turn over as in cooking

lie-down = FLOAT

    Float (on water)

FLOOR (LEVEL)

    Floor; story (of a building); level

FLOWER

    Flower

FLOWER +

    Flowers

FLOWER "ROW"

    A flower bed; a flower garden

FLY

    To fly (an aircraft)

FLY +

    Airport

FLY = noun +

    An airplane; aircraft

FLY = noun + **SMALL**

    A very small airplane

FLY = here

    Fly here

FLY = there

    Fly elsewhere; fly to a given place

FOLLOW

Follow; adhere to

FOR

For; to (as an infinitive)

FOR   ME

For me

FOR   CONTINUE

To be; to remain as it is

left = FOREARM

Left forearm

FORESEE

Foresee; predict; forecast

FORGET

Forget; slip one's mind; forgot

FORGET = not

Don't forget!

FOUR   YEAR

Four years

we = FOUR

We four; the four of us

those = FOUR

Those four; the four of them

FRANCE

France; French

FREE

Free; freedom; liberty; state of being free

FREEWAY

Freeway; expressway; super highway

FREEZE

To freeze; frozen

FREEZE + +

A freezer; the freezer

FRIDAY

Friday

FRIEND

Friend

FRIEND +

Friends

FROM

From

FULL = eat

Full from eating; "stuffed"

FUN

Fun

FUNERAL

A funeral; funeral service

FUNNY₂ +

Comics; humorous; comical

FUNNY‿ YOU

You are the funny one; you sure are funny!

FUTURE

The future; at some point in the future; future time

near = FUTURE

The very near future; very soon; before very long

GARAGE

Garage; carport

GALLAUDET   UNIVERSITY

Gallaudet University

GAME +

Games

GEAR-SHIFT

(Sign is made according to type of shift)

    Gear shift

GEAR-SHIFT   object = PULL-DOWN

    Shift gears downward

GERMAN

    German; Germany

GET-IN-VEHICLE

    Get in or board a car, bus, train, plane

GET-IN-VEHICLE + +

    Several persons boarding a car, bus, train, or plane at the same time

GET-OFF-VEHICLE

    Get off or out of a vehicle

GET-UP

    Get up; arise

$GIFT_2$

    A gift; a present

$GIFT_2$ +

    Gifts

$GIFT = him_1$

    Give (something) to him

$GIFT_2$ EXCHANGE

    Gift exchange; to exchange gifts

GIRL

    A girl

GIRL +

    Girls

GIVE = me

    Give to me; gave me

GIVE = you/him/her

    Give to you/him/her

GIVE = you $FINISH_1$

    (I) already gave (that) to you

$GIVE_2$

    Give (something)

GLORIA (arbitrary name sign)

    Gloria

GO

    Go to

GO +

    Go to regularly; attend

group = GO

    Go in a group

GO = down

    Go downstairs

GO-OUT

    Go out; go; gone

GO-OUT $FETCH_1$

    Go fetch; go get something or someone

GOD

    God

GOD "THERE = poetic"

    God in heaven

GOLD

    Gold; California

GOOD

    Good

GOOD

    That's very good!

GOOD L-U-C-K

Good luck

GOOD‿THING

It's a good thing

GOOD‿TIME

A good time; have a good time

GRANDPA

Grandpa; grandfather

GRASS

Grass

GREEN

Green

GRIEF

Grief; to grieve; to bear anguish

all=GROUP

The entire group; the whole bunch; a group

GROUP=together

To come together as a group or gang

GROW(+)

Grow; raise; growing

GROW=noun+

Spring; springtime

GROW-UP

Growing up; grown up

GULLIBLE

Being gullible; "swallowing a fish"

GYM

A gym; gymnasium

GYM NEW+

A very new gymnasium

HAMBURGER

Hamburger

HAPPEN

Happen; occur

HAPPEN+

Be; happening; happen; occur; take place

HAPPEN

If; in the event that; in case

HAPPY

Happy; glad

HAPPY‿YOU ?

Are you happy?

HARD

Hard surface; hard in the sense of difficult

HARMONIZE

Work out; fall into place; mesh gears; integrate well

HARMONIZE

Really work out very well; work very well together

HATE

Hate; despise; strongly dislike

HAVE

Have; possess; own

HE/HIM

He; him

HEADLIGHT-OFF$_2$

Turn headlights off

HEAP$_2$

A lot of; a pile of; a stack of; a whole lot of; a heap

HEAP₂ + >

    Bushes; hedges

HEARING (PERSON)

    A hearing person; one who can hear

HEART

    One's heart

HEARTBEAT

    One's heartbeat

HEART⌒HIT

    A heart attack

HEART‿LARGE

    Having a big heart; being very generous and understanding

HEART‿NEEDLE-WRITE

    An electrocardiogram; an EKG

HELP

    To help; help

HELP = around

    To help all around; to help everywhere

it = HELP = you

    It will help you

HELP = her/you, etc.

    Help her; help you

HELP = me

    Help me

HELP = them NEEDY

    Help those who are in need

HERSELF

    She; her; herself

"HEY"

    "Hey" as an attention-getter

HI

    "Hi, John/Mary" (or whoever)

HIM/HE

    Him; he

HIMSELF

    He; him; himself

HIS

    His

HIS +

    his; his own

HIT

    Hit; strike

HOE

    A garden hoe; to hoe

"HOLD = mouth"₂

    Keeping a tight lip; being close-mouthed about something; a double "shut-up" or clamming up about something

HOME

    Home

HOME HER +

    Her home; her house; her place

HOOD-OPEN

    A raised car hood

HOPE

    Hope

water = HOSE

    A garden hose; a water hose

HOSPITAL

    A hospital; in the hospital

HOT-DOG

    Hot dogs

HOTEL

    A hotel; an inn

HOUR

    An hour; an hour's time

HOUR + +

    Hours and hours

one = HOUR

    A full hour

one = HOUR

    A *solid* hour

three = HOUR

    Three hours; three hours time

HOUSE

    House

big = HOUSE

    A large house; a mansion

HOUSE   PRETTY

    A pretty house; a lovely house

HOW

    How?

HOW + +

    How is (that) done; how do (they) do it?

HUMBLE

    Humble; humility

HURRY

    Hurry; hurry up; make haste; hasten

HUSBAND

    Husband

"I-LOVE-YOU" +

    I love you; I really care about you!

ICE-CREAM

    Ice cream

IDEA

    Idea

IDEA   GOOD

    It's (that's) a good idea

IDLE

    Being idle; having nothing to do

#IF + +

    If; in case; should it happen

IGNORE = him

    Ignore him; pay no attention to him

IMPORTANT

    Important; importance; significance; worth

IMPRESS = me

    Impress; being impressed by something

IMPRESS = you

    Impress; impressing someone else

IMPROVE

    Improve; get better; become better than before

IN

    In

IN +

    Inside

all = INCLUDE

    All at once; all at the same time; inclusive; "kill two birds with one stone"

INCREASE +

    To increase; to gain; increasing

INFORM = me

    Inform me; let me know; keep me informed

INFORM = you/him, etc.

Inform you/him; let you/him know

INSTITUTION

Institution; state school

INTELLIGENT

Intelligent; intelligence

INTEND

Intend; intention; purpose

INTEREST

Interested in; interesting

INVESTIGATE

Investigate; check; check out

INVESTIGATE ‿ FINISH₁

Having investigated; checked; already investigated or checked out

INVITE$_A$

Invite several people

IRON

To iron

ITS

Its (possessive pronoun)

ITS +

Its own (possessive pronoun repeated for emphasis)

JACK-UP

Jack up a car; raise vehicle by means of a jack

JANE   (arbitrary name sign)

Jane

JEALOUS

Being jealous or envious; envy; jealousy

JENNIFER (arbitrary name sign)

Jennifer

JIMMY   (arbitrary name sign)

Jimmy

JOT-DOWN

Write down; put down; jot down

JOT = list

Jot down a list; make a list

JUMP = stand

Quickly jump up to a standing position

JUMP = up +

Very happy; filled with joy; jump for joy

KEE-KONG   (arbitrary name sign)

Kee Kong

KEY

Key; a key

KITCHEN

Kitchen

KNACK

Having a certain expertise or skill

KNOW

Know

KNOW +

Know

don't = KNOW

Don't know; not knowing

KNOW ‿ FINISH₁

I knew it!

KNOW ME

I know that!

KNOW = noun +

Knowledge

KNOW THAT ?

Did you know that; did you know about that?

KNOW YOU

You know!

"KNOW YOU"

You know that!

plane = LAND

An aircraft in the act of landing; a flight landing or touchdown

LARGE

Large; big in size

LARGE-JEWEL = *ring*

A large jewel set in a ring; indicative of the size of a certain jewel such a diamond

LAST

Last; the last one; the last thing

LATE

Late; not yet; haven't

LATE

Being very late

LATER

Later; after a while

LATER + +

Later on; after a while

LAUGH + +

Laugh and laugh; laughter

LAW

The law; a law

against = LAW

Illegal; against the law; forbidden

LAWRENCE (arbitrary name sign)

Lawrence

LEADER

Leader

LEAF +

Tree leaves; bush leaves

LEARN

Learn

LEARN +

Learn about; learning

LEARNER

Learner; student; one who learns

LEARN = noun +

Education; learning

LEARN = noun + BETTER

Better education

LEAVE +

To leave be; to be left in place

LECTURE

A lecture; a speech; an address

LEFT

Leave; what's left; remainder

LENGTH

Length; from here to there

LET'S-SEE

We'll see; see if . . .

LETTUCE

Lettuce

LICENSE

A license; a license plate

LIE = talk

Lie; to tell a lie or a falsehood

LIE-DOWN

Lie down; to lie in a state of rest

LIE-DOWN = continuously

To be bedridden; to be unable to get up

LIE-DOWN LOOK-AT

To view a body lying in state or in a coffin

LIFE

Life

LIGHT$_2$> ITS CHRISTMAS

Christmas lights

LIGHT-ON-OFF$_2$+

Flashing lights; lights blinking on and off repeatedly

LIGHTNING

Lightning; electrical flashes in the atmosphere

LIGHTNING STORM

Electrical storm

LIKE

Like

LIKE

Really like; like intensely

LIKE ME

I like that

don't = LIKE

Don't like

LIMIT

To limit; a limit; the limit

up = LIMIT

Up to a certain limit or amount

LIMIT NEED

An absolute limit; must limit

LINCOLN

Abraham Lincoln; also a Lincoln car

LINE = forward$_2$

A line (of people) moving forward

car = LINE-UP$_2$+ +

A line of cars; cars backed up or backing up

LION

A lion

LIPSTICK

Lipstick; chap stick; lip balm or cosmetic

LIST

A list; to list

LISTEN

To listen; to hear

LITTLE-BIT

A little bit of; a small amount

LIVE

Live

LONELY

Lonely; lonesome; to be alone

LONG

Long (in time)

LONG-AGO

Long ago; a long time ago; way back in time

LONG-AGO

Long, long ago; far into the past

LOOK-AT$_2$

To look at; to take a look at; to watch

LOOK-AT + +

To look at different things, one after another; to watch

LOOK-AT = ahead$_2$ +

   To look ahead; to look forward to

LOOK-AT = around$_2$ +

   To look around at; to look over

LOOK-AT = *around-mouth*

   To examine mouth

LOOK-AT = down = around$_2$

   To look at something in the area below you

LOOK-AT = each-other

   To look at one another

LOOK-AT = noun$_2$

   Observation (area)

LOOK-AT = outside

   To look at or observe as through a window

LOOK-AT = past$_2$

   To look back upon; to recall from the past

LOOK-AT = *ring* +

   To admire a ring or diamond

LOOK-AT = us$_2$

   Look at us; watch us

LOUSY

   Lousy; rotten; no good

LOVE

   Love

LOVE ME

   I love (that) very much!

LOVE   BEST

   Love the best of all

LOWER = body = in-ground

   To bury; to lower casket into grave; to be "six feet under"

LUCKY

   Lucky; fortunate

MAIL = me

   Send me; sent to me; mailed to me

MAIL = it

   Send or mail something; sent by mail

MAMA

   Mama

MAN   (formal)

   Man; a man; men

MAN   (informal)

   Man; a man; men

MANY +

   Many, many; a large number

MANY$_1$?

   How much?

MANY$_2$?

   How many?

MARRY

   Marry; get married; married

MASK = nose

   Being given gas or ether; being given an anesthesia through the nose; a nose covering or mask

catholic = MASS

   The Mass or Eucharist in the Catholic Church

tooth = MASSAGE

   Rubbing or massaging a sore gum

MATERIAL

   Material

MAYBE

Maybe; perhaps

ME

Me; I

ME+

Me; I

"ME = poetic"

Me

ME⌣WANT

I want (to do this or have that)

MEAN

Meaning; definition; (I) mean

MEAT

Meat; flesh

MEDICINE

Medicine; medical

MEET

Meet (on a one-to-one basis)

MEET = around

Meet (others) all around as at a convention

MEETING

A meeting; a convention; a conference

MILK

Milk

MIND⌒FREEZE

Shocked; speechless; at a loss for words; thoughts immobilized temporarily

MINUTE

A minute's time; in a minute

MISSING

Missing; absent or gone

MIX

Mix; stir

MOMENT

A moment

MONEY

Money

MONEY

Lots of money; having money; being well off

MONEY SPEND₂

Money (we) spent; the amount (we) spend

MONEY⌣STACK

A stack or pile of money (saved)

MONKEY

A monkey; monkeys

MONTH

A month; one month

MONTH + +

Monthly; every month

MORE

More

early = MORNING

Early in the morning

late = MORNING

Late or later in the morning

MOST

Most

MOTHER

Mother

MOTOR

Motor; engine

MOTOR   object = run = ROUND + +

Motor running

MOTOR   object = turn = ROUND +

Motor turning

car = MOVE = forward

A car moving forward; a car moving up; a car proceeding; a car's pickup

MOW = grass +

Mowing; mow the lawn; cut the grass

MUCH

Much

MUSTARD

Mustard

MY

My; mine

MY +

My; mine

MYSELF

Myself

NAME +

One's name; a name

NAME = verb

Named; called

NAME ∨

A list of names

NAPKIN

Napkin

NEAR +

Near; nearby; close to

NEED +

Need; necessary

NEED + +

Needs; necessities

NEED

Must; have to

NEED = "soft"

Should

NEEDY

Needy; poor; not having much; scant

NERVOUS

Nervous; jittery

NEVER

Never

NEVER

Absolutely never; never at all

NEW

New

NEW +

New not long ago

NEW + +

Very new; recently new

NEW

Brand new

NEW‿DIFFERENT

New and different; stylish; changing

NEW   CLOTHES

New clothes

NEW-YORK

New York City; New York

NEWSPAPER

Newspaper; print; printing

NEXT

Next

NEXT-DOOR

Neighbor; people next door; next door

here = NEXT-TURN = there

First here and then there; next in place

this = NEXT-TURN = that

First this and then that; next in line

NIGHT

Night; nighttime

all = NIGHT

All night; all night long

NO

No (negative response)

"NO-NO"

That's a "no-no"; taboo

NO-MATTER

It doesn't matter; nevertheless; however; although

NONE₁

None; having none

NONE₂

None at all; having none at all

NONE

Absolutely none at all

NOON

Noon; at noon; at 12:00; at the noon hour

NOT

Not

NOT ALLOW

Not allowed; not permitted

NOT BAD

Not bad

NOT BAD IDEA

Not a bad idea

NOT EXPECT

Not expected at all; unexpected

NOT TRUE

Not true; not real; not sure

NOTHING

Nothing

NOW

Now; presently; currently; the present time

NOW+

Right now; just now

NOW

Right now; right away; right at this moment

NOW AFTERNOON

This afternoon

NOW DAY

Today; this day

NOW MORNING

This morning

NOW NIGHT

Tonight; this evening

NOW OLD FIVE

Now five years old; now age five

NOW YEAR

This year; the current year

NUMBER

Number

NURSE

Nurse; a nurse; the nurse

O-K

OK; okay

O-K$_2$

That's OK; that's all right

O-K + +

Okay, okay; that's just fine

OF-COURSE

Of course; naturally

pedal = OFF = little

Take foot off accelerator a little; let up on the gas a little

OFF-POINT

Off the point; deviate; change subject

OFF-WORK

Off work

OFF-WORK +

Vacation; being off work for a period of time

OFF-WORK + +

Loafing; doing nothing

OFFICER$_2$

Officers; officials

OFFICER$_1$

Officer; official; boss; captain; general

"OH-I-SEE"

I see; I understand

OLD

Old; age

OLD +

Old; aged; not used any more

OLD FIVE

Age five; five years old

OLD   INCREASE +

The older you become; as age increases

OLD   MANY$_1$ $\wedge$?

How old; what age?

ONCE

Once; one time

ONCE-IN-A-WHILE

Once in a while; occasionally

ONCE-IN-A-WHILE

Once in a great while; seldom(ly)

ONE

One

ONE-PAST = head$_A$

Things passing by on each side when traveling on surface (by car or train)

ONE = forward   FIVE = forward +

They go forward together with me

ONE   MORE

Just one more

ONION

Onions

"OPEN-NECK"   COAT   PANTS

A casual suit

OPERATE = mouth

Oral surgery

OPERATE = right-side

Surgery on right side of body

stomach = OPERATE

Surgery on abdomen or stomach area

OR
> Or

OTHER
> Other

OTHER +
> Other; other things

OUR
> Our

OUT = me
> From within me

OUT +
> Outside

OWE = her/him
> Owe her or him; a debt to her or him

OWE = me
> Owe me; a debt to me

head = PAIN
> Headache

stomach = PAIN
> Stomachache; abdominal pain; bellyache

tooth = PAIN
> Toothache

PAINT +
> Paint (a house, a wall, an object)

PAINTING
> A painting

"PALM-SIZE"
> Small; about the size of a palm; capable of being held in palm of hand

PANCAKE +
> Pancakes; flapjacks

PAPER
> Paper

PAPER   ON = object
> Put or place paper (pattern) on top

PAPER   on = WALL
> Wallpaper

PAPER‿THIN = object
> A bulletin or brochure; a pamphlet

car = PARK
> Park the car

car = PARK + +
> Parking

PARTY
> Party; a party

PARTY   EAT$_A$
> A dinner party

PASS
> Pass; pass by

PAST
> The past; in the past

PAST +
> Before; some time in the past

PAST + +
> Way back in the past

PAST‿NIGHT
> Last night

near = PAST +
> Recently; not long ago

near = PAST + +
> Very recently; just a little while ago

PAST SATURDAY

   Last Saturday

PAST+ two = MONTH

   Two months ago

PATIENT = verb

   Tolerate; abide; bear; having patience; being patient; tolerating

PATRONIZE

   Repeatedly go to a certain place or person

PAY-CASH

   Pay cash for; pay in full

PAY = her/him

   Pay her or him

PAY = me

   Pay me

PEACE

   Peace; tranquility; peaceful; tranquil

PEDAL$_A$

   Foot pedal

PEEL

   Peel; pare with paring knife or peeler

PEOPLE

   People; mankind

PERFECT

   Perfect; without flaw or error; perfection

"PERFECT"

   A common gesture meaning "just right" or "perfect"

PERFUME

   Perfume; cologne

PERIOD = (.)

   A period (.); decimal point

PERSUADE

   Persuade; urge; cajole

PHILADELPHIA

   Philadelphia

PICK-UP$_A$

   Pick up one thing and then another

PICKLE

   Pickles

PICNIC

   Picnic; outing

PIE

   Pie

PIN+

   Straight pins

PIN+   STICK = around +

   Sticking in straight pins to attach pattern around a piece of cloth

PITY+ +

   Really pity; feel very sorry for; really sympathize with

PLACE+

   Places

PLACE-IN = me

   Put me in (as being placed or put in a hospital)

PLAN

   A plan; to plan; to prepare

PLAN+

   Plan for; prepare for; get ready for

PLAY

   Play

PLAY-POOL

   Pool game; play pool or billiards

PLEASE

Please

PLEASE +

Please; "pretty please"

PLEASE = noun₂ +

Pleasure; enjoyment; entertainment; enjoy; entertain

PLUS

Plus; in addition; also

POINT + +

Points

POLICE

Police; police officer; cops

POOR PEOPLE

Poor people

POP

Soda pop; soft drinks

POPCORN

Popcorn; popping corn

POPULAR

Popular; well-liked

PORTION-OFF + +

Pay in regular installments; pay part at a time

POSTPONE + +

Put off consistently

POTATO

Potatoes

POUR = around + +

Pour (coffee, etc.) for each person

PRACTICE

Practice

PRACTICE + +

Practice over and over; rehearse; rehearsal

PRAY

Pray; prayer; say a prayer for

PREDICT

Predict; prophecy; foresee

PREFER

Prefer; like best

PREGNANT

Pregnant

PRESIDENT

President; superintendent; head

PRETTY

Pretty; attractive

PRETTY

Very pretty; very attractive

PRETTY DRESS

Pretty dress; attractive dress

PRIDE

Pride; proud

PRIEST

Priest; clergyman

PROBLEM

Problem

PROCEED

Proceed; go ahead; move on; continue

PROMISE

Promise; pledge

PROMISE

Guarantee; guaranteed

tooth = PULL

    Tooth extraction; pulling a tooth

PULL-UP$_A$

    Pull up first one and then another

pedal = PUSH +

    Pushing a foot pedal, in this case an automobile accelerator

pedal = PUSH   car = MOVE = forward **SLOW**

    Poor pickup when accelerating

PUT$_2$

    Place or put in place on something

PUT = around$_2$

    Put or set (dishes, etc.) around; place around

PUT-AWAY$_2$

    Load up; act of loading, as in putting baggage on a plane

PUT-IN$_1$

    Put or place in (something)

PUT-IN +

    Put or place in (several things)

PUT-IN = ignition

    Put or place (key) in ignition

baggage = PUT-IN$_2$

    Check baggage

PUT-IN$_A$

    Pack up; put in many different things, one after another

PUT-IN = savings + +

    Save (money) regularly; add to savings over and over

PUT-IN$_2$ DRY‿ROLL$_1$ +

    Put or place in dryer

PUT-IN R-E-F/FREEZE

    Put or place in refrigerator or freezer

PUT-IN-OVEN‿POTATO

    Baking potatoes

PUT-OUT$_2$ +

    Place outside; put outside

PUT-UP$_2$ +

    Put up; put in place

QUESTION + +

    Ask questions (of someone or about something)

RACE

    Compete; run for; competition

RACE = noun (See SPORTS)

    Sports

RAIN +

    Rain; continuous rain

RAKE

    To rake; a rake

RAKE = around +

    Rake all over; rake an entire area

READ +

    Read and read

READ = *my-finger* +

    Read my fingers; read my fingerspelling

READY < >

    Ready in the sense of everything being prepared

READY > >

    Ready in the sense of being ready for something

REASON

    Reason

RECEIVE

Receive; get; obtain

RECENT

Recent; not long ago

near = RECENT

Recently; a short time ago

near = RECENT

Very recently; not very long ago

RED

Red

REDUCE

To lessen; to reduce; reduced; to lower (in cost, for example)

REGULAR

Regular; with regularity; at regular intervals

REINDEER

Reindeer; any deer in general

RELAX

Relax; take it easy

RELIEVED

Relieved; feeling relief

REMEMBER

Remember; recall

REMEMBER +

Memory

REMOVE

Remove; take out; extract

REPAIR

Repair; fix

REQUIRE

Require; take; insist

RESERVE

Reserve; reservations; act of making reservations

RESIGN

Resign; quit

RESPECT

To respect; to have respect for; to look up to

RESTAURANT

Restaurant; eating place

REVENGE

Revenge; getting even; getting back at (someone)

RIDE

Ride; rides

RIGHT

Having a right or rights

RING

A ring

RIVER

A river

ROLL = pastry

Flatten pastry dough with a rolling pin

"ROLL"

Something rolled up as an "egg roll"

"ROW"

A row, here meaning a (flower) bed or row

RUB-ON = floor‿SHINY₂

To wax or polish floor surfaces

RULE +

Rules

RUN

To run; to hurry to (a place)

R-X

A prescription; an Rx

SAD

Sad; unhappy; not happy

SALAD

Salad

SALAD FINISH$_2$

The salad is finished; the salad is ready

SAME

The same; no difference

SAME$_2$

Just the same as before

SAME‿YOU

You are no better; you are no different; the same as you

SAME = around$_2$

The same everywhere; like everywhere else

SAME = continuous$_2$

The same thing over and over

he = SAME = she

He and she are alike; he and she do the same things

me = SAME = you

Me, too; me also; I'm the same

me = SAME = you$_2$

It's exactly the same with me as with you

this = SAME = that

(Objects) exactly alike or the same

those-two = SAME = them

(People) exactly alike; they do the same as them

SATISFY

Satisfied; content; contented

SATURDAY

Saturday

SAUSAGE

Sausage

SAW-OFF

Cut off with a saw

limb = SAW-OFF

Saw off limbs or branches as with a pruning saw

SAVE

Save

SAVE

Really save

SCHOOL

School

SCRAMBLE (EGGS)

Scrambled eggs

SEARCH

Search; look for

SEARCH = around

Search around; look around for

SECRET

Secret; personal

SECRETARY

The secretary; a secretary

SECOND

The second thing; in the second place

SECOND = you

Agree with you

SECOND = you

(I) agree with you 100%; (I) completely agree with you

SEE

    See

SEE = you

    See you

SEE‿ME

    See me

SEE‿FINISH₁

    Having seen; saw; already seen

SEEM +

    Looks like; appears; seems; apparently

SELL

    Sell

SELL = noun +

    Store; market place

SELL‿REDUCE

    Sale; on sale

SEND-TO

    Send to; sent to

SERVE

    Serve

SEVERAL

    Several; a number of

SET = noun + +

    Set up certain objects in place

SEW +

    Sewing (by machine)

SEW = hand +

    Sew by hand; hand sewing or stitching

stomach = SEW = hand +

    Stitch or sew up (suture) stomach after surgery; stitches

SEW MACHINE

    Sewing machine

SEW +   TABLE

    Sewing table

SHAPE = body

    Bodily shape or figure

SHE

    She; her

SHELF + + ∨

    A set of shelves; shelving

sun = SHINE + + ∨

    Sunbathing; sunning

SHINY₂

    Bright; shiny and clean; polished lustre

SHINY = *ring*

    The brightness or sparkle or glow of a jeweled ring

SHINY = tooth₂

    Clean, bright, and shiny teeth

SHIRT + +

    Shirts or blouses

SHOCK

    Shock; extreme surprise; shocked

SHOE

    Shoes; a shoe; a pair of shoes

SHOE MONEY‿REDUCE

    A shoe sale

SHOOT = arm

    Administer a shot or vaccine or local anesthetic into arm; an injection into arm

SHOOT = cheek/gum

Inject a local anesthetic into gum and cheek; a novocaine injection

SHORT

Short; brief

SHORT + +

Very shortly; very briefly; soon

SHOW

To show; to expose

SHOW = you

Show something to you

SHRIMP

Shrimp

SICK

Sick; ill

SIGHTSEE

To sightsee; to go sightseeing

SIGHTSEE = around

Going sightseeing; seeing the sights

SIGN

Sign; signing; Sign Language

SILLY~A~

Being foolish; fooling around

SISTER

Sister

SIT = around~2~

Sit around (a table); sit in a circle or semicircle

car = SKID

A skidding car; a car going into a skid

SKILL

Skill; skilled; having skill

SKYSCRAPER +

Skyscrapers; very tall buildings or other structures

SLEEP

Sleep

SLEEP +

Sleepy

SLEEP-HARD

Fall fast asleep; being sound asleep

SLEEP‿SUNRISE

Oversleep; sleep past sunup

SLIDE = door~2~

Sliding doors

SLOW

Slow

SMALL

Small in size or shape

SMALL-MEASURE

Short in length or small in measurement

SMILE

Smile; smiling

SMOOTH

Smooth; fluent; fluency

"SMOOTH-LIP"~2~ +

Tease or take advantage of someone by playing tricks on them or fooling them

"SNUGGLE-UP"

Snuggle up; sit very close together; act of snuggling up

SOFT‿BOIL (EGGS)

Soft-boiled (as eggs)

SOME

Some

SOMEONE

Someone; somebody

SOMETHING

Something

SOMETIMES

Sometimes

SON

Son

G-R-A-N-D SON

Grandson

SONG

A song; to sing a song

SONG SIGN

To sign a song; to give a rendition of a song in Sign

SORRY

To be sorry; to feel sorrow for

SOW-SEED

To sow seeds; to plant seeds

SOW-SEED‿AROUND

A garden; a garden plot or area

SPADE

A spade; to spade or turn over earth with a spade

P-L-U-G SPARK

Sparkplugs

"SPELL-OUT"

Give out the questions, information, etc.; spell out a word or words

SPEND

Spend; pay out

SPEND$_2$

Spend a lot of money

SPORTS (See RACE = noun +)

Sports; athletic competition

SPRAY-CONTAINER

An aerosol; a sprayer

SPREAD = globe

Spread out over the earth or world

STAND ∧

Rising or moving upward in a standing position as in an elevator or lift

START

Start; begin; initiate

START REFUSE

Refuses to start; refuse to begin

STATE-SCHOOL-FOR-THE-DEAF

(See DEAF INSTITUTION)

State school or institution for the deaf

STATUE

A statue

STAY

To stay; stay put; remain

STEP

To step; a step forward

STETHOSCOPE = around

Check with a stethoscope

STILL$_2$

Still; continuing

STIR + +

Stir up or mix as in making a cake or pancake batter

STOMACH = big

Heavy with child; very pregnant

STOP + +

Make several stops; stop over and over

STORM

A storm

STORM LIGHTNING

An electrical storm

STORY-TALK

Talk and talk; tell a story

STRADDLE = back-and-forth

Unsure of; unable to decide or make a choice right away; being "on the fence about something"

STREET

A street

"STRETCH = leg"$_2$

Slightly recline and stretch out legs to relax

STRICT

To be strict or unyielding

STRIKE-CHANCE

A lucky strike; a lucky break or chance

STRIKE-CHANCE FIND

To find by a stroke of luck; a lucky find

STRONG

Strong; powerful

STRONG GROUP

A strong group; a power group

"STUCK"

Stuck; having a problem and not being sure how to solve it

STUDY FINISH$_1$

Studied; having finished studying; already studied

"STUPID"

Not knowing how to do something because of a lack of experience or ignorance

SUBTRACT

Subtract; take away from; minus

SUBWAY

Subway; a subway system

SUCCEED

Succeed; success; successful

SUNDAY

Sunday

SUNSHINE

Sunshine; sunny weather

sun = SHINE + +

Sunning or sunbathing

SUPPOSE

Suppose

SUPPOSE + +

Suppose; if

SURPRISE

Surprise; surprised

SURPRISE

Very surprised; astonished

SUSPECT

To suspect; suspicion; being suspicious

SWEET‿YOU

    You are sweet; you are a doll

SWIM + +

    Swimming; to swim and swim

TABLE

    A table; the table

TABLE$_2$

    A table; the table

TAKE-CARE

    Take care of; watch after

TAKE-DOWN = object

    To take down something; remove something

plane = TAKE-OFF

    An aircraft taking off or lifting skyward; take off

TAKE-PILL +

    Take pills; the act of taking medication by pill or capsule

TALK = each-other

    Talk to one another; exchange views

TALL-STRUCTURE$_A$ +

    Many tall buildings or other structures everywhere

TAP = him

    Tap (him) on the shoulder or body to get (his) attention; get (his) attention; remind (him)

TASTE +

    Taste or preference; prefer

TEA

    Tea

TEACH = me

    Teach me; instruct me

TEACH = you/him/her

    Teach you/him/her; instruct you/him/her

TEAM

    A team; teamwork

TEARS-FLOW$_2$

    Flowing tears; heavy crying from grief; grief-stricken

TEASE = him/her/you

    Tease him/her/you

TEASE = me

    Tease me; teased me; the act of teasing me

TELEPHONE

    A telephone; to phone or telephone; to call

TELEPHONE NUMBER

    A telephone number; what number to call

TELEPHONE POLE

    A telephone pole

TELL = me

    Tell me; told me

TELL = you

    Tell you; told you

TELL = them

    Tell them; told them

TEMPERATURE

    Temperature; fever

time = TEN

    Ten o'clock; at 10:00

TEND

    Tend to; having a tendency toward something

TERRIBLE

    Terrible; very bad

TEST

A test; an exam

TEST+

Tests; testing

THANK-YOU

Thank you; thanks

THAT

That

THAT

Exactly that

THAT = there

That one; that particular (object or place)

THEATRE

Theatre; a movie house

THEIR

Their

THEIR+

Theirs

THEIR = around

All theirs

out = THERE

Out there

over = THERE

Over there; at that particular place

up = THERE

Up there; above somewhere

THERE = far

Very far off; a great distance away; far into the distance

THERMOMETER = mouth

An oral thermometer

THEY

They; them

THEY = deaf

They, the deaf

THING+

Things; objects

THINK

To think; a thought

THINK‿YOU ?

Do you think so?

THIRD

The third thing

THIRSTY

Thirsty

THIRSTY₁

Very thirsty; crave something; a craving or strong temptation to do something

THIS

This

THREE

Three (3)

we = THREE

We; we three; the three of us

those = THREE

Those three; the three of them; they

THROUGH

Through

go = THROUGH

Go through

come = THROUGH

Come through

go = THROUGH , come = THROUGH

Through and through; throughout; to go through an entire building or place thoroughly; be thorough

THROW-AWAY

Throw away; discard

THROW-IN +

To throw into a container; to discard

THURSDAY

Thursday

TICKET

Ticket; any kind of ticket for travel or entertainment

TIME +

Time; clock time; time of day

TIME

It's time now!

TIME NEAR +

Time drawing very close

TIME-PERIOD

Times; a span of time; a period of time

TIME‿EIGHT

Eight o'clock; at 8:00

TIME‿FOUR

Four o'clock; at 4:00

TINY-BIT + +

Tiny bits or very small pieces of something

TIRE

Tires; a tire

TOGETHER = around

All together; in unison

group = TOGETHER

all together; the whole group together; coming together as a group

TOILET

Toilet; bathroom; lavatory; rest room

TOM   (arbitrary name sign)

Tom

TOMATO

Tomato

TOMORROW

Tomorrow; the next day

TOMORROW‿MORNING

Tomorrow morning; the next morning

TOMORROW‿NIGHT

Tomorrow evening; tomorrow night; the next night

TOO-MUCH

Too much; over the acceptable or allowable limit

TOOTH = plural

Teeth

TOUCH

Physically experiencing

TOUCH + +

Physically experiencing several places or things

TOUCH = around + +

Travel all over touching or experiencing many places everywhere

heart = TOUCH

Touched in the heart; emotionally touched

TOUCH‿FINISH₁

Having been to a certain place; having experienced a given place

TOUCH‿FINISH₂

    Having been to a certain place already

TRADITION

    A tradition; traditional

TRAFFIC

    Traffic, whether vehicular or pedestrian

TRAIN+

    A train

TRAIN>

    Go by train

TRAIN   TICKET

    A train ticket; a railway ticket or fare

TREASURER

    Treasurer; money keeper

TREE

    A tree

TREE++

    Trees; woods; a forest; many trees around

TREE‿limb=FALL

    Fallen tree limbs or branches

TRIM+

    To trim or cut with large pruning shears

TRIP

    A trip; travel

TROUBLE

    Trouble

TRUE

    True; real; sure

TRUE+

    That's true; (I'm) not kidding

TRUE ?

    Is that true; is that so?

TRUE

    That's very true!

TRUE **RIGHT**

That's right, no mistake about it.

TRY

    Try; try out

"TRY-ON"++

    Try on different dresses or gowns

TURN-OFF=ignition

    Turn off the ignition; "kill the motor"

TURN-ON=ignition

    Turn on the ignition; attempt to start the motor

TWO

    Two (2)

TWO=approximate

    Approximately two o'clock; around 2:00

TWO=forward+

    Walking together, side by side

object=TWO

    The two things just mentioned

we=TWO

    We; the two of us; we two

you=TWO

    You; the two of you; you two

those=TWO

    They; the two of them; those two

alternate=TWO=*two*

    One or the other; either one

UNDERSTAND

    Understand

UNDERSTAND + +

    With the understanding that; being understanding

UNITY

    Unity; being united; all together as one

UP‿DOWN+

    Fluctuate; go up and then down; rise and fall

VACUUM

    Vacuum clean; to vacuum

VALUE

    Value; worth; cost

VARIOUS

    Various; variable

VISIT

    Visit

VOLLEYBALL

    Volleyball

"VOMIT"

    Hate; detest; can't stand; strongly dislike, etc.

VOTE

    Vote

VOTE+

    Vote; voting

VOTE=noun+

    Election; the vote

WAIT

    Wait

WAKE-UP

    Wake up; awaken; open eyes

WAKE-UP   FINISH₂

    Woke up; already awakened

WALK

    Walk

"WALK"=around

    A gesture meaning to walk around to a certain spot; to saunter over to a particular place

WALL

    A wall; walls

paper=WALL

    Wallpaper

WALLET

    Wallet; billfold

WANT

    Want; desire

WANT+

    Really want or desire

WANT‿YOU

    Do you want this?

WANT+   YOU

    Do you really want (to do) this or that?

don't=WANT

    Don't want

don't=WANT

    Don't want at all; will have nothing to do with

WARM

    Warm; cozy; warmth

WASH=object=clothes

    Wash clothes; launder; laundry

WASH=object=chicken-breast

    Wash off pieces of chicken breast

WASH = object = potato

    Wash off or scrub potatoes (before cooking)

WASH = object = wall

    Wash walls or wall surfaces

WASH$_A$ WINDOW

    Wash windows; the act of washing windows

WASH$_A$ WALLS

    Wash walls; the act of washing walls

WASHING-MACHINE

    An automatic washer; a washing machine

WASHINGTON

    Washington, D.C.; (George) Washington

WASHINGTON SKYSCRAPER

    The Washington Monument

WATER

    Water

WATER radiator-cap = GUSH

    Water gushing from overheated radiator

water = WAVE

    The ocean; waves

WEAK

    Weak; not strong

WEAR-OUT

    Worn out; falling apart; coming to pieces

WEATHER

    The weather

WEDDING

    A wedding; a marriage ceremony

WEDDING WHEN ?

    When is the wedding; what is the wedding date?

WEDNESDAY

    Wednesday

one = WEEK

    A week; one week

two = WEEK + +

    Every two weeks; every other week

three = WEEK

    In three weeks

WEEK + +

    Weekly; every week

WEEK = ahead

    Next week; the week ahead

WEEK = past

    Last week; the past week

two = WEEK = past

    Two weeks ago; the past two weeks

WEEK⌢END

    Weekend

WEIGHT

    Weight; weigh; pounds

WELL QUICK

    Quick recovery; get well quickly

WHAT ?

    What?

"WHAT"

    What; what's that?

"WHAT"$_1$

    What; what's that?

#WHAT

    What?

WHAT-FOR

What for; why?

WHAT'S-UP

What's up; what's going on

WHEEL-BUMP

Wheel not turning smoothly, but with a bump or thump

WHEN ?

When?

WHERE ?

Where?

WHEW

Whew!

WHEW+

Whew! WOW!

WHICH ?

Which?

WHICH

Or; whether

"WHIFF"

A sniff or a strong smell of something

WHILE

While; during; at the same time; as

WHISKEY

Whiskey; liquor

WHITE

White

WHITE‿COVER = face

Pale; a blood-drained face

WHITE   HOUSE

The White House

WHO ?

Who

WHO

Who; whom

WHY ?

Why

WHY + +

The reason for; because

WHY‿NOT

Why not; there's no reason not to

WIFE

Wife; a married woman

WILL

Will

WILL   ME

I will; I would

WILL   SHE/HE

She will; he will; she would; he would

WILL   THEY

They will; they would

WILL‿THURSDAY

This Thursday; this coming Thursday; next Thursday

WILL‿SATURDAY

This Saturday; this coming Saturday; next Saturday

WIND

The wind; blowing winds

WINDOW

A window; windows

WIN   EASY

Easily win; win without any trouble; win without a doubt

WINE

Wine

WINE   ITS   WHITE

White wine

WIRE

Wires, such as ignition wires or other wires

WIRE = me⌣T-T-Y

Call me on the TTY

WIRE = her/you⌣T-T-Y

Call her/you on the TTY

WISE   (+)

Wise; a very good idea; wisdom

WISH

To wish or desire; a wish

WITH

With

me = WITH = you

I'll go with you; I'll accompany you

you = WITH = me   ?

Will you go with me; accompany me?

WITHOUT

Without; not having

WONDER

Wonder; think about

WONDER$_A$

Wonder about; contemplate carefully

WONDERFUL

Wonderful; great

WONDERFUL

Marvelous; fabulous; fantastic; extremely pleasing

WORK

Work; job

WORK +

Work and work

WORK = around +

Work around; work everywhere

WORK = continuously

Work and work and work; a workaholic

WORK⌣FINISH$_1$

Having finished or completed work; having done a job already

WORK   NOTHING$_2$

Doing absolutely no work at all

WORRY

Worry; be mentally concerned

WORSE +

Worsen; become worse

WORTH   MANY$_1$ ∧

How much is (it) worth; what does (it) cost; what's the value?

WRAP = object = potato

Wrap potatoes (as wrapping in foil for baking)

WRITE

Write; write something

WRITE = between

Write notes back and forth

WRITE = note

Write notes

WRITE = page

>Write out a page

test = WRITE = page

>A written test; to take a written test

color = WRITE = book +

>Coloring books

WRONG

>To err; to be wrong

WRONG +

>A mistake; an error

WRONG

>As it happened; as it turned out

X͡ SNAPSHOT

>X ray or X rays; X-ray photos

YEAR

>Year; a year; years

YEAR = ahead

>Next year; in the year ahead

one = YEAR = ahead + +

>Annually; yearly; every year

two = YEAR = ahead

>Two years from now; in the next two years

two = YEAR = ahead + +

>Every two years; biannually

three = YEAR = ahead + +

>Every three years; triennially

YEAR = past

>Last year; during the past year

YEAR = recent-past

>Just this last (past) year

YES

>Yes; an affirmative response

YESTERDAY

>Yesterday

YOUNG

>Young in age; youth

YOU

>You

YOU = around

>All of you

YOUR +

>Yours

ZOOM

>Leave very quickly; disappear rapidly in the distance; take off quickly

Additional Vocabularies